Praise for *Bo...*

"This book is a must read! Dr. Elkin's perseverance and ... ...ty and health related issues is extraordinary. A daunting chain of events took place that led to the realization that you must listen to your body and be proactive. Constantly learning and thinking outside the box is his key to overseeing your health.

His philosophy on sound nutrition and exercise are key factors to a healthy lifestyle, as there is no magic pill. He focuses on prevention and lifestyle management versus pharmaceuticals except when necessary.

Dr. Elkin has given us permission to take charge, ask questions, and be better informed no matter what. Knowledge is power and staying connected to your body is paramount. Having been the doctor and the patient has opened his eyes. He is an expert in his field as well as an empath who truly desires to help his patients heal by giving them the necessary tools for success.

This is a sincere account with selfless words of wisdom in his endeavor to change the medical field for the better, and to empower all of us to be our own '*Medical Advocate*'."

LISA NUNZIELLA
Life Fitness Coach
Partner/Producer, Alumbra Films

"Being an RN for over 40 years, has had one major drawback: always being present for others, while putting myself last.

This book has empowered me to both change and set new priorities. What I have learned is that we must Plan for Wellness, while Focusing on Prevention.

Dr. Elkin provides us the tools and roadmap to do this.

We must take the driver's seat!

Dr. Elkin is an excellent role model, sets a good example and motivates us to take charge NOW.

Everyone who reads this book will surely benefit."

AMY KAUFMAN, RN

"This is not simply another "how to take care of your heart" book! In a most engaging, self-effacing, and inspiring sharing of the considerable physical and emotional stresses life has dealt him, Dr. Elkin compellingly illustrates the need for patients to be respected, and how patients can successfully take charge of their health by becoming their own '*Medical Advocate*'.

With the inclusion of inspiring testimonies, coupled with Dr. Elkin's honest sharing of difficult health situations as both physician and patient, this becomes a book that offers readers every tool to effectively enable them to push to attainment their own health goals."

David Stetson
Musician and Teacher

"The information that Dr. Elkin provided around this book has been unquestionable and, admittedly, what made me both eager to get my hands on it and terrified to read it. I mean, what if I was to be the one person that being your own best health care advocate didn't apply? However, with the relevancy of the information that this book provides, I knew this one was a must-read, so I was ready to set my fears aside and dive in.

That said, I had an altogether more personal, ulterior motive for wanting to read this book. Dr. Elkin personally guided me through my own health recovery journey, through using his proven methods. This has led me now to the healthiest point in my life!

This book will give you the cheat codes on how to avoid being a hamster in a wheel in the medical system.

Thank you, Dr. Elkin, for your knowledge, and thank you for being in the forefront of a revolution that is for the patient!"

Ralph Abitbol, DC

"Dr. Elkin's book is a real eye opener when it comes to seeking professional medical opinions and care. His experience, strength and unstoppable drive make this read not only educational, but inspirational for the road to achieving wellness."

Joey Feldman, Artist

"This is a real-life human-interest book with something for everyone. It's the Real Deal. In his book, Dr. Elkin points out that no one is immune from health issues, not even a physically fit cardiologist who suffers a heart attack, and 19 months later emergency back surgery.

Dr. Elkin is the Real McCoy. He's been there. He knows what it's like to be a doctor, and then suddenly when the tables are turned, becomes a patient. Through personal examples, Dr. Elkin relates his own health story and the struggles and obstacles he encountered along the way needed to regain his health and become his own '*Medical Advocate*'.

I found myself not wanting to put the book down, but eagerly wanting to know what was in the next chapter. I feel encouraged. Now, I want to become my own '*Medical Advocate*'."

JOE HUCKEBA, currently retired
Former Contracts Specialist,
Space Shuttle Programs

"In this book, Dr. Elkin provides us with the tools necessary to take charge of our own wellness to create the best strategies for our overall health. Due to the rise in medical specialists, most of us have a "team" of doctors that is not being managed well. No one seems to be in charge! Sadly, it is rare to find a medical care provider that has the integrity and sincerity of Dr. Elkin. He fully understands "both sides of the table" as he has lived it both personally and professionally. His journey includes conventional medicine coupled with the support of alternative therapies.

This book is a must read for those of us who demand a higher standard of health. Realistically, the only way through this health care crises is to take charge and manage our own self-care and become our own '*Medical Advocate*'. This book provides the information we all need to attain vibrant health throughout our entire lives."

RUSS PFEIFFER, Rolfer

"As a patient of Dr. Howard Elkin for the past six years, I have learned firsthand what it means to be my own *'Medical Advocate'*. It has been life changing for me!

This book so clearly demonstrates how stress and unknowns can creep into our lives and suddenly derail our health and entire life!

Fasten your seatbelt and get ready for an intense ride through this book! It is packed with expert advice and resources from the Authentic *'Medical Advocate'* himself, Dr. Howard Elkin!

You will walk away with quite a comprehensive "to do list" to take your life & health to the next level!!

As I have heard him say.... "Just put one foot in front of the other and move forward."

A gut-wrenching story of life and amazing advice on "taking charge" and Living Your Very Best Life!!

With Gratitude to Dr. Howard Elkin..."

Roberta Pierce, currently retired, Former President, York Employment Services, Inc.

"Dr. Elkin has delivered a powerful message with his authentic writing. He has brought us into the vulnerable reality of being a patient, and has taken us on his health journey, which was not always easy. His ability to draw you into his emotional side while cultivating empathy for those around him is uniquely written.

In the book, he tells his story of how he has overcome obstacles with strength and has wisely curated a medical dream team to surround him, empower him and to help him meet his goals.

Leading by example, Dr. Elkin, in turn, gives us the blueprint for doing likewise in becoming our own *'Medical Advocate'*. We all encounter health challenges throughout our lifespan. This book is invaluable in not only in guiding us but encouraging us to live vibrantly."

Michele K. Cazares, DPT, OCS
Professional Physical Therapy

FROM
BOTH SIDES
OF THE
TABLE:

When Dr. Becomes Patient

Become Your Own Medical Advocate

Howard K. Elkin, MD

HEARTWISE .PUBLICATIONS

From Both Sides of the Table: When Doctor Becomes Patient
by Howard K. Elkin MD, FACC

© 2022 Howard K. Elkin, MD

www.heartwise.com

Published by Heartwise Publications

All rights reserved. No part of this book may be used or reproduced by any means without the written permission of the author except in the case of brief quotations embodied in critical articles and reviews.

Editor: Jack Barnard

Cover Design: Anthony dos Santos

Author Photos: David LaPorte

Photo Finishing: Joan Wood

Book Design: Book Savvy Studio

ISBN: 978-0-578-34766-0

First Edition

Printed in the United States of America

PLEASE READ: This book details the author's personal experiences and opinions about general health, prevention of disease, nutritional supplements, and/or exercise. The author is not your healthcare provider.

Howard K. Elkin, MD, and Heartwise Publications and Medical Advocate, Inc. are providing this book and its contents on an "as is" basis and make no representations or warranties of any kind with respect to this book or its contents. The author and publisher disclaim all such representations and warranties, including for example warranties of merchantability and healthcare for a particular purpose. In addition, the author and publisher do not represent or warrant that the information accessible via this book is accurate, complete or current.

The statements made about products and services have not been evaluated by the U.S. Food and Drug Administration. They are not intended to diagnose, treat, cure, or prevent any condition or disease. Please consult with your own physician or healthcare specialist regarding the suggestions and recommendations made in this book.

Except as specifically stated in this book, neither Howard K. Elkin, MD, or Heartwise Publications, or Medical Advocate, Inc., nor any authors, contributors, or other representatives will be liable for damages arising out of or in connection with the use of this book. This is a comprehensive limitation of liability that applies to all damages of any kind, including (without limitation) compensatory; direct, indirect or consequential damages; loss of data, income or profit; loss of or damage to property and claims of third parties.

Understand that this book is not intended as a substitute for consultation with a licensed healthcare practitioner, such as your physician. Before you begin any healthcare program, or change your lifestyle in any way, you should consult your physician or another licensed healthcare practitioner to ensure that you are in good health and that the examples contained in this book will not harm you.

This book provides content related to physical and/or health issues. As such, use of this book implies your acceptance of this disclaimer.

*To my mother Lillian for her gift of
determination, groundedness, and goal setting.*

*To my father David Aaron (Archie) for his gift of
creativity, bravery, and risk-taking.*

CONTENTS

Acknowledgements	xi
Foreword by Stephen Sinatra, MD, FACC	xv
Foreword by Suzanne Somers	xix
Introduction	xxi

PART ONE : MY JOURNEY

Chapter 1	Denial – It Ain't Just a River in Egypt	1
Chapter 2	The Cath Lab Experience	7
Chapter 3	Life as an Inpatient	11
Chapter 4	Coming Home	17
Chapter 5	Learning to Thrive	23
Chapter 6	No One Is Immune	27
Chapter 7	A New Year: Moving Right Along	31
Chapter 8	18 Months Later—WHAM!	35
Chapter 9	My Worst Nightmare	41
Chapter 10	The Unexpected Road to Recovery	47
Chapter 11	Light at the End of the Tunnel	55
Chapter 12	Cruising Through Rehab	59
Chapter 13	The Journey Continues	65
Chapter 14	The Turning Point	71
Chapter 15	Renewing Hope	75
Chapter 16	The Unexpected Happens	79
Chapter 17	Making the Most of A Lousy Situation	85
Chapter 18	Good Isn't Good Enough	91

PART TWO: THE MEDICAL - WHERE AM I?

Chapter 19	Heart Facts: Why Me?	97
Chapter 20	Where Do I Fit In?	117
Chapter 21	The Real Question: Why Not Me?	131
Chapter 22	Stress: The Misunderstood Risk Factor	139

PART 3: BECOMING A MEDICAL ADVOCATE

    Chapter 23 | Stay in the Driver's Seat   149

    Chapter 24 | My Heroes   153

    Chapter 25 | My Dream-Team   175

PART 4: THE MEDICAL ADVOCATE'S GUIDE TO WELLNESS

    Chapter 26 | The Key to Vibrant Health   193

    Chapter 27 | The 5 Dimensions of Wellness   199

    Chapter 28 | You Are What You Eat   209

    Chapter 29 | Supplement Your Health   251

    Chapter 30 | You Gotta Move   275

    Chapter 31 | You Gotta Breathe   285

    Chapter 32 | Avoiding Aging Ungracefully Ever After   293

PART 5: THE JOURNAL (Life Without an Outline)

    Preamble to the Journal   318

REFERENCES   339

ACKNOWLEDGEMENTS

WRITING A BOOK IS TRULY A MONUMENTAL TASK. As early as the beginning of this century the idea hit me. I saw what was happening to health care in this country, and it seemed antithetical to my own belief system. I felt the need to make a paradigm shift and I figured I was going to use my voice to make that happen.

But it wasn't as easy as all that. I literally had to be hospitalized not once, but twice, to fully appreciate what I had to bring to the table as I evolved into the role of *The Medical Advocate*.

I didn't do it all alone. I was fortunate in having many wonderful folks assist me in my endeavor.

This book is dedicated to my parents, David Aaron (Archie) Elkin and Lillian Elkin Levitt. My father who died many years ago gave me the gift of creativity and adventure. If it were not for my dad's influence, I would probably never had gone out on a limb and taken various risks in life. My mom has given me the gift of groundedness. I gleaned from her discipline, focus, and an unparalleled work ethic. I am forever grateful for their combined gifts.

I'm also grateful for my three siblings. Although we are all quite different, the love and respect we have for one another allows us to appreciate our differences.

My children stand out as giving me unbridled support as both a dad and teacher. It's a two-way process. We have truly learned from one another.

Having been blessed with so many great teachers throughout my long and arduous education, I give thanks to those who appreciated my need to speak up and be heard.

Meeting and working with Stephen Sinatra, MD, during my anti-aging training and beyond on the *Earthing* study was truly pivotal in my own career as I embraced integrative cardiology. He was my teacher and mentor. Sadly, Dr. Sinatra left us in June 2022 after battling a serious but short-lived illness. I respected and admired him greatly, and his teachings will remain indelibly in my memory

Suzanne Somers, whom I have the fortune of knowing personally, did all of us a great favor with her book, *The Sexy Years*. I say this with great intention, as it made my work in treating menopause and perimenopause a much easier task. Being a male did little to help me identify with the plight of so many women suffering in the throngs of menopause. No longer did I have to print various one-sheets for patients. Instead, all I had to say was, "Just read Suzanne's book."

As I developed my own *Dream-Team* which helped propel me to my current state of health and wellness, I started working with Dr. Ralph Abitbol, an esteemed chiropractor who had retired in 2008. Ralph single-handedly assumed the role of my dream-team director. Post back surgery and a relapse a mere seven months later, his role proved invaluable in providing me guidance and direction. He continues in that role today.

I also give thanks to my other Dream-Team members: Dr. Glen Cloud, gifted chiropractor who literally saved me with years of decompression therapy for my ailing back, Dr. Gale O'Kieffe, acupuncturist par excellence, and Russ Pheiffer, the ultimate Rolfer who taught me everything I know about walking and movement. Two later additions who proved invaluable were Dr. Michele Cazares owner and director of Professional Physical Therapy in Whittier, California and Tony Molina of Rewire Project and, most recently, Arete LifeLab in Santa Monica. Tony continues to challenge me beyond belief and has introduced me to various forms of biohacking that I have since embraced. With both Michele and Tony, everything is positive and possible.

Special thanks go to my dear friend Barry Bruder who has always believed in the work that I do and who sat with me for hours early on, helping me develop a blueprint for my book.

Thanks to Sandra Gluckman who had the unglamorous role of transcribing interviews with my dream-team members as well as the heroes discussed in this book.

ACKNOWLEDGEMENTS

I honor and thank my dear friend, professional dancer, and life coach par excellence Lisa Nunziella, who never gives up on me, and who remains by my side while relearning some of my dance moves, essential to my confidence, performance, and overall wellness.

I also give thanks to my long-time friend Helen Rahder who graciously assumed the role of head proofreader of my final edit.

My entire HeartWise staff must be commended for all that they do for both me and my practice. Mary Sullens, my dear friend and office manager, has always believed in me. I can't thank her enough for her dedicated service.

Invaluable describes my long-term friend Angela Winter, RN, BSN. Angela became the nurse coordinator for my newly formed lipid clinic twenty plus years ago. An incredible educator and organizer, she was my right-hand assistant for the EARTHING study and its effect on hypertension. The study was eventually published.

Berkeley Stewart, my web designer, has gifted me her enormous talent for which I am most grateful. Her handling of my branding has been nothing short of fantastic.

James D. Rosenthal played an vital role as a collaborator. He helped me create the vision for the big picture of how this book could tell a story that was personal, inspirational, and groundbreaking in its genre.

One of the most pivotal roles in my career, and especially this book, goes to my editor and speaking coach Jack Barnard. Jack was the one who branded me *The Medical Advocate*. I credit Jack with upping the ante as it relates to my speaking. Furthermore, he introduced me to a more current way of writing, using shorter sentences and paragraphs.

I thank my loving partner Anthony Santos who clearly took a back seat over the last several years while this book became my major "part-time" project, second only to my busy practice. Tony played a huge role in the artistic design of my Instagram posts, as well as various HeartWise videos. I am most proud and grateful for his cover design for this book. His support and patience in dealing with me has been vital. Sadly, Tony left us on 11/28/22 after a long and valiant battle with advanced kidney cancer. His contribution remains indelibly present in this book and in my heart forever.

Finally, a special thanks to all my patients over the years. They have been amongst my greatest teachers. Their faith and support in me have been invaluable and greatly appreciated.

FOREWORD

By Stephen Sinatra, MD, FACC

THERE IS NO DOUBT ABOUT IT! Heart disease (HD) remains the Number One killer of both men and women in 2021. So, when a board-certified cardiologist writes a book about his own heart attack, we need to seriously listen and take in the personal message. And indeed, *From Both Sides of the Table: When Doctor Becomes Patient* is not only personal, it is full of hope, inspiration, and vital messages that can save your life.

Not only is the author an expert on HD, he developed the very same acute event that he tries to prevent in his very own patients. In fact, I know of no other board-certified cardiologist who performs delicate invasive cardiac procedures on a day-to-day basis who succumbed to what we call an acute myocardial infarction (MI). And I have been in the field of invasive cardiology for decades! It must have come as the biggest shock to the cardiologist himself: Dr. Howard Elkin, a busy, well-renowned heart specialist treating countless cardiac patients in Los Angeles County.

Is Dr. Elkin a Medical Advocate? Of course! How difficult to be the ultimate advocate--as well as an expert in everything related to the heart--and abruptly find yourself on "the other side of the table" as the patient. I resonate completely with my fellow colleague as he describes what this "role reversal" has been like for him. For just a simple example he shares that, instead of being the physician performing an angiogram on his own patient, he finds himself the patient having another physician doing the procedure on him!

Talk about a mind-blowing turn of events! Imagine being on the other side of a surgical procedure you have performed routinely for decades. Imagine listening as one of your colleagues explains the status of your own coronary arteries. Psychologically, "role reversal" is an understatement! The emotional and physical suffering that Dr. Elkin experienced first with his heart attack, then with relentless back pain and subsequent surgery, is a testimony to the ultimate endurance of the human spirit.

As a cardiologist myself, I can attest to what Dr. Elkin and I have both faced in our lengthy and demanding medical training. The long hours, endless night call with little-to-no sleep, the harmful radiation of emergency procedures, and the emotional grief and turmoil dealing with life-and-death situations in emergencies: it is all sometimes overwhelming. It can and does impact the core of our beings.

So, when this author describes his journey from healer to patient facing painful, tedious, and meticulous rehab challenges, he again speaks from both sides of the aisle: from that of both the patient and the physician point-of-view.

Offering genuine pearls of wisdom gleaned from his pain and suffering, Elkin states, "embrace your power and trust your thoughts and intuition." At one point during his hospital stay he was "incredibly stressed, paralyzed post-surgery while on opiates" and yet having to do the work of the hospital staff in obtaining authorization from his insurance company to gain transfer to the physical rehab unit.

"I was truly my own Medical Advocate and unfortunately I had to battle it alone."

Later in the book he reiterates how being on both sides of the table reinforced his insights.

"As a physician and patient, I trust that the body can heal. I believe that my higher power is the ultimate healer."

Again, profound words of wisdom with which any patient—any doctor—can resonate. Later, more words of wisdom follow as this physician explains his "secret sauce" as to how you can become your own best Medical Advocate. His personal message of how he came to healing the mind, body, and spirit becomes realized in subsequent pages of the book.

For example, as a physician who has embraced the Mediterranean diet for decades, I was delighted that Dr. Elkin had similar

FOREWORD

recommendations. His approach to nutritional supplementation is not only accurate but complementary to his overall wellness program. Of course, I am always delighted when another boarded cardiologist strongly suggests CoEnzyme Q10 in the care of his patients. Dr. Elkin's anti-aging advice is yet another pearl as is his hormonal recommendations. In fact, this book offers vital recommendations for men and women, as well as for young and old.

To summarize, this doctor has delivered a very important book with multiple words of wisdom. I agree with most, if not practically all of the content. If you take in his insights and recommendations, I strongly believe you will "raise your own vibration" in thwarting off illness and suffering.

I hope you enjoy this very personal book from the heart of a cardiologist who has not only sacrificed and suffered, but who now offers a solid blueprint and plan for wellness…and perhaps for longevity as well.

— Stephen Sinatra, MD, FACC

Sadly, Dr. Sinatra passed away on June 19, 2022. He left us with an amazing legacy.

FOREWORD

By Suzanne Somers

THE HEART IS THE 'ENGINE OF THE BODY'. Without a well working heart there is no life quality, yet our biggest killer is heart disease. Clearly, the present allopathic paradigm needs changing.

Enter Dr. Elkin, a cutting-edge integrative cardiologist with a new option; a major emphasis on prevention using the best of alternatives. With so much misinformation regarding cholesterol and things we thought held the answer, we continue to die. Overuse of statins, blood pressure medicine and diuretics have tremendous deleterious side effects. How about approaching heart health in a new way that doesn't include pharmaceuticals unless there is no other option?

Dr. Elkin is an integrative cardiologist focused on prevention rather than waiting for a catastrophic event and then climbing uphill. This is the kind of doctor I seek for the care of my heart.

And when your doctor also becomes the patient, as Dr. Elkin did, you benefit from his or her experience because the physician has been 'there'. Dr Elkin is a cardiologist who had a heart attack. As his patient I knew Dr. Elkin would 'rethink his approach' as a result of his own personal experience.

I already knew that he was integrative but I wondered what he learned from his experience as a patient. I am very satisfied with the end result—this fine book.

I admire Dr. Elkin, and I truly appreciate his journey. As you will read, it has not been easy, but he has made it work for him. A negative turned into a positive.

ENJOY, SUZANNE SOMERS

INTRODUCTION

HAVING PRACTICED CARDIOLOGY FOR OVER THIRTY YEARS, I have witnessed quite a bit of change in the way medical care has been provided in this country. Along with computerization and automation come many time-saving graces. However, with technology comes a certain degree of depersonalization. I embrace technology. We are living in a fast-paced world that demands expedient results.

But what are we losing in return? Over a span of many years, surveys have repeatedly shown that the number one complaint patients have with their medical providers is that they don't feel heard. "My doctor always has one foot out the door," is a frequent quote from patients. With the advent of HMOs and large group practices, especially in this climate of specialization, patients often feel slighted.

This is nothing new. I saw the writing on the wall in the first few years of my solo practice. Patients were flocking to HMOs because of financial reasons. But over time, many of them returned. They opted for more personal care.

In 1994 I created HeartWise Fitness Institute to address a more holistic approach to health care delivery. I hired a nutritionist and an athletic trainer to assist me with this endeavor.

This was natural progression for me since I had been an athlete and diet and exercise were always huge components of my lifestyle. We took members of the community to supermarkets and taught them how to shop and how to read food labels. We held programs at local restaurants that obliged with healthy menu preparation. We stress tested our patients and subsequently wrote exercise prescriptions for them.

Additionally, I became interested in the teachings of "alternative" physicians such as Andrew Weil, M.D. and Bernie Siegel, M.D. The former nebulous term "healing" took on a different meaning for me.

By the end of the 90s I knew inwardly that I just had to write a book. I possessed this voice that needed to be heard. I even had a preliminary title: *Reclaiming the Soul of Medicine*. There was a purpose behind this book. These were the objectives:

1. To encourage patients to tap into their intrinsic ability to heal
2. To motivate and mentor patients to adopt a consciousness of wellness
3. To foster healing on physical, mental, emotional, and spiritual levels
4. To train patients to take responsibility for the state of their health
5. To encourage patients to look "outside the box" and to explore an integrative and alternative approach when appropriate

These are the same tenets I use today when speaking about those who become their own Medical Advocate. Such individuals remain in the driver's seat when it comes to their health.

But I wasn't ready to launch my book at that time. There were a few missing pieces. The funny thing was that I was unsure where these loopholes resided. Everything came to a halt, an impasse.

First, I needed to learn more than what I had been taught in medical school and in all my postgraduate years in both internal medicine and cardiology. I became interested in the anti-aging movement. Suddenly things started falling into place. The year was 2000 and we were entering the new millennium.

My interest in integrative medicine really took off and I held my first weekend retreat in Santa Barbara in the spring of that year: *The Power of Healing: Healthy Tools for the New Millenium*.

Although most of the attendees were my own patients, it didn't much matter. I saw the positive effect of this event in bringing together integrative medical providers. It was so well received that

INTRODUCTION

I held a second event a year later in Palm Desert.

From there I took the fellowship sponsored by the American Academy of Anti-Aging Medicine. I underwent the requisite and rigorous educational modules, and the appropriate board examinations. Subsequently I became board-certified in anti-aging and regenerative medicine.

Here I was introduced to the concept of functional medicine; learning what causes what, as opposed to treating patients with a Band-Aid approach. In medicine we may not always have the answer, but we can't be content without attempting to learn the cause and effect. That's how I define functional medicine.

My practice has grown considerably over the last few years. Today I utilize an integrative body-mind approach. Whether it's a cardiac patient, a menopausal patient on bioidentical hormones, or someone with a functional bowel disorder, I endeavor to find the cause and treat it accordingly.

This is not a cookie-cutter approach. It often requires an enormous amount of time. We perform advanced laboratory testing which aids in honing in on a specific diagnosis and treatment.

But this is what accounts for the difference between my solo practice and the large, highly automated group practices. One is not necessarily better than the other. But there is a tradeoff. It's all about filling the needs of the individual patient. One size clearly does not fit all. This is how I choose to practice medicine.

So, I've learned a lot. But there was one missing piece. I needed to become an actual patient!

I was hospitalized emergently for two unrelated conditions in a nineteen-month span. Becoming a patient was probably the most humbling experience of my life.

It clearly has made me a better doctor. I am certainly more empathic as I truly understand the plight of the individual patient striving to recover from a serious illness.

Most importantly, I learned where the current medical model fails. Our individual health lies in our own hands.

Yes, we must continue to expect nothing but excellence from our physicians, nurses, and hospitals. But make no mistake about it; if you think your doctor, your health provider, your hospital, your insurance plan or Medicare is going to save you, you will clearly be disappointed.

As a patient who sustained an unexpected complication from back surgery, I learned that I had to truly step up to the plate. As a result of these two hospitalizations, I learned that the onus was on me to achieve optimal health and wellness.

Being an inpatient twice in a short period of time sets the stage for this book. Oddly enough, the objectives set forth from my original title, *Reclaiming the Soul of Medicine* remain equally relevant today. But again, it's as if I had to become an actual patient for all this to gel.

The title changed to *From Both Sides of the Table: When Doctor Becomes Patient*. Whenever I perform a cardiac catheterization or a physical exam on a patient I am generally on the right side of the examining table. But this time was different. I was actually *on the table itself.* This is not where a physician normally wishes or expects to be!

During both hospitalizations and thereafter, I continued to do the utmost to stay in the driver's seat when it came to my health and wellness. As incredible as it may sound, I'm still doing it. My work on myself never ends.

I eventually became known as The Medical Advocate. Yes, I did the necessary work to obtain this position. Now it's your turn. It's not enough for me to be your Medical Advocate. You have to step up to the plate and do the same.

That's what this book is all about. It's about you taking the lead and becoming your own best Medical Advocate. It's both possible and doable. But there's no free lunch here. Although it requires work on your part, the rewards are immeasurable.

INTRODUCTION

The book is divided into five parts:

PART 1 is my actual story. I'm a cardiologist who happened to sustain a mild heart attack. Being clueless at the time, I was in complete denial. How did that happen? How can I prevent a future cardiac event? What can you do to prevent such a mishap?

Seventeen months later I was back at Cedars-Sinai Medical Center in need of emergency back surgery. My surgery was complicated by permanent nerve damage. I was very much broken. I worked hard to recover, but I didn't do it alone. I assembled my "Dream-Team" and aimed for the stars. It's not about looking back, but about pushing forward.

PART 2 is the medical or factual component where you will learn about the various risk factors for heart disease, both major and minor players. The less appreciated risk factor, *stress*, will be highlighted in detail.

PART 3 introduces the concept of the Medical Advocate. You will read about individuals who did what was necessary to take control of their health. This underscores the fact that you don't need to be a doctor or medical professional to be your own best Medical Advocate. Furthermore, there is a section on assembling your Dream-Team. *You don't have to do this alone.*

PART 4 is the "how to" portion where I describe both a patient's bill of rights *and* a patient's responsibilities. Knowledge of both is essential when transforming oneself to the role of the Medical Advocate. When speaking about medical advocacy, I discuss the importance of the 5 dimensions of health:

- Physical well-being
- Mental well-being
- Emotional well-being
- Spiritual well-being
- Social well-being

Chapters on nutrition, supplements, exercise, stress management and longevity follow. All these topics are crucial when seeking optimal health and wellness. I attempt to separate fact from fancy. The chapters in this section are not meant to be isolated subjects. You will discover how all of this is intertwined.

PART 5 is the unexpected part that was not supposed to happen. In May 2015, I experienced a serious setback, a major blow to both my unstable spine and my pre-existing nerve damaged right foot and ankle. This was truly the unplanned part of the book. It certainly was not part of my outline. Its content is written extemporaneously in a journal-type style.

Truly a work in progress, I never really know what tomorrow may bring. But I know one thing. Giving up is not an option for me. My zeal and passion are not unique to me. All of you have it to some extent. My wish is for you to tap into that energy and your individual resources to become your own best Medical Advocate.

After all, whose body is it? It's your body. I ask you to give yourself permission to embark on a healthy adventure in this short journey that all of us share, called LIFE.

Yours in health,
HOWARD K. ELKIN, MD, FACC

From Both Sides of the Table
When Doctor Becomes Patient

PART ONE

My Journey

CHAPTER 1

DENIAL – IT AIN'T JUST A RIVER IN EGYPT

Only in Hollywood do you find valet parking at the emergency room. As I screeched up to the curb, I simply told the valet captain, "Please take my car." He tore off a ticket stub, shoved it into my hand and said, "Park over there, pay the fee, then come back and give me your keys." I turned to him and impatiently yelled out, "Buddy, I'm having a heart attack!"

I awoke at 2:00 that morning with what I thought was heartburn. This was a rather unusual sensation for me, and I figured it was a late-night meal that had interrupted my sleep. It lasted approximately five minutes, and I was able to doze off again.

I subsequently reawakened at 5:00 with a similar sensation. This was a bit more intense than the first episode. This time the discomfort lasted longer, more like fifteen minutes in duration. I actually became frightened at this point. I got out of bed to search my medicine cabinet to see if there was some relief in a bottle such as Mylanta or Pepto Bismol.

To my dismay there was none, which wasn't too surprising since I rarely, if ever, experience heartburn. I went back to bed, did some deep breathing to calm myself, and fell back asleep.

The next thing I knew it was 8:00 am. I felt fine at this point with no discomfort whatsoever. I showered, shaved, dressed, and headed to the office. I thought it wise to skip breakfast until my digestive system caught up with last night's dinner.

Per my usual routine, I saw patients, wrote in charts, prescribed medications, and scheduled cardiac tests. Suddenly at 11:30, I broke out in a cold sweat. I attributed this to hypoglycemia, since I hadn't had breakfast. But what was different about this episode was that I wasn't jittery or nervous, as I usually am when I am low in blood sugar. There was no pain or discomfort, just an intense cold sweat. I yelled out to my nurse, "Heide, can you perform an EKG on me?" The tracing was unremarkable, and the sensation passed within minutes. I went on with my day, leaving the office at about 2:00 pm, as Thursday is normally a half day for me.

I proceeded to drive to Golds Gym Venice on the west side of town for my standing appointment with my trainer. I figured at least I would be in close proximity to my physician if any further symptoms occurred!

The workout went well, with no additional discomfort of any kind. My trainer, however, looked at me in a strange way and muttered, "Are you ok, Doc? You don't seem your usual self." To that I replied, "I'm fine, Charles. I'm just a little stressed today."

Encouraged by my workout, I decided to linger in the gym a bit longer to work my abdominals on one of those ubiquitous ab benches. Suddenly, a new sensation developed. Both arms felt incredibly heavy. There was no chest pain, no more heartburn, but a feeling that I had never experienced before.

The discomfort wasn't persistent, and somehow, I managed to climb the stairs to take a shower. In the locker room while getting dressed, the "heartburn" returned. Being ravenously hungry since I had not eaten in eighteen hours, my likely explanation was stomach acid caused by intense hunger.

I had a plausible explanation for every symptom!

My prescription: head straight to the nearest restaurant and order the biggest item on the menu! So, I made a pit stop at the Firehouse, a bodybuilder's hangout where healthy food is served. Waiting at the counter for my buffalo burger to arrive, the arm heaviness returned with vengeance.

There I was all alone at the bar stool trying to fuel my appetite while experiencing intense heaviness down both arms. This time I

CHAPTER 1: Denial – It Ain't Just a River in Egypt

was scared. I'm a cardiologist, experiencing intermittent heartburn and heaviness in my upper limbs.

I had run out of excuses for my symptoms.

What do I do now? I called my best friend Barry. "Barry, something is wrong. My arms feel as if they weigh fifty pounds each."

I am a competitive bodybuilder. This seemed to be no surprise to Barry. "Howard, your arms do weigh 50 pounds each!"

I replied fearfully, "No Barry, this is real!"

He said, "For God's sake, Howard, this sounds like a medical problem. You need to phone your doctor right away."

I phoned my personal physician who advised me to go to Cedars-Sinai Medical Center post-haste. His exact words were, *"It would look pretty ridiculous if a cardiologist dropped dead of a heart attack without being evaluated."*

I don't know if it was because I felt comforted by my physician or what, but suddenly all my symptoms seemed to vanish. Finally, I had a plan: to get to the hospital as per my doctor's orders.

But wait, I had to make one final stop before getting on the freeway. I decided to pay a quick visit to one of my favorite coffee houses, the Urth Café in Santa Monica. I just had to have a large cappuccino and a triple chocolate cookie for the road!

This was a weekly treat for me. I actually recall saying to myself, "Gee, I don't know when I'll be back here, so I might as well indulge myself before battling the traffic."

There was no rationale for any of my actions. I don't know what I was thinking.

Hell, I wasn't thinking! This had to be the most surreal experience of my life.

Making my way through rush-hour traffic at 4:30 pm on the 10 freeway, it took ninety minutes to travel the fifteen miles from Santa Monica to Beverly Hills.

As I inched my way across town, I decided to make three important phone calls. The first was to my eldest daughter DeAnna. I said calmly "Honey, meet me at the Emergency Room at Cedars. I think

I'm having a heart attack."

She replied, "Dad, are you driving? Pull off the road and dial 911!"

I told her I wasn't about to leave my Mercedes on the side of the freeway.

"Forget about your car! What would you instruct your patients to do?"

I resisted and next phoned my older sister Renée in New Jersey. Again, I muttered, "Renée, I'm on the way to the hospital. I might be having a heart attack."

Her immediate response was, "Well, did you take an aspirin?"

"No," I said, "I don't carry aspirin with me!"

"You're a damn doctor, Howard. Everyone knows you're supposed to take an aspirin if you think you might be having a heart attack."

Since I didn't like those two responses, I decided to go for call # 3: my good friend Monte in Palm Springs.

Again, the words just seemed to come out glibly without full realization of their meaning. "Monte, I think I may be having a heart attack and I'm driving myself to Cedars-Sinai."

"Did you take an aspirin?"

I barked back impatiently, "What is it with you guys and aspirin? I don't carry aspirin with me and I'm not going off the freeway to find some. I'll call you later after I make it to the hospital."

Within five minutes of hitting the front door of the Emergency Room, I was put on a gurney and evaluated by the ER physician who had me chew an aspirin. It tasted so bad that I thought I was going to vomit. In amazement I blurted out, "What about oxygen and an intravenous line?"

Her reply: "Only after you chew that aspirin whole."

An EKG was subsequently taken. Unlike the one taken in my office earlier that day, this second tracing was clearly abnormal. Fifteen minutes later I was seen by the cardiology fellow who informed me I was going to the cardiac catheterization laboratory for an emergency angiogram.

I was concerned, but somehow the day's events had yet to make

CHAPTER 1: Denial – It Ain't Just a River in Egypt

complete sense to me. I couldn't imagine that in my great shape I could be a candidate for a heart attack. I didn't smoke or drink. I ate well, exercised regularly, had normal blood pressure and cholesterol, and had no familial history of heart disease.

Heart attack? Not ME!!!

My daughter DeAnna did make it to the Emergency Room and indeed she was a great source of comfort. Everyone else around me had the look of doom and gloom. I kissed her good-bye as I was wheeled to the cardiac cath lab.

After being transferred from the gurney to the cath lab table, I started to look around. I was in familiar surroundings. I looked to my right and to my left. I saw the X-ray tube, the camera, the graphics screen, the monitoring chamber, as well as all the physicians and nurses.

It suddenly dawned on me, "Seriously, Howard. This is no false alarm. You *are* having a heart attack!" I'd been a practicing cardiologist for nearly twenty-five years. I've done this procedure on countless patients.

Usually, I'm the operator at the right side of the table. Now, I was no longer on the right side, but on the table itself—the wrong place for a practicing interventional cardiologist!

I found myself in a completely new role. I went from doctor to patient in a matter of minutes.

At this point there was a moment of realization. *I took in a deep breath and completely surrendered.* I was calm, collected and pain-free. Furthermore, I knew I wasn't going to die. It just wasn't my time, and I knew I was in excellent hands.

The nurse asked if I wanted to be sedated. I replied, "No, thank you." After all, I felt perfectly comfortable. I then said to the entire cath lab staff, "I want to be awake for my procedure, and I'd like to have a role in deciding what type of stent I receive!"

There was no more denial. This event would drastically change my life.

CHAPTER 2

THE CATH LAB EXPERIENCE

So here I was in the cardiac cath lab on the evening of November 16, 2006.

When it dawned on me that this was not a false alarm, I realized that I was in the throngs of a heart attack.

And this is where I needed to be at this precise time.

It was late 2006. There was quite a bit of controversy at that time as to whether a stent should be bare metal or drug-eluting (coated with a drug) in the setting of an acute heart attack. The staff, including the attending cardiologist seemed amazed when I calmly stated I wanted to be awake during the procedure.

I'll never forget the moment when the cardiologist injected dye from a catheter lodged in my right groin into my coronary artery.

WHAM! The first camera shot shocked us.

He suddenly exclaimed, "Wow! Did you see that?"

Hell yeah, I saw it...to my chagrin. It was a *huge blood clot* in the most important of the three coronary arteries, the left anterior descending (LAD), commonly known as the *"widow maker."*

Being that I was completely awake, calm, and resplendent with all my mental faculties, he asked, "Mind if we extract that ugly looking clot?"

My response: "By all means, be my guest."

It was like an out-of-body experience. Surreal. As if it was happening to someone other than me. Rarely would I describe myself, as a low-key, complacent kind of guy. This time around, however, nothing seemed to bother me.

The interventional cardiologist and I had full discourse during the entire procedure. Despite being a patient, he treated me as a colleague. He extracted that huge clot with what is known as a thrombectomy catheter.

Then he collected it in a mesh-like container and showed it to me. It wasn't pretty. He asked me, "Doctor, how successful have you been in extracting a clot *this big* during an emergency procedure?"

"Not often," was my response. This was the largest blood clot I had ever seen. It occupied about 95% of the cross-sectional area of the artery. In other words, had it been any larger, the artery would have been completely filled with clot, and I would have suffered a massive, possibly fatal, heart attack.

Yet, just a few hours earlier, I had shunned the advice of my sister and friend when they begged me to take an aspirin. Let's be real here. These lay people were more helpful to me in the throngs of a heart attack than I was to myself!

Indeed, *aspirin is ALWAYS administered* during an acute cardiac event to keep the platelets, a component of blood, from clumping together. I don't know what I was thinking, other than getting to the hospital through rush hour traffic on one of LA's busiest freeways.

I certainly didn't ask myself *what a reasonable cardiologist would do* in this case. Nor did I even consider that *my life was in imminent danger.* I was acting as many of my male patients have over the years.

With regard to my symptoms…**I was in complete denial.**

Following the extraction of the clot, the affected artery was open, and I was out of danger. I was left with a blockage that appeared to be less than 50% in severity. This is often the case with acute heart attacks.

However, to hopefully avoid any recurrence, the artery was subsequently stented. The end result was an artery that looked entirely normal in appearance.

For the record, "we" decided on a bare metal stent only because my arteries were huge, the size of a six-foot-five-inch football player. At that time drug-eluting stents did not come in my size! That seemed pretty surprising to a man who stood five feet nine inches on a good day.

CHAPTER 2: The Cath Lab Experience

Then it was all over. The entire procedure lasted less than an hour. A huge blood clot had been extracted from my LAD, and in its place was a stainless-steel wire mesh, commonly known as a stent.

This procedure saved my life, and it was the mere beginning of a long journey. I would subsequently learn how to become my own best **Medical Advocate** *by taking charge of my health,* and essentially *my life.*

CHAPTER 3

LIFE AS AN INPATIENT

The Start of My Journey

UNDER NORMAL CIRCUMSTANCES a patient is admitted from the Emergency Room (ER) to either Critical Care or the hospital floor. Not so in the case of someone experiencing a heart attack.

We make a life-saving detour from the ER directly to the cath lab. Surviving the intervention, we are then transported to the Critical Care Unit, where we have to lie flat with a catheter lodged in our groin for several hours.

Fortunately, we are living in an age when coronary intervention is not only possible, but is the preferred emergency treatment for someone in the throngs of a heart attack. When it comes to survival, this is one area where Western medicine is unequivocally superior.

However, the above *only holds true if one makes it to the ER alive.* The reason why there has been such hoopla about getting to the hospital shortly after symptom onset is this: TIME IS MUSCLE— heart muscle, in this case!

Being that I was not in touch with the severity of my symptoms, it was a miracle that my outcome was so positive. I was quite lucky, as I was experiencing a "stuttering" heart attack with symptoms that were intermittent. The majority of victims experience symptoms that are incessant and more obvious.

Mine was a disaster waiting to happen.

The fact remains: one should never sit on their symptoms as I did. There is no time to wait and ponder. It's all about getting to the hospital as fast as possible.

Being safe is a lot better than being sorry!

After the emergency intervention in the cath lab where the blood clot was extracted and a stent deployed, I was happily transported via gurney to a true hospital bed in the CCU. By this time, it was after 10:00 pm and I was pretty exhausted from the day's activities.

Being a Patient. It didn't take me long to realize how life would be as an inpatient. My sleep was constantly interrupted by nurses taking my vital signs, drawing vial after vial of blood, taking electrocardiograms (EKGs) and probing me to see if I had any recurrence of chest pain.

Then they repeatedly asked if I needed something to help me sleep or relax. I refused any such medication. Truthfully, I never have a problem sleeping—except for when being awakened by the nursing staff! Given the setting, I was as relaxed as any person could be.

Feeling perfectly fine after my procedure, I was hoping to be discharged the very next day. To my dismay, I learned that my cardiologist wanted to keep me another two days.

I then discovered that taking a shower was a privilege, not a right. Imagine having an aid accompany me to the bathroom while waiting for me to complete my shower. I felt as if my independence was suddenly stolen from me.

It wasn't fun. One day I'm training at Golds Gym in Venice, and the next day an aide has to walk me to and from the shower room.

I did receive some very positive news that first day, post-procedure. While carefully observing the ultrasound technician perform an echocardiogram on me, I saw with my own eyes the condition of my heart. There was *no evidence of any heart muscle damage* as a result of my coronary event.

My ticker was just fine and I was a very lucky man.

As I previously mentioned, I felt surprisingly relaxed in my hospital bed, just bored out of my mind. I'm certainly not one used to a sedentary existence, much less lying in bed all day. Being hooked up to EKG wires in the CCU, the most distance I could walk was a mere fifteen feet. What kind of challenge was that?

CHAPTER 3: Life as an Inpatient

With all that time on my hands, all I could realistically do was either get lost watching television, or do some serious work on myself. Not being a TV kind of guy, I chose the latter.

I was determined to make the most of my hospital stay. I worked on my breathing…I meditated…I prayed…and I asked both God and myself how in the hell did I end up here? The funny thing is that it took me no time to figure this out.

The stress I had incurred over the past five years was enormous. It took a major toll on my health and well-being. This was no accident. It was a major wake-up call!

I knew that work had to be done, and that the time was ripe.

Naturally, my office staff was worried about me as was my eldest daughter. I reassured them that I was fine and that I would take the next week off from work. I would use that time to simply relax and regroup. This decision was an easy one since it was Thanksgiving week and there were only three full workdays.

But I did have one very difficult task at hand. What was I going to say to my seventeen-year-old daughter who was in an adolescent residential unit for eating disorders?

I was split. Part of me was extremely worried because she was still in a fragile state. I certainly didn't want any negative repercussions.

But another part of me came to the realization that enough was enough. I was unable to withhold this information from her. She had to know that her father had taken ill, and that *he could no longer hold the whole world on his shoulders.*

While still in the hospital I phoned her therapist and we mutually decided that she would be the one to inform my daughter that I was in the hospital. The last thing I wanted was for her to feel compelled to visit me. When confronted with this issue, Marisa emphatically said to her therapist, "I want to go see my dad. Can you please bring me to the hospital?"

Within two hours my daughter was driven to the hospital to visit me. There was her big strong father in bed wearing a hospital gown. What a heartfelt visit that was. It was if my daughter forgot about her own problems long enough to place her dad first.

I don't have to mention that this was major for any adolescent, especially an inpatient with a serious eating disorder. This was a *turning point for both father and daughter.* She realized that she had to pull it together, and that dad had some limitations now.

She went back to the unit where she resided for the previous two months and worked incredibly hard. Within one month, she was discharged and was able to return to school, while attending therapy sessions as an outpatient.

Sunday, November 19, was my date of discharge. I shall never forget the words of the attending cardiologist as he said good-bye to me. "Dr. Elkin, I have to say that I have never been, nor will I ever be in the physical shape that you are in right now! I don't even know how to counsel you about cardiac rehabilitation and exercise, since you could obviously teach it. So, I have to conclude that you are on your own here."

I was baffled, but looking at him and then looking at myself, I knew that he was correct! "Hmm," I muttered to myself, "guess I'm up to the challenge."

But then he ended the conversation with something that absolutely floored me. "But everything is going to be just fine. You have a new stent in that artery, and you are going to do great."

As he left, a thought flashed in my mind that would forever change how I care for myself and how I manage the care of my patients: if everything is fine and I'm going to be great with this new stent, what do I have to do to stay in this "great condition"?

I knew inwardly that although he meant well, this BS was absurd! Seriously, I was already in great shape as he quickly pointed out. How did I get here in the first place and, most importantly, how was I going to prevent a recurrence?

Little did I know that *this was truly a new beginning for me.* Yes, receiving that stent and the excellent care at Cedars-Sinai Medical Center saved my life. But that certainly was not going to be the end-all-be-all.

CHAPTER 3: Life as an Inpatient

As a cardiologist, I knew quite well that *coronary heart disease can be a malignant disorder.* One heart attack and a stent can lead to another heart attack and another stent. Furthermore, one bypass procedure can certainly lead to another. I've seen this scenario too often in my practice.

It would definitely be *up to me and not the medical establishment* to avoid future recurrences. This was the very beginning of *me taking control of my health,* and *remaining in the **driver's seat.***

Eventually this would be the philosophy that I would instill in my patients—as I became known as the **Medical Advocate.**

CHAPTER 4

COMING HOME

Now the Work Begins

A MERE FIVE MINUTES after my cardiologist discharged me, informing me that I was going to be "just fine" with my new stent, my eldest daughter appeared in my hospital room to drive me home.

Prophetic as it may seem, she had a writing tablet in her hand and she said enthusiastically, "Dad, it's time to write your book! The world needs to hear your story."

I figured I was up to the challenge that literally began that day.

Fifteen minutes after arriving home, I was sitting alone at my kitchen table wondering what I was going to do over the next week. How was I going to use my time? What was my next move? I certainly had never had this much time for myself to do absolutely nothing.

Design Your Own Rehab. The words of my cardiologist kept echoing in my head. "When it comes to rehab, Dr. Elkin, you are on your own. You could teach the subject."

Well, he wasn't wrong. When I was a senior fellow in the department of cardiology at Northwestern University in Chicago, I helped supervise an out-patient program in cardiac rehab. Moreover, when I was employed by a large multi-specialty group in Southern California the year following my fellowship, I worked with a team to formulate cardiac rehab programs.

I knew what I needed to do, but suddenly I was in the role of patient and I had to comply with a program myself.

This apparent no-brainer was no easy task. Cardiac rehab programs incorporate progressive exercise while one's heart rate and rhythm are monitored. Then there is emphasis on a healthy cardiac diet along with stress management. But most patients enrolled in a formal program are considerably older than I was at that time. Furthermore, they are most often overweight, have poor eating habits, and haven't done any form of exercise in years.

This explains precisely why the doctor said I would have to invent my own program. Being in a typical cardiac rehab program would not only have been a waste of time for me, but it also would not have met my specific needs.

It would have set me into a tailspin, a terrible depression. Furthermore, I had no discernible heart muscle damage. From a prognostic standpoint, this placed me in the most favorable position; therefore, there was no real need for me to be monitored while performing progressive exercise. I didn't really need any instruction on a healthy heart diet since I had been following such a diet for years.

In addition, I was in that 50% group of individuals who had *sustained a heart attack with normal cholesterol levels*. Surely, I needed cardiac rehabilitation. Change was clearly in order. But I didn't need a formal out-patient hospitalized program when I was generally in better physical shape than the nurses and exercise physiologists supervising these programs.

So, this was my challenge: How was I actually going to design my own individual cardiac rehab? Slowing down both physically and emotionally was clearly needed.

For the next week I decided to place my work as a physician on hold. That meant answering no phone calls and tackling no patient-related problems. That was difficult since I had always been so involved in my work.

I realized that *a change in mindset was necessary*. Therefore, I made the conscious decision that this WAS indeed going to be vacation of sorts, a reprieve from my regular lifestyle. It would also be a valuable time to regroup. I remember saying to myself, "What would I recommend to an athletic, youngish, middle-aged male who had sustained a similar event?"

CHAPTER 4: Coming Home

I had to step outside of myself to find the appropriate answer.

A Step at a Time. "Walking...why that is the basis of any physical rehabilitation program, isn't it?" That's what stood out in my mind. So, I decided to begin walking twenty minutes twice a day, increasing by five minutes daily as tolerated.

I was fortunate to be living in a beautiful neighborhood in a rather hilly area with spectacular views. Walking suddenly took on a new meaning. I had always been an athlete, more specifically a runner, so this was the first time that I remember walking in my neighborhood.

Taking a casual stride initially, I had time to experience the scents of the flowers, the colors, chirping birds, barking dogs, water running from automatic sprinklers, the visual beauty of the gardens, and my neighbors.

I finally understood what it meant to "slow down and smell the roses."

I continued with my walking twice a day for the next month, changing routes ever so slightly for a little variety. Endurance was never a problem for me. Unlike many cardiac patients, I was easily able to increase my activity by five minutes twice daily. I eventually leveled out at forty-five minutes twice a day.

What I noticed to be most uncanny was that I was clearly in the present moment during these periods. Work-related problems, as well as financial and personal stress seemed to somehow vanish. Without even trying I was in that zone that folks often talk about.

This was no small detail for a guy who only seemed to know the fast lane. Prior to this, I had never even realized that a gray zone existed. Formerly, everything had to be either black or white. As a result, I was often unyielding and impatient in dealing with both myself and others.

Relax...Breathe. The next feat was to start a regular meditation practice. I call it a feat simply because it was not a natural phenomenon for me. Interestingly enough, I had been teaching patients for years how to deep-breathe, how to meditate, and how to perform body scans and visualizations.

I was a very effective teacher. I had taken numerous workshops on mindfulness training and participated in retreats that focused on both emotional release and meditation. Also, I had read everything I could from all the great spiritual leaders.

Previously, I had often commenced a meditative practice, but I would simply give it up after a few weeks. There was just no time to sit and meditate with so much going on in my life. At least that was what I said to myself.

I was not only wrong, but I was also a big fraud. I was not practicing on a regular basis what I had been preaching for years. I got burned as a result. Being driven to the max while thinking I could do it all was simply faulty thinking.

> *My cardiac event was my **wakeup call**, an **epiphany**.*
> *I discovered the need to slow down.*

Taking that week off from work, I reread *Wherever You Go, There You Are* by Jon Kabat-Zinn. Then I went to Barnes and Noble and purchased audio books by Thich Nhat Hahn. Knowing the pitfalls with my attempts in the past, I decided to make the process easy for myself. Failure was not an option.

I started my meditation practice as soon as I awakened, before even getting out of bed. I timed myself for ten minutes and repeated the practice at night before bed.

Although I have made numerous changes in my practice over the years, I kept to this regimen without deviation for the first two months following my cardiac event.

I would simply focus on one thing: *my breath.*

The logistics of my meditative practice, which is really just an exercise in deep breathing, are very simple. I knew back then that it was essential to my health and well-being. I have continued this practice on a daily basis, and I teach it to my patients as well.

From this point on I became the doctor who "walks his talk."

CHAPTER 4: Coming Home

In essence, the rehab program I developed for myself included simple, mindful walking and a regular meditation practice.

Bless My Stress. But there were other issues to address. Let's not forget what was going on at the time of my heart attack. The stress certainly did not fade away because of my illness! It was up to me. *I had to adapt to the stress at hand.*

The most significant source of stress was my youngest daughter who was in a residential facility for adolescents with a serious eating disorder. The changes in her were monumental.

My illness motivated her to take responsibility for her own healing. Her entire demeanor had changed. I didn't even have to say, "Dad can't do it all anymore, honey." It was if she could read me.

She worked arduously over the next month. She was able to be discharged from the in-patient service by Christmas vacation. She set her goal high and she accomplished it. She returned to her senior year of high school after the first of the year thirty pounds heavier.

Then there was the never-ending saga of settling my ex-wife's estate with my eldest daughter. Under the influence of legal authorities, she fought me all the way until the final settlement. This battle was more divisive than the entire divorce process.

What made it especially difficult was that two of us had always been so close. But the heart attack did change this sordid situation. She came to my aid immediately at the time of my event.

In turn, I made a conscious decision to yield to certain financial constraints. My heart attack taught me that my savings mattered little since I still had a fair amount of time left in my career to recoup the losses. Moreover, keeping the family infrastructure seemed much more important than any dollar mark.

Lastly was the issue of the economics of my cardiology practice. By mid-2004 changes were aplenty in the medical world. I was certainly not immune to these changes.

I had always had a thriving practice, but employers and patients alike were gravitating to Health Maintenance Organizations (HMOs) in Southern California in efforts to reduce medical costs. Having formerly contracted with the major HMO in my area, I was suddenly terminated as an independent contractor, as they began to employ their own cardiologists.

Suddenly my invasive cardiology practice started to diminish, as my service was no longer needed. This loss was not insignificant.

In addition to the legal bills surrounding the divorce and the ongoing battle with my eldest daughter over her mom's estate was the financial drain of my ex-wife's experimental cancer treatment —which was not covered by insurance.

I had certainly experienced some rough financial times prior to my heart attack. Undoubtedly this had a negative effect on my mood and disposition. I had nothing but love for my patients and the practice that I had created since late 1986. But being human, I cannot say that I was unaffected by the change in the economic climate.

After my heart attack I knew inwardly that personal change was necessary for me to not just survive, but to thrive. Before I even stepped back into my office after my recuperative week at home, I configured a new, healthier attitude.

Out went any negative thoughts.

I saw myself in a new role: *a true facilitator of healing who holistically treated the entire patient...body, mind, and soul.*

It's not that my practice standards had changed. I had always taken pride in how I treated my patients as individuals with physical, mental, emotional, and social concerns. But now I saw how vital a role I actually played in their lives.

There was no such thing as a boring patient, an irritating patient, or an overly needy patient. Folks came to me for a reason, to fulfill a need.

In truth, I took an even greater interest in my work, and this really came about quite naturally. It was this change in mindset that prompted my healthier attitude. I believe that my heart attack and my experience as a patient profoundly affected my medical practice.

It had made me a *better doctor,* certainly *more patient* and *empathic.*

CHAPTER 5

LEARNING TO THRIVE

The First Month Out

IT WAS A RATHER EASY DECISION to recuperate at home the first week post hospitalization. Feeling fine physically, it gave me the opportunity to regroup and to orchestrate my individual cardiac rehab program.

Thanksgiving was a simple but lovely affair. My youngest daughter was granted the holiday off from rehab. We celebrated at home with a couple of family friends. This was a holiday where thanks were clearly in order, indeed more than ever before. Having both my daughter and me back home one week after my heart attack was truly a double treat.

The Patient-Doctor. Returning to work the following Monday, I felt ready physically, but somewhat anxious emotionally. There was this sense of ambiguity that seemed so foreign to me. I was about to go from patient back to doctor. Was I truly ready to return to work as caregiver to all the folks who needed me? Did I need more mending or more time?

In truth, I was a bit fearful about relinquishing my sick role!

It seemed odd...concerns like this had never before entered my mind. In the past I had not suffered from work-related anxiety. Parking my car, I suddenly noted this weird, uncomfortable feeling.

I ascended a flight of stairs to my office suite. For the first time ever, I took notice of the sign to the right of my door which read, "Howard K. Elkin M.D., Cardiologist." That's when it hit me. "That's me...and I'm ready to move on!" I recalled the words of my wise mother: "No looking back."

I march forward from this moment on.

My first week was uneventful. My energy was solid, and I continued my daily walks. My first walk took place in the early morning before leaving for work. After arriving home in the late afternoon, I would go out once more.

The anxiety that I had briefly experienced quickly vanished as soon as I entered my office door that Monday. Switching roles was easier than I thought. I truly saw myself in a more vital position as a physician and facilitator of healing. There was merit in every *procedure* I performed, every *question* I answered, and every *prescription* I wrote.

I was learning to appreciate my work more than ever before. It was as if I had to actually get sick to see how important a role I played in people's lives. This was truly a turning point for me, an added bonus in my quest to self-heal.

Out with the Old. That first month post-event proved to be of immense benefit. It set the tone for a new, healthier lifestyle that allowed me to slow down and take notice of my environment. Prior to this I had been so driven that I was unable to enjoy the simple pleasures of life.

Most importantly, I relinquished some of my old stubborn ways which made dealing with family and personal matters a lot less problematic and a lot less dramatic. For example, I started noticing how easy it was for me to get upset over the simplest things such as misplacing my wallet, accidentally dropping something, or tying a knot in my sneakers prior to my daily walk.

I tended to say, "Damn, I can't believe I did something so stupid" ...followed by a few four-letter words that need not be repeated here. Suffice it to say, it didn't take long to realize not only was this *totally ridiculous*, but it was a *complete waste of energy*. It dawned on me that I had adopted this pattern years before my heart attack.

This was anything but self-soothing!

So, out went the negative. Before long I would catch it—before

CHAPTER 5: Learning to Thrive

turning three shades of red—and say to myself, "Stop, cancel, delete… Is this life threatening? Is this really worth getting upset about?"

The answer was always the same. A definite NO!

Oddly enough, I had registered for a life-altering weekend seminar at the recommendation of my voice coach and good friend William, a mere three weeks prior to my heart attack. The timing was obviously uncanny, definitely meant to be. This weekend program, *Insight Seminars*, was a self-healing venture held at the University of Santa Monica.

I vividly remember registering for this seminar, which was more like a weekend retreat in an urbanized setting. It was this description from the website that spoke to me: "Insights Seminars serve to awaken people to the natural beauty, strength, and capability of who they really are. We believe we can help transform the world into one in which everyone wins through increased awareness, loving and personal accountability."

So here I was entering this strange new adventure of personal growth. I knew none of the other attendees or the staff. Moreover, it was a mere two weeks after my heart attack.

Nervous? You bet I was. I may be quite at ease competing at an athletic event or addressing an audience, but that's about performance. I'm a Leo, a natural performer. That is well within my comfort zone.

In actuality, I tend to be a shy introvert, and here I was choosing to put myself in an atmosphere where personal awareness and change was to reign. It was pretty damn scary!

The first exercise involved getting up in front of the room and addressing an audience of fifty or more attendees plus eight staff members. We were asked to describe ourselves in two minutes and to state what interested us in this retreat.

I was sweating bullets. "God, what am I going to say when they call on me?" Fortunately, they asked for volunteers, but after the first ten folks spoke, I couldn't handle the anxiety any longer, so I waved my arm feverishly. I was then chosen to speak.

I remember just standing there in front of the microphone and out came these words: "Hi, my name is Howard. I'm a cardiologist and I actually had a heart attack two weeks ago." After a round of "oohs" and "aahs", the room became so quiet you could hear a pin drop.

Then I blurted out, "but it's okay because I know CPR!" I have no recall of what I said after that, but the audience burst out in both laughter and cheers. I suddenly became the darling of the retreat. It was really nothing more on my part than a spasm of nervousness and the need to come completely clean.

And I think it was the truest moment of my life!

That introduction was the ice breaker. This particular seminar, entitled *Insights I* was one of the most moving personal growth experiences in my life. We were placed in an atmosphere where we could unplug, recharge, and reconnect with ourselves. No cellphones, emails, faxes, and the like.

The subsequent individual and group exercises we did were truly rigorous...and quite mesmerizing as all of us exposed ourselves in a safe and caring environment.

Choice...that was the take-home lesson for me. By taking personal responsibility for my individual life experiences, I felt empowered in every aspect of the word.

My weekend at *Insights* proved to be a gift beyond measure. The fact that it took place just two weeks after my heart attack seems surreal to me today. But there are no accidents. It rounded off the first month of my recovery, and it gave new meaning to my life, in a very real and optimistic way. It not only reshaped some of my career goals, but also changed how I value my role in personal relationships.

All of us can benefit from life-altering healing experiences such as this. I encourage you to do some valuable self-seeking for yourself.

But take heed, you don't have to sustain a heart attack or a life-threatening condition to embrace *Change and Choice*.

CHAPTER 6

NO ONE IS IMMUNE

EVERYTHING JUST SEEMED TO FLOW after the *Insights* seminar late November 2006. Any anxiety I had about surviving a heart attack, while lacking all the usual risk factors, seemed to vanish. *Insights* taught me to forgive the past and to embrace a positive future, one that was predicated on choice, my choice.

Continuing my home-walking program and meditation practice, I did make a few alterations at the beginning of the fourth week post heart attack. Being a competitive bodybuilder since 1998, I was beyond excited to get back in the gym.

My *cardiac rehab program was designed solely by me* for my purpose. So, it was I who decided to take a four-week hiatus from lifting to give my mind, body, and soul a chance to mend.

Now, feeling positive about my progress, I decided it was time to get back into strength training. But first I needed to undergo a stress echocardiographic study, a noninvasive evaluation of potential cardiac risk.

The results could not have been more favorable. There was no discernable heart damage whatsoever. My exercise tolerance was way above average. Furthermore, there was no sign that my heart was deprived of oxygen.

It was time to return to the gym, to my passion, bodybuilding. Normally in the gym four days a week with my trainer, I opted for three days the first week, to ease myself back into the groove. I continued my walking program but limited it to one forty-minute session daily.

Everything just seemed to flow. My strength returned in no time. Indeed, I was very happy being back in an atmosphere which was like a second home to me. The following week I was back to training four days in the gym. It felt as if I had never left.

Life Without Heide. But all things came to an abrupt halt Christmas Eve when my beloved nurse Heide suddenly became deathly ill. The week before Christmas is often a bit slow as people prefer to use that time shopping, rather than visiting their physician!

I recall casually sitting in my office joking with Heide and my good friend Monte early Friday afternoon, December 22. All the patients of the day had been seen. We shared a few fun, joyous moments.

On Tuesday, December 26, I received the most shocking news of my life. My office manager phoned and informed me that Heide was hospitalized Christmas Eve after sustaining a massive stroke. She was in deep coma, critically ill.

Heide had been in church Christmas Eve with her daughter and granddaughter. Suddenly she was unable to move her right leg, and within a minute or so she was unable to speak. She subsequently went into coma and was rushed to a nearby hospital.

She never regained consciousness. She lay in coma for a full two weeks before being transported to an extended care facility, otherwise known as a nursing home. Within several hours she expired.

The only fact I could gather from her attending neurologist was that she had sustained a massive hemorrhage in her brain. The chance for any gainful recovery was next to nil.

My entire office went into mourning. For a day-and-a-half we remained closed because my office manager was out of town visiting family, and my right-hand nurse was gone, totally absent. I looked at my remaining staff in bewilderment and said, "What are we going to do without her?"

Patients, pharmaceutical reps, and office staff from other physicians' offices in the building were all shocked. It was unreal. Patients were truly worried. "Dr. Elkin, are you going to be able to manage without Heide?"

Heide was no ordinary nurse. To this very day I say that having a nurse like Heide was a gift, a blessing of a lifetime. Equally comfortable in both back and front office, Heide could essentially run the entire office. There was nothing she couldn't do or fix. Working in a busy office where emergencies and last-minute calamities can occur, she always brought a sense of calmness to the scene. Often while feeling pressured, I would say, "Heide, I need this or that."

Her response was always the same: "I'll handle it."

And she always did!

My youngest daughter was about to be released from the residential facility for eating disorders. She was terribly saddened. She had worked in the office part-time during summers. Heide had become a maternal role model for her, following her mother's death from cancer.

I'll never forget her words, "Daddy, if there really is a God out there, why does He take good people like Mommy and Heide?"

How do you answer that question from a teenager? My only response was, "Honey, God has a master plan, and it is not our job to be privy to it. It is beyond our understanding."

I'm not so sure she could comprehend this any better than I could. But it dawned on me that with loss of loved ones, we simply have to forgive the *whys* in life.

Heide's untimely death really brought out my spiritual side, which of course was a major part of my healing process. Heide was about as healthy as one could be. In her late 50's, she had normal blood pressure and cholesterol levels, and she had only been hospitalized in the past for childbirth. She had no known medical maladies and complained of nothing. She brought her own homemade healthy lunch every day and never imbibed on junk food or sodas. Furthermore, she was extremely athletic. She had been an avid hiker, downhill skier, and tennis player.

Most extraordinary, in seven years she never missed a day of work. I recall asking her jokingly one day, "Heide don't you ever catch a cold or flu?"

Her response was a glib, "I'm German. We never get sick!"

To this day, her death remains a mystery to me. Perhaps she had an aneurysm or a type of vascular malformation in her brain that could have conceivably lead to a massive bleed. But even that is a bit unusual because she never complained of any headaches or neurological symptoms.

I think Heide's death was a greater shock to me than my own heart attack. I was completely stumped and tried earnestly to make sense of her demise. My daughter's question echoed in my own mind, but eventually I, too, had to accept the loss of this beloved woman.

Her short-lived illness and death took place a mere six weeks after my own heart attack. For me, there was a take-home lesson. I learned to be appreciative for my health and well-being in this incredibly bountiful but short journey we call *life*.

I could never again ask, "Why me?" As I learned just a few weeks back, none of us is immune to a life-threatening illness.

This added new *value, gratitude* and *meaning* to my daily prayer and meditation, a practice that I continue to uphold to this very day.

CHAPTER 7

A NEW YEAR: MOVING RIGHT ALONG

THE LAST TWO MONTHS OF 2006 proved to be more tumultuous than I could ever imagine. Prior to this I was the type of man who simply kept running and performing. I had an insatiable drive that seemed boundless to many.

But *there are no accidents.* Chaos either brings about *disaster or change.* Having sustained a minor heart attack that could have cost me my life was one trauma. Losing my right-hand nurse to an unexpected massive stroke a mere five weeks later was even more traumatic.

I'm proud that I quickly adapted and made cogent changes that would forever shape my life.

I was never more elated to start a new chapter, so I decided that 2007 was going to be a year of abundance for me. My drive was still limitless. However, I was now ready to embrace a new life. It was time to live within my limits and boundaries, while relinquishing any notion that I was Superman.

I could no longer do it all.

By January 2007 things were proceeding quite nicely. My youngest daughter was back home and was able to complete her last semester of high school along with her classmates.

It was a busy but productive time as we toured various college campuses together. We wanted to find a school that would be academically challenging, but also comforting. After all, it had been a mere 1½ years since her mother's death.

I continued seeking self-growth and inner peace. After *Insights* I changed my meditation practice a bit. The emphasis was still on *breathing* and *letting go of the little things* in life. I came to believe that much of what we encounter on a daily basis is pretty small. Every Monday and Friday morning I would include a series of affirmations, which was a carry-over from the INSIGHTS program.

A few simple examples:

"I am special."
"I enjoy excellent health."
"I am intelligent."
"I am a gifted physician."
"I am a wonderful parent, brother and friend."
"I am a magnet in attracting terrific people."
"I create abundance in everything that I do."

Now these quaint phrases are not mere euphemisms to feed my ego. They are simple reminders that *I am fortunate* and that *my life is good.* With all the everyday hustle bustle, we often find ourselves living in the fast lane.

We ALL need to take a little time out
and be reminded how fortunate our journey is in life.

Physically, I was in the best shape of my life. I was back at Golds Venice, lifting heavy weights again. However, I was careful not to forfeit my cardio endurance training.

I was overjoyed with my ability to recover. I was lifting more like a man in his mid-thirties than a man in his mid-fifties.

A little over the edge? Perhaps, but as my own Medical Advocate I finally learned to respect my body and to watch for any unusual symptoms. After all, it was my attending cardiologist at Cedars-Sinai who said I would have to incorporate my own cardiac rehab program—since I was anything but the norm!

But I wasn't foolish. I took a beta blocker to protect my heart muscle for the first year after my heart attack, along with a statin to get my LDL (lousy) cholesterol in the 70 range. Incidentally, this became the new norm for those with a previous cardiac event.

CHAPTER 7: A New Year: Moving Right Along

By the way, remember that aspirin that everyone was chiding me about at the time of my presentation? It became a vital part of my daily regimen from day one! Indeed, aspirin for life is *de rigueur*.

The Challenge of Being a Doctor. I felt as if I was beginning this year in a favorable light. What was lacking, however, was how to deal effectively with the changing environment of medical practice.

With many patients gravitating to HMOs, along with the markedly decreasing reimbursement from third party payers, my financial crunch was more real than ever. Then there was the barrage of bureaucratic red tape and restrictions where physicians no longer had the upper hand in patient care.

We were clearly entering a new era, one in which we physicians had less and less autonomy than ever before. It seemed as if doctors everywhere were burning out rapidly.

I didn't undergo fourteen years of higher education to dislike my profession. Upon taking the advice of my good friend Barry, I enlisted the services of a premier business coach, Patty Dedominic, who brought me to a whole new level of career success.

After our initial meeting, Patty said, "I think you really enjoy what you do, and I don't see you working for some big corporation or doing anything else." From there she had me do a series of exercises which included one-year and five-year goal setting. Then my task was to design a plan to achieve these goals.

Patty and I worked together weekly for several months via telephone. The results were astounding. By changing my mindset and actually visualizing my success, my monthly production increased markedly. This was purely based on internal marketing.

2007 was a good year, mainly because I put my best foot forward and made the conscious decision to create a life of *happiness and abundance*. Gone was negative thinking, predicated on self-pity and regrets.

But I didn't do it alone. I chose to be around positive-minded, successful people who enjoyed life. In less than a year from that fateful day in November 2006, my life had changed favorably. I let go of the "stuff" that I couldn't control, and instead focused on what was possible and positive in this great journey we all have.

*It's called **LIFE.***

CHAPTER 8

18 MONTHS LATER—WHAM!

WITH ALL MY POSITIVE THINKING AND REPROGRAMMING, I had convinced myself that 2007 was going to be a year of true abundance. And it was for the most part. My *practice was thriving*, my *health was excellent*, and I was *back in the gym* getting my beta-endorphin high.

But there were issues... I had made financial concessions with my two daughters, as their mother's estate eventually went through probate. These yields were not trivial in the least, but I felt it more important to maintain the family structure. I certainly was not going to return to the battlefield and allow my health to falter as it had in late 2006.

There was no room for negative energy. I made the conscious decision to accept my financial losses and to work hard to recoup them.

Although my youngest daughter was accepted to some very fine colleges, she felt clear in midsummer 2007 that she was simply not ready to leave home. So, we altered her plans. She enrolled at Santa Monica College, which has a fine matriculation rate to UCLA.

Because the commute was too far from where we lived, she decided to move to the Westside of Los Angeles and live with her older sister. Little did I know that her sister rarely slept there, as she had moved in with a "friend" in Venice, California.

This was the beginning of a new disaster. Suddenly Marisa was given complete freedom to do whatever she wished. By mid-fall she had made new friends and subsequently entered the drug scene. It wasn't long before she dropped out of college.

Eventually it became apparent to me what was happening. I witnessed her slipping, but at age 18, there was little I could do to force change. As a result, I often felt hopeless as a parent.

I also knew that I could not allow this to adversely affect my health.

Despite my greatest efforts, I could never really rest comfortably knowing that she was going down another dark road, from life-threatening anorexia nervosa to drug addiction. I felt inadequate.

There was nothing I could do about it.

The Lure of Bodybuilding. But I kept on my path and continued to work diligently on both my career and on my level of physical and emotional well-being. As 2008 rolled around, I decided it was time to return to the bodybuilding stage. This was going to be my big comeback at the national level, as my last showing was in 2005.

With the exception of the first month post heart attack, I had never truly taken a break from training. However, I chose not to compete in 2006 so that I could fully focus on my role as single working dad. Then, I decided to forgo competition in 2007 because of the need to recuperate from the heart attack itself.

I had learned a lot from my prior experience of overdoing it while not listening to my body. Making the conscious decision to not subject myself to the duress of contest preparation was an easy one in 2007. But as 2008 rolled in, I felt inwardly that the time was ripe.

Generally, I start my contest preparation anywhere from twelve to fourteen weeks prior to the actual contest. For those of you not familiar with the rigors of this aspect of bodybuilding, let's just call it *extreme* to say the least!

Working this hard to obtain body fat levels of less than 5% is not terribly healthy. Furthermore, it borders on insanity. But being an over-the-top, determined individual, I generally make a goal and keep striving to reach it. After all, it had been a year-and-a-half since my cardiac event.

I felt ready both physically and emotionally.

People often ask me why anyone in their right mind would choose to sacrifice to the extent necessary to place in a bodybuilding contest. Well, in a strange sort of way, it was akin to returning to medical school. In med school one learns from the onset that sacrifice is compulsory. Because of the academic demands placed on the medical student, there is little or no time for leisure.

Fortunately, the sacrifice was worth it, as I sincerely love what I do.

I've always considered myself a strength athlete. With a background in gymnastics, bodybuilding seemed like a natural progression. I entered a bodybuilding contest upon the persuasion of my trainer in 1998. He felt I had the requisite "genetics" to place high. So, in my mid-forties I entered my first contest and placed fourth. I guess you can say that I became hooked.

I moved up in placement and within two years I placed first in my age group in the heavyweight division. I maintained that position for an additional year. I was subsequently encouraged to move from regional contests in Los Angeles where I had reached my zenith to the national level.

What a difference that shift in competition made. I quickly learned that politics are very much involved as one ascends the national level. After all, in what sport other than bodybuilding can one be both a promoter and competitor?

At my first Masters National competition in Pittsburgh in 2002, everyone thought I should have placed fifth or higher. However, I was up against a well-known former competitor/promoter of that particular contest. He was attempting a national comeback. It was pretty strange. Here he was with his cheering squad of young adoring females, as well as with a new fitness magazine that he was hoping to launch. Needless to say, I placed sixth while he placed fifth. Something very similar occurred a year later in 2003, and still later in 2005.

But like medical school, one chooses to partake in this activity because of love, rather than individual placement. At least that's how I see it. Of course, I want to place high and be rewarded for my effort, but that isn't my main focus. With each contest that I entered, I always felt I was a winner, and that I repeatedly came on stage in the best possible condition.

Did I tell you I was a Type A? For me, it's more than just sacrifice. It's about achieving something so dear to me, that I will not stop short of achieving that goal. It's about sheer will and determination.

Interestingly enough, one of my trainers, professional bodybuilder Pedro Baron once said that in my case M.D. means more than Doctor of Medicine. It also stands for "Mr. Determination." So that's me. I don't necessarily think that my way is the best way or even the healthiest way. *It clearly borders on the extreme.* But it does define who I am, and I've grown to be quite comfortable with myself.

I understand the plight of those who feel that they must climb Mt. Everest, despite the attendant sacrifice and risks. They take on a mission that could not only cost them their lives, but if it did, they'd leave loved ones behind.

All this to fulfill a given pursuit.

Some call this insane and selfish. Climbing Mt. Everest isn't exactly my goal, but I understand and appreciate the passion of those who attempt this feat.

I've always felt that I should have been a professional actor, athlete or opera singer, not because of talent, but because I understand and appreciate the mentality that goes along with this passion.

It's a never-ending drive to achieve a given goal in life.

When young competitors come up to me and ask whether I think they should compete, I always utter these words: "You have to dig deep within yourself to find that answer. I can't give it to you." My belief is if you have to question this, you probably lack the passion.

Posing a Problem. So, after sitting out for 2006 and 2007, I was definitely ready to return to the posing stage in 2008. I embarked on this path fourteen weeks out by drastically reducing my carbohydrate intake and increasing my cardio or aerobic activity.

People are often amazed when they discover that my overall caloric intake isn't ridiculously low during this period. But remember, I am slowly but surely increasing my cardio or aerobic exercise, along with maintaining heavy weight training. In addition to this, I am forever practicing my posing.

All this exercise burns an incredible number of calories. Therefore, to avoid losing all that hard-earned muscle, one must ingest a fair amount of food. The emphasis is maintaining a high protein intake.

This process progresses fairly rapidly over the course of fourteen weeks. Performing a lot of cardio is also necessary during this period. Typically, I begin my mornings on a treadmill, elliptical, stair climber or stationary bicycle. This is done on an empty stomach to help mobilize my fat stores. Before long, I find it necessary to add an evening session.

There was no time to give into fatigue. I simply couldn't go home after a long day in the office seeing patients or performing procedures in the hospital. Instead, I had to make a *second* trip to the gym for my *second* cardio session of the day.

Maybe you've heard this one: one should lift lighter weights and perform more repetitions while dieting. Misinformation! Nothing could be farther from the truth. It's as if one is saying, "Well, I guess I don't need all this hard-earned muscle after all, so I'll lift lighter and work on *toning*."

I've never heard a good definition of the word toning. According to Webster, it is a transitive verb which means *to strengthen*. I can guarantee anyone that *lifting lighter will not strengthen*. Period.

Secondly, despite the need to combat fatigue because of ever-diminishing carbohydrate ingestion, an arduous program of heavy lifting must be maintained.

I mention all this not because I am trying to interest you in competitive bodybuilding, or in my particular pre-contest regimen. I've outlined here a few basic tenets to illustrate the stress it imparts on the body over a relatively short period of time.

Wham Bam. Tuesday May 27, 2008, after Memorial Day Weekend, I'm ready to start my day with my morning cardio on an empty stomach. Sitting at the kitchen table, feeling just fine, I merely bend down to tie my sneakers. *Wham!* It felt as if I was hit by a Mack truck.

A horrendous back spasm overcame me. I was literally stopped in my tracks. I sat there for several moments. Eventually I waddled out of my home to my car. It was clear that any cardio exercise that morning was out of the question.

Little did I know how incapacitated I would become over the next ten days. The mental anguish was incredible, as I blamed myself. My reasoning: *To have this much pain, I must have done something wrong.*

Suddenly, it was if all my hard work with positive thinking and affirmations over the previous eighteen months had vanished.

The Downside of Determination. I was in both physical and emotional pain. But I was still resolute, not yet willing to give up the prospect of competing. This was supposed to be my comeback year. Nothing was going to stop me from achieving my goal.

Even though I was compelled to place my cardio on hold, I somehow mustered the *energy and will* to continue strength training. Furthermore, I maintained my strict diet, even though it was incredibly difficult to stand in my kitchen weighing my food portions and preparing my meals. The pain in my back was that bad.

Being pro-active as well as determined, I sought immediate chiropractic treatment and physical therapy. Unfortunately, I never experienced any significant relief.

I recall standing and giving a PowerPoint presentation to a group of about fifty people later that week. The topic was stem cell therapy and its potential usage in cardiology. This was a mere two days after the onset of my back pain.

Somehow, I persevered and managed to complete my twenty-minute lecture as well as the subsequent question and answer period. But all I could do was pray to be relieved of enough pain so that I could *continue standing* long enough to finish my presentation.

Nothing seemed to help. I eventually had to take a few days off from my strength training, but I continued dieting and bargaining with myself. "If I get better, I'll still be able to compete."

Those were my words. Who was I fooling?

Saturday, June 7th, was the turning point. Absolutely nothing could have prepared me for what occurred just before midnight on that fateful day.

CHAPTER 9

MY WORST NIGHTMARE

DESPITE MY GREATEST EFFORTS, everything went downhill after Memorial Day Weekend 2008. *My competition days were over.* The back pain that I endured in late May was the beginning of the end.

Despite physical therapy, chiropractic treatment and bodywork, nothing seemed to work. I recall vividly that last treatment on Saturday June 7th. Instead of experiencing relief, I could barely make the fifty-foot trek from the door of my chiropractor's office to my car. I was simply bent over at the waist.

Feeling Defeated. At this point I went home and tried my best to relax. That evening I lay in bed reading a novel to distract any negative feelings.

Just before midnight, I attempted to get out of bed and proceed to the bathroom. Suddenly this strange, new feeling overcame me. *I was numb below both knees.* When I attempted to stand and bear weight, I plunged right to the ground. I couldn't support my own weight. I tried to prop myself back up by leaning onto my bed. But there was no way to make a meaningful move. From that point on, I was relegated to a crawl.

The events of the next few hours seem a blur to me today. I do recall getting to my computer where I was able to use the strength of my upper body to climb onto the chair. I simply sat there at the screen trying to regain some sort of focus.

Then it came to me crystal clear. *I was in deep trouble.* I had paralysis in my lower limbs. Certainly, the competition was out for sure.

Worse, I had to face being hospitalized once more.

It was 1:00 in the morning. Feeling very much alone, I was truly scared. I was hoping that my legs had simply fallen asleep, but there was no let up. I lay on the floor bare-naked after crawling back to my bedroom to get my cell phone. Who could I phone at that hour? I was in no mood to dial 911.

I just lay there on the floor in pain until 6:00 am when I phoned my closest friend Barry. It was Barry who rescued me. With his assistance I was able to somehow make it back into bed. That was no easy feat when you consider that I was 220 pounds with legs of rubber!

We phoned Carol, my office manager, who promptly came to my home with a wheelchair. I somehow managed to position myself in her car.

We were off to Cedars-Sinai Medical Center in Los Angeles. This was a mere nineteen months after my previous hospitalization.

I was dumbfounded. While making that trek to Cedars-Sinai, I had no idea what was up. I was clearly unable to support my own weight, much less walk. What I did know was that I just threw seven weeks of contest preparation down the drain.

By the time I was lifted out of the car and placed in a gurney in the Emergency Room, I was writhing in pain. I soon received my first intravenous injection of Dilaudid, which makes morphine seem pale in potency. This suddenly became my new best friend.

I don't remember much after that. My eldest daughter met me in the ER, just as she had done in November 2006. I was whisked to the MRI suite for imaging of my lumbar sacral spine. Three men were needed to move me from the gurney to the exam table. But I needed more pain relief, so I was given an extra dose of Dilaudid.

I remember being a bit hysterical at this point, and unable to fully cooperate with staff. The pain was unremitting. Without my daughter's calming, suggestive voice, I don't know how I would have been able to complete this exam.

Finally, back in the ER, I received word that my internist was away and that I would be assigned a hospitalist who would supervise my care. That along with the fact that I would have to be hospitalized was anything but pleasant news.

CHAPTER 9: My Worst Nightmare

Feeling Helpless. But I had to face the truth. *I was unable to walk.* Shortly thereafter I was admitted and given a verbal report. The results of the MRI read, "critical spinal stenosis."

Having had a diagnosis of severe spinal stenosis since my first MRI in 1996, nothing seemed preposterous or unexpected. My past history of back pain had been marked by long periods of complete remission, following painful relapses that would last up to three months. But now, it went from severe to critical.

The news was not good, and I was at my wit's end.

It was all a blur for the next 3-4 days. The only thing I had to look forward to was my intravenous injections of Dilaudid. I made sure to not miss a single dose. Despite my clouded brain, I kept track of each injection, and would ring for the nurse each time I was eligible for my next shot of this opiate.

I don't recall if the pain ever went away completely, but I did experience a moment of bliss following each injection. *I actually remember smelling fresh flowers and hearing birds chirping.* It was if I had transcended to the other side.

This had to be pretty damn serious if death suddenly seemed inviting!

Those injections were my only solace. I truly understand and appreciate how folks get addicted to opiates. Pain in itself is such a strong motivator that any action or substance that relieves it is indeed welcomed.

I was evaluated by a neurologist the next day. He wanted to see if I would improve with bed rest. He was also quick to mention that surgery was a distinct possibility. I recall lying in bed virtually paralyzed. Attempting to walk was out of the question. Being constipated from the narcotics actually had a redeeming quality, as it minimized the times I needed to ask for a bedpan!

Disappointing & Demeaning. I found the entire experience terribly laborious. Waiting to see if I would improve seemed fruitless. I continued to lie there for three days, unable to function in any meaningful way. I had little interactions with the doctors. The nurses' role was to take my vitals, empty out my urinal, and give me my injection of Dilaudid every three hours.

The only test performed on me was an EMG (electromyograph), a painful nerve conduction study whereby the electrical activity of the muscles is recorded. Imagine being in pain and unable to move your legs as the physician pokes your extremities with several needles and then administers a series of electrical shocks. What was being tested was the nerve conduction down my legs. A muscle simply can't contract without nerve stimulation.

As a physician, I am all about getting the necessary testing to clinch a diagnosis, especially if the results might impact a given choice of therapy. But all I was thinking was, "Really? I CAN'T MOVE!"

It was pretty obvious that the nerve to muscle connection was simply not there. The physician administering the test was cold and non-empathic. At the conclusion of the test, I politely asked him about the results.

He uttered, "You have to take that up with your physician."

"But I'm a doctor," I replied.

He then said, "But you aren't the ordering physician."

The grand moment came when he said, "OK, I'll give you a hint. You have a motor neuropathy in your legs."

I literally said, "No S--- Sherlock." Seriously, it didn't take a degree in medicine to figure that out!

By Wednesday of that week, it was obvious that I was showing no signs of improvement. The neurologist said I would require surgery. I definitely didn't want to go there, but I knew inwardly that I had no viable choice.

I requested "the absolute best neurosurgeon on staff." Early that evening a tall, attractive woman entered my room. She said, "I'm so and so, Dr. H's physician's assistant, and I am here to examine you for Dr. H prior to surgery."

By this time, I was fed up with the treatment I had been receiving. For those of you who think doctors get special treatment while hospitalized, that clearly was not true in my case.

I didn't expect special privileges. What I did expect was better communication between myself and the medical team responsible for my care. I promptly dismissed this young woman, letting her know once and for all, that the doctor-patient relationship in this case must commence with the neurosurgeon and me, the patient.

Ten minutes later my appointed neurosurgeon entered my room and bluntly told me that I had little option at this point. Proceeding with surgery was mandatory, lest I be relegated to a wheelchair for the rest of my life.

Although he wanted to give me a little time to "think about it," I promptly called his assistant informing her of my decision to proceed. Surgery was set for Friday the 13th of June. I was content and at rest with the decision. I simply wanted it to be over.

Therein marked the beginning of yet another journey.

CHAPTER 10

THE UNEXPECTED ROAD TO RECOVERY

FRIDAY THE 13TH OF JUNE was the date of my surgery. I recall waiting in the holding area after being evaluated by the anesthesiologist. I had no fears at that time. I simply wanted to get this over with so that I could move on with my life.

Good News, Bad News. Just minutes prior to being transported to the operating room, my surgeon came by my bedside. He wanted to prepare me for what was to transpire post-surgery. "I have both good news and bad news for you, Doc."

"Tell me the good news first."

"Because you are in such good shape physically, your recovery will be much faster than the average person."

That was certainly music to my ears, even though I knew inwardly it was true. Then I muttered, "Ok, so what's the bad news?"

I will never forget his words: "Because you have so much muscle mass, you are going to have severe muscle spasm post-operatively as your body attempts to deal with the insult of surgery."

That was anything but promising, but I simply put that on the back burner, as just a few minutes later I was whisked into the operating room.

The next thing I remember was that I was in the recovery room and a male nurse was attempting to comfort me, reassuring me that it was all over. I sat there literally crying as this was a moment of cathartic relief for me. Imagine after experiencing nearly two weeks of agonizing pain and five days of complete immobilization, it was all over.

At least that was what I thought!

I was so drugged with pain killers that the next twenty-four hours are a complete blur to me. I don't remember how long I was in the recovery room, or even when I was wheeled to the VIP post-op surgical suite where I spent the next two days.

OK, I did receive one special perk. Because I was a physician, they gave me a large, lovely room reserved for the elite, complete with a fantastic view. But what a waste, as I was unable to even makes it out of bed into the chair, much less to the bathroom.

Forget What Was. Much to my dismay I must say that the surgeon was correct. Absolutely nothing could have prepared me for the pain I experienced post-operatively. Again, all I could do was lie motionless in bed. The surgery was over. It was *successful* according to my surgeon, who bragged while saying, "It was a cinch. Ninety minutes…Skin-to-skin."

But a complex surgery done expeditiously meant nothing to me. I felt even worse than I did pre-operatively! Prior to surgery I couldn't move. Now I could move my legs, but every muscle hurt, as I experienced one shooting pain after another. There was no end to the pain killers, and again I made sure not to miss a single dose.

The day following surgery, a physical therapist came to evaluate me. It literally took her and two nurses to position me at the side of the bed so my legs could dangle. I burst into tears, as I had never felt so miserably helpless.

This is What is. "This is my recovery?" I cried. The therapist looked at me and uttered these words that I will never forget, "Listen, forget what was. This is what is."

I knew from that moment that recovery was going to be a major obstacle course. I was going to have to suck it in and acknowledge that fact. There would be no shortcuts this time around. Being a strong athlete meant absolutely nothing. It was one day at a time, and it seemed completely out of my control.

The next two days proved to be increasingly frustrating. All I

CHAPTER 10: The Unexpected Road to Recovery

remember was the pain while attempting to sit up by the side of the bed with assistance. I had yet to take my first step.

We then noted that I was completely unable to *dorsiflex* my right foot. Bending my foot backward at the ankle was simply impossible. The left ankle and foot were also impaired, but not nearly as severe as the right side. This was anything but good news. By Monday the 16th of June, it was obvious to all that I was in no position to be discharged.

I was subsequently evaluated by the rehabilitation team who thought rehab was my only true therapeutic option. But it wasn't as easy as all that. While attempting to get the necessary authorization from my PPO insurance, initially, I was flatly turned down.

Instead, my insurance company decided unilaterally that a convalescent home with a physical therapy staff on site would be their choice for me, as it was considerably less expensive. This was incomprehensible and completely unacceptable to me.

Unfortunately, the discharge planner was of little help. As a registered nurse, her job was to make all necessary provisions for discharge. However, she felt as if this was out of her hands and that there was nothing she could do.

Being My Own Medical Advocate. As I had done nineteen months earlier when I devised my cardiac rehab program, I took matters into my own hands. I spent the greater part of that Monday afternoon *convincing* and then *demanding* that authorization be granted for me to be admitted directly to the rehab unit.

Imagine being incredibly stressed, unable to move, drugged on opiates, and having to do the work of the hospital staff. I was truly my own Medical Advocate here and, unfortunately, I had to battle it alone.

Never in over twenty-five years of treating hospitalized patients had I ever encountered such a situation. I have always worked closely with the nursing staff to ensure that my patients be given the most effective discharge treatment.

So again, to those who believe that doctors get preferential treatment, I am here to say that this was simply not true, at least in my case.

By early evening on the 16th, I was transferred to the rehab unit where my work truly began. What a rude awakening it was when my admitting nurse flatly told me that intravenous pain meds were not administered on this unit. So, my first course of action was to transition from IV Dilaudid to the oral formulation.

The following day I met with both the physical therapist (PT) and occupational therapist (OT) to whom I was assigned. Being in the inpatient rehab unit was hard work without frills. I had both a PT and an OT session in the morning, and then two additional sessions after lunch. In between I would take a much-needed nap. I was thoroughly exhausted by day's end.

I couldn't eat enough while in rehab. Prior to my hospitalization I had been dieting for a contest for nearly eight weeks. It didn't much matter that the food was not entirely healthy (yes, even at Cedars-Sinai). I simply ate everything in sight. I would even ask for two portions at a given meal!

Because I had sustained neurologic damage as a result of my surgery, progress was much slower than I could ever imagine. With a dropped foot on the right, I could not even place that foot in front of my left. Even with assistance and a walker, I could barely walk ten feet.

I was instructed to wear sneakers to rehab, but I quickly discovered, that I had sustained, also as a result of surgery, a total lack of proprioception with regard to the right foot.

Proprioception? Proprioception is *the unconscious perception of movement and spatial orientation arising from stimuli within the body itself.* I didn't have it!

I couldn't tell what direction my foot was heading in a closed shoe. I could not distinguish if my big toe was hitting the top or the bottom of the shoe. It simply would not go. So, my daughter went out and purchased open-toe sandals so that I could actually *see* what direction my foot was going.

The first few days were terrible. I wasn't mobile enough to even go to the PT department and work in the gym. Just learning to proceed from a sitting to a standing position took a great deal of

CHAPTER 10: The Unexpected Road to Recovery

effort. Besides, I was still suffering from a lot of pain from ongoing muscle spasm.

Then I had to be monitored in order to take a shower. The nursing staff and the therapists were fantastic, but it still seemed like jail to me. I felt as if all my independence had suddenly been stripped away. I clearly remember a sign on the wall opposite my bed which read, "STOP...DON'T BEND, TURN OR TWIST. CALL FOR HELP!"

One Calamity after Another. By the end of my first week in rehab I had broken out in a terrible rash, from chest-to-back, and from buttocks-to-groin. I didn't know if it was the detergent they used or the crummy bed sheets. Eventually I needed antihistamines to control the itching, as well as topical lotions.

Then there was great difficulty sleeping, a problem that was completely foreign to me. Generally, I am one of those who falls asleep within five minutes of getting prone. But because I was relegated to lying flat on my back, it was difficult to find a comfortable position.

Moreover, the rehab unit was far from quiet at night with patients constantly buzzing and screaming for their pain meds. Next, we needed to add *sleeping medications* to the mix which included *antihistamines* to control the itching from the rash, *pain meds*, meds to control *muscle spasm*, and *anti-anxiety meds*.

The list just grew. As an inpatient, you literally are a depot of medications.

On the 5th day post-op, I noticed tremors and severe fatigue. By this time, I was just a bit curious as to what meds I was actually taking. I asked the charge nurse to give me a complete list, but naturally, she had to obtain authorization from the medical staff. Again, it didn't matter that I was a physician. I seriously felt that I had a right to know what meds I was prescribed.

Well, I learned I was taking Gabapentin, otherwise known as Neurontin. Side effects include drowsiness, loss of coordination, and tremors, just to name a few. All I needed at this point was a medication that would further impede my progress by robbing me of energy and coordination!

Wasn't dealing with the pain, immobility, and the neurological damage from the surgery itself enough?!

I immediately phoned my rehab physician to ask why I had been prescribed a medication indicated for neuropathic or nerve pain. His reply was that it would hopefully control my pain. "Besides," he said, "it's routine for post-op spine patients."

Well, this really went against my grain. Anyone who knows me is aware that I don't generally believe that one size fits all. But I get it. This seems to be the sine qua non methodology utilized in clinical medicine these days.

I politely asked him to withdraw this medication from my list because of the adverse effects I was experiencing. Besides, I didn't think I was suffering from nerve pain, but pain from intense muscle spasm. He complied, and needless to say, these nagging side effects resolved within 48 hours.

WHEW! Talk about being my own Medical Advocate while laid up in bed simply relearning how to walk!

It was living hell that first week in rehab. I actually dreaded the next PT or OT session. I simply wanted to be left alone in my room. Towards the end of the first week, the staff urged me to join the other spine surgery patients in the recreation room for lunch. I wasn't too keen on the idea.

Being social was the farthest thing on my mind.

Feeling a bit pressured, I acquiesced, but was I ever sorry. Imagine me being wheeled into this large room complete with books, magazines, and a large screen television. There were seven other patients, all of whom were female.

The first question I was asked was, "How many back surgeries have you had?" Without hesitation I replied, "This is my first and last!"

One woman who was about my age responded, "Yeah? That's what we all said." She had three surgeries, another had four and all the rest had been under the knife at least twice. This didn't include all the epidurals and procedures performed for nerve stimulation

CHAPTER 10: The Unexpected Road to Recovery

devices to help control chronic back pain.

I called for the staff to wheel me out of there, as this was anything but a therapeutic atmosphere for me. This was not my thing.

By the start of my second week in rehab I was very depressed. Progress was at a snail's pace. I was sent to another group outing in the recreation room for a little Chi Gong. I thought, "REALLY?" I can barely get from a sitting to a standing position, much less perform any gainful exercise.

But it was part of my therapy, so I complied. Suddenly a traumatic event overcame me. At one point my legs were suspended while sitting in a chair. Without warning I went into such a muscle spasm that my shriek frightened both the staff and the other patients.

Thoroughly disgusted by this point, I tried to meditate—while deep breathing—in my bed. I had become so proficient in this form of relaxation after my heart attack that I thought for sure this would serve me well, as it had in the past.

Wrong again! It's as if I suddenly forgot a craft I had clearly perfected over the previous nineteen months. And one I had also taught my patients.

I sat in bed crying and I asked to be seen by the rehab psychologist for help in instructing me how to simply relax.

I felt so diminished by this time. Surely someone as strong as me could overcome a ninety-minute back surgery that had left me neurologically impaired. There just had to be a missing link somewhere, but what would it take to discover it?

My answer came later that evening on the 23rd of June when my eldest daughter came to visit me. It was if she was sent by my higher power, because what transpired was an experience so profound that it completely obliterated my *black cloud*.

It was absolutely pivotal to my healing.

CHAPTER 11

LIGHT AT THE END OF THE TUNNEL

On June 22, as I lay in my bed attempting to meditate—while praying for an answer or some relief—my eldest daughter DeAnna came to pay me a visit.

My prayer was about to be answered.

DeAnna was barely 23 at the time, and was always much wiser than her years, at least from a spiritual standpoint. I swear this child was born a saint. As a little girl her biggest pleasure was pleasing her parents.

She possessed a clear sense of God that must have come from within. I'll never forget one evening long ago when she was no older than six. I sat with her in her bed about to read a good-night story when she broke out in smiles and said, "Daddy, I'm so excited!"

The moment seemed so surreal because I recall vividly that I was anything but in a good mood that particular night.

"Why honey?" Then she said something that absolutely floored me, a statement that I will never forget. "Because I just know tomorrow is going to be a beautiful day! God told me so!"

Such an unusual child, she was always there to spread happiness in a household that was often times chaotic and dysfunctional. When her mother was diagnosed with stage-four breast cancer, she elected to be the primary caregiver at age seventeen, forfeiting an opportunity to attend college.

She was clairvoyant and she knew from an early age that her mom would succumb while she was still a teenager. Even at her mother's deathbed, she chose to lie with Nanci as she witnessed her last breath. Most nineteen-year-olds would find this very difficult, but DeAnna felt the need to be alone with her mom as she transitioned to the other side. She actually described this last moment with her mother as a healing experience.

Back to me and my misery. A week into rehab, I was still dependent on oral narcotics. My progress was ridiculously slow, and my morale was at an all-time low. But in walked my smiling daughter with a snack, a book on healing, and a boom box with some relaxation CDs.

She helped me into the bathroom where I had to sit on an elevated commode, since I was unable to stoop low enough to actually sit on the toilet stool. Because this particular commode was suited for a person much taller, my feet could not reach the floor. Another intense muscle spasm overcame me.

I had no choice but to let out a yell, a shriek that could be clearly heard throughout the entire rehab unit. Three nurses came to my rescue and assisted me back into bed. I was very emotional and riddled with pain. I was hysterical beyond belief. This was the closest thing to a panic attack that I had ever experienced.

Time for Magic. The next two hours spent with my daughter were amongst the most intimate moments spent with anyone in my entire life. With my eyes shut, we proceeded to really focus on deep breathing. It was a means to keep my mind on the present, and away from all my pain and emotional turmoil.

Next, she put me through visualization where I imagined myself walking on the beach and then hiking in the local mountains. I saw myself in prime form once again, without pain and without a dropped foot. I had been transported to another place and time.

Misery was replaced with bliss.

Within a span of thirty minutes, memories of the bathroom scene fiasco had completely disappeared. But this was just the beginning. She played a few calming discs on her CD player. There we were, chanting and working within our chakras—creating a serene, safe place for ourselves. It was a shared experience that I will never forget.

CHAPTER 11: Light at the End of the Tunnel

After the music stopped, she sat next to me in my hospital bed, and we reminisced about our family life and her youth. Somehow it segued to my relationship with her deceased mom. The remarkable thing was that we only focused on the fun and positive memories. There was absolutely no room for negative talk.

Finally, we delved into my own youth and I found myself opening up in the presence of my older daughter, telling her things that had formerly been "family secrets." It just happened without a plan. The time seemed so ripe. I guess I needed to disclose stuff that had been hidden deep within my memory. It was one of those rare conversations that occur once or twice in a lifetime.

We laughed and cried together, and she said, "Daddy, I have never felt so close to you as I do tonight."

Suddenly, without warning, *music popped out of nowhere.* It had been over forty-five minutes since the last song ended. I was completely stupefied at this point.

"DeAnna, do you hear that music? Do you have a remote in your hands?"

She replied, "Dad, I'm sitting here in bed with you. I have no remote. I didn't turn on that music!"

As incredulous as this may seem, she walked to the corner of the room where her CD player was situated. Then she emphatically said "Dad, I don't know what to say, but if that song is selection number 2, it's Mom!"

It was selection 2. I was beyond spooked. "DeAnna, this is nuts. No one would believe us."

I subsequently learned that DeAnna had repeatedly played that particular tune for her mom the last week of her life. She wanted to provide comfort to her mom in the terminal stage of her disease. This occurred at the same hospital on the oncology floor exactly one flight above us.

It was as if Nanci had sanctioned a time for healing, not only for me, but for the family as a whole. It was the most amazing moment of my life. To this day I can't readily explain what happened and how, but I know deep inside that there are no accidents.

I had witnessed a truly baffling healing phenomenon.

What I can tell you is that my pain vanished that particular night. From that point on, I was able to fully embrace my healing.

My progress took off like a rocket! .

CHAPTER 12

CRUISING THROUGH REHAB

JUNE 24 MARKED A NEW BEGINNING for me in rehab. Pain-free at last, I was determined to soar. There would be no turning back.

Both physical and occupational therapy staff members were amazed at my newly-found energy and sense of positivism. Within a day or so I was allowed to go to the PT gym and use their equipment. In no time flat I was able to walk within the parallel bars... back and forth with ease.

Sure, I had my powerful upper body strength to help bolster my steps, but finally I was able to walk somewhat normally, placing one foot in front of the other without pain. Before long I could get in and out of a chair without assistance. Eventually, I was able to walk twenty-five feet with the aid of my walker.

But I didn't stop there. Walking twice a day between my assigned therapy sessions, I made it a point to increase my distance by a minimum of ten feet with each round.

Don't forget, after my heart attack, I was encouraged to design my own rehab program. This time around as an in-patient, I had the exceptional support of the rehab professionals at Cedars-Sinai.

Still, it was *ultimately up to me* to keep pushing while expanding the limits of my infirmity.

Forget What Was. Therapy sessions were no longer grueling and demeaning. I actually found pleasure in my ongoing progress. I recalled vividly what that physical therapist had advised me the day following my surgery, *"Forget what was; this is what is."*

I decided that the best attitude I could take from this point on was to remain in the *present moment*. It no longer mattered to me that I was a former athlete and that six weeks prior to my surgery,

I was prepping for a national bodybuilding event.

It was time to go easy on myself. Yes, I had been through hell. *Emergency back surgery* was one thing, but I had to deal with horrendous *post-op muscle spasm*, magnified by the large amount of *muscle mass* I was carrying. Then there was the *neurologic damage* I had sustained as a complication of the surgery itself; a *complete dropped foot*, and an inability to walk or even position my right foot in front of my left.

I was on a roll. I took the same vim and vigor used in preparing for a marathon, a triathlon, or a bodybuilding competition and socked it into my rehabilitation. I mastered how to bathe myself within the safety-equipped shower. I learned how to manipulate in the OT lab's mock kitchen.

At this point I was unstoppable and determined to be home by the first of July.

Continuing to journal my progress, I never once turned on the overhead television set. Even the Democratic primaries and upcoming National Convention meant little to me. My only concern was my progress. I was back on track with my meditation practice. I worked on deep breathing and visualization daily—upon arising, after lunch, and before bed.

Much to the surprise of both medical and nursing staffs, I had a friend supply me with my favorite supplements. These were clearly not a part of the therapeutic regimen at Cedars-Sinai.

They included Coenzyme Q10, vitamin D, fish oil, various antioxidants such as vitamins C, E and alpha lipoic acid, and finally minerals such as magnesium and zinc.

I had a shoebox full of these supplements at my bedside. I'll never forget the perplexed look on the faces of the medical staff as they made their daily rounds; "What are these, Doc?"

I fell into the role of teacher. "Well, fish oil helps with inflammation. Let's not forget I just had major surgery. Then we have zinc which helps to boost my immune system and also aids in wound healing."

I kept on, but I could tell that they didn't get it. Finally, I blurted

CHAPTER 12: Cruising Through Rehab

out, "Don't you guys learn about this stuff in medical school? I'm over twenty years your senior!"

These weren't just medical students, but residents, fellows, and attending physicians. I'll never forget their response. "Oh no, on this unit we only concern ourselves with pain meds and physical rehabilitation."

I threw my hands in the air and uttered, "Whatever!" It was obvious I wasn't going to put a dent in their education.

Progress came with each new day, as I was able to walk further in the hospital corridor, and even proceed up and down the narrow, crowded aisles in the hospital gift shop.

Armed with my walker, I was truly unstoppable.

I even took delight in the playful bantering of the medical staff as they poked fun at me during their daily rounds: "There's the big bodybuilder doctor with all his supplements."

But I knew I would have the last laugh: "Yeah, that's right. And you just wait; this big guy is getting out of here in record-breaking time!"

I knew I was pushing my limits when I approached the staff with one final request as an in-patient. I wanted to go off-site, in a specially equipped vehicle, to attend the musical *A Chorus Line*.

> *"Kiss today goodbye and*
> *point me toward tomorrow"*
> From *"What I Did for Love"*... A Chorus Line

Months before, I had purchased matinee tickets for my daughters, my office manager, and her daughters for what I believed to be one of the greatest musicals ever. Of course, I didn't expect to be recuperating in the hospital after back surgery.

Because of my amazing progress, I was determined not to relinquish these tickets and forgo my favorite show. When I made the initial request to take the afternoon off from rehab in order to practice my survival skills in the real world, I was flatly refused. I was told how preposterous this request was, especially because it had never been done in the past.

But I don't yield that easily. Besides, just because it had never been done before didn't mean it couldn't be safely done now! With my tenacious persistence, I was able to win this political battle and obtain the necessary authorization.

First, I had to sign a disclaimer in the low likelihood that something might happen to me while away from the medical center. Then I had to prove to the staff that I had the endurance to perform what they considered to be a rather unusual feat.

With the support of my physical therapist, I was able to ascend the ramp to and from the hospital mezzanine to the employee parking deck, back and forth, a total of four times. Admittedly, this did push my limits, as it was a bit exhausting. However, I never once showed an ounce of fatigue. I ended our escapade by asking her, "Shall we make another run of it?" Seemingly more tired than me by this time she replied, "No, I think that's enough. You pass."

But there was one more task to perform. Using my walker to descend to the hospital lobby via elevator, I had to approach the parked automobile that would deliver all of us to the performance. Next, I had to show finesse in getting in and out of that car without assistance.

Mission accomplished! I was bound to the Ahmanson Theater on Sunday June 29 to see *A Chorus Line* with my family and friends. But I had completely forgotten one surprising detail. Not expecting to be handicapped, *I had not purchased wheelchair tickets.* We had seven seats in the middle section of the first balcony—excellent seats to view this particular show.

But when the usher saw me on a walker, he said, "What do you think you're doing? Walkers aren't allowed in the seating area. You should have purchased wheelchair seats like everybody else."

He was anything but sympathetic. "You'll have to walk down fifteen steps and then across ten seats to find your place, which is dead center."

CHAPTER 12: Cruising Through Rehab

Well, I certainly didn't make all this effort to fail at the last moment. I said, "Sure thing. Take my walker. I'll pick it back up at the end of the performance."

With the brute strength I had from years of competitive bodybuilding along with a determined attitude, I used my arms to hold onto the chairs on both sides of the aisle. Like Tarzan, I swung down all fifteen steps and then ten seats to my right.

Folks clamoring to get out of my way, I heard gasps from all angles. When I got to my seat everyone clapped. It was the perfect prologue to a truly terrific musical production.

Thank God *A Chorus Line* is a one act play with no intermission, as it was obvious that I was going nowhere until it's conclusion!

It was an incredible performance. Having seen this show four times previously, including the original production in 1976 on Broadway in New York, it seemed uniquely special this time around, because I was able to share it with my children and staff.

And perhaps, what made it especially meaningful were the hurdles I had to jump in order to make this day trip a reality.

After a lovely dinner in the restaurant below the theater, I was driven back to the hospital where I spent the next day-and-a-half prior to my discharge.

I kept to my original promise, which was to be home by the first of July, 2008.

CHAPTER 13

THE JOURNEY CONTINUES

Home Again

Keeping to my goal, I was discharged from the physical rehabilitation unit at Cedars-Sinai Medical Center on Tuesday, July 1, 2008. I had resided there a total of twenty-two days, a bit more than two weeks after my actual back surgery. My good friend Mary drove me home to surroundings that seemed less than familiar to me.

Sure, I was happy to be out of the hospital, but I immediately experienced a sense of helplessness and loneliness in my own home. I recall sitting by my walker at the kitchen table trying to muster what would be my next move.

This was the same feeling I had experienced the day my daughter drove me home from the hospital post heart attack, nineteen months earlier. The difference was that I wasn't living alone at that time. She was living with me. Furthermore, at that time, I COULD MOVE AROUND!

Imagine how cumbersome it was to shuffle around in my home with a walker every step of the way. At that time, I couldn't walk ten feet unassisted. Fortunately, I remained pain-free, but it was as if I was a prisoner in my own home.

But foolish I wasn't. Realizing my incapacity to fully care for myself, I had made all the necessary arrangements in advance to make life tolerable. I had a portable elevated toilet seat in my bathroom along with a urinal by my bedside. Then I had safety bars strategically placed in my shower for much-needed support. This was similar to the shower at the hospital, replete with a portable chair so that I could sit while sponging myself.

Demeaning? Not at all! I quickly learned how to humble myself, meandering from one life skill to another. Wasting no time, I had one of my employees drive me to my first session of physical therapy the day following my arrival home. After an hour of some very basic exercises, I was completely wasted, but I made sure to never miss a session.

I had scheduled three weekly therapy sessions for the next three months, so this would be my home-away-from-home for a while.

Mom to the Rescue. I was beyond fortunate in having a mother who was alive and well at age eighty-two. She traveled from West Palm Beach, Florida to help assist in my care. I was blessed by her presence for nearly two weeks.

Mary drove me to LAX where we picked up Mom on Saturday, July 5th. She was amazing. There was never a question as to where my siblings and I inherited our boundless energy. She was able to do for me what I couldn't do for myself.

I guess this is what they call a *gift from God!* She shopped and she prepared my favorite meals—including her famous brisket, which was just what this doctor needed, *Jewish comfort food!* She helped schlep me to and from PT. Most important, she was excellent company as we watched old movies on TV and her favorite-CNN. She even cooked and entertained a couple of my friends who paid me visits during my convalescence.

Adapting to my infirmity, I was amazed at my newly found self-acceptance. I literally took one day at a time, while continuing my physical therapy and my meditation practice. I never lost my desire to get better.

Back to Work. I was adamant about returning to work on Monday, July 7th, This was literally less than a month from my admission to Cedars, exactly three weeks and two days from my actual back surgery. I wasn't really trying to set any personal record. I simply felt inwardly that it was time to resume my work as a practicing physician.

CHAPTER 13: The Journey Continues

Many thought this was pretty incredulous, since the average absence from work after back surgery is often several months. But I wasn't just anyone. Besides, a week at home being pampered by my Jewish mother was about as much as this guy could handle!

So here I was on that Monday morning back in the office seeing patients with walker in hand. It didn't bother me that I was less than perfect. I was able to do my thing, utilize my medical judgment, and move around pain-free.

A good friend asked me, "Gosh, isn't it a bit embarrassing having to see cardiac patients with you on a walker?" My reply: "Absolutely not. What is there to be ashamed of? I'm not some god-like figure who is immune from illness or injury."

I found it a humbling experience that brought me even closer to my patients. I didn't have to be perfect or in optimal shape. My skills as a physician had never left me. I was certainly capable of resuming my work, and was happy to do so.

We're All Just Human. Actually, I believed it was a good thing for my patients to see me in a different light. I always felt uncomfortable with the idea of doctors being viewed as figures on a pedestal. I prefer being known as a man humbled by my humanness, a genuine person, who just happens to be a physician interested in caring for others.

Besides, it was a cute scene as I handed my patients' chart to them at the conclusion of a visit. I then asked, "Could you kindly?" After all, I needed both hands on the walker as I maneuvered myself out of the exam room.

Their help was invaluable. Chart in hand, they waited for me to open the door and walk out of the room. They subsequently followed.

I think they appreciated that I promptly returned to work to serve their best interests.

Rehabilitation was no simple process. Although I was pain-free and able to get around fairly well on a walker, I felt like a total klutz. It seemed forever before I would graduate to a cane. I tried multiple times in PT to make this transition, but I was never quite able to make the grade. Because of the nerve damage, my right foot was simply too limp at times. Moreover, I simply lacked the coordination.

Getting Needled. It really does take a village. I also underwent acupuncture from the gifted Gale O'Keffe to enhance my overall rehab. I sought optimal wound healing and an enhanced sense of centeredness.

It doesn't matter whether it's an incision along the midline of the chest, the abdomen, or in my case the back; the body is traumatized and inflamed post-surgery. The right and left sides of the body are truly discombobulated.

Although my neurosurgeon and physical rehab physicians at Cedars-Sinai didn't necessarily subscribe to this theory, I felt acupuncture was an essential component of my healing. This made even more sense when you consider that the nerve damage I had sustained greatly affected my balance, an impediment to my progress.

Requiring the use of a walker for nearly five weeks, I was finally able to transition to a cane. I was a bit wobbly at first, but it didn't take long to master the skill.

It was great to be able to use a cane while working in my office. Now I was actually able to carry the patient's chart in my left arm while holding onto my cane with my right. Funny how such a seemingly small boost in activity level furthered my progress, both physically and emotionally.

Entering my third month of rehab in early September 2008, I was progressing by leaps and bounds with each PT session. I begged my therapist and certified athletic trainer to allow me to go from balancing on the ground with a huge medicine ball to some mild resistance training.

I was hungry to pick up weights again after an absence of over two months. I felt as if I was back home and my strength came back predictably, adding credence to the fact that *muscle has memory.* This could not have been truer for me.

But my coordination was still not up to par. Besides, any attempt to straighten my core while on the floor working with that huge

CHAPTER 13: The Journey Continues

medicine ball just didn't cut it for me. I could barely get on and off the floor.

The energy expended in doing those basic maneuvers simply exhausted me. I'm not some four-legged animal. I don't know who responds best to this sort of therapy, but it sure wasn't me! Working on the floor did nothing for me.

So, I was compelled to go back to the drawing board.

I went to the local YMCA. They had a warm therapy pool where the temperature was ninety-two degrees Fahrenheit. I had learned a series of exercises for back stabilization from my physical therapist back in 1996, when I first developed back pain and disability.

So here I was back in the warm therapy pool, flexing, extending, and side-bending while whipping my legs doing "eggbeaters." The effect of all this was to work my core. It did just that.

I returned to the pool 2-3 times weekly for the next several weeks. Progress wasn't fast, but I steadily improved. Besides, it felt good. Being weightless in water, I felt much more agile and less clumsy.

Gym Rat. After three months of PT where I graduated from a walker to a cane, and while working on strengthening my core, it was time. I made the conscious decision to return to Gold's Gym in Venice, the Mecca of Bodybuilding.

It was October. I had to be totally prepared this time around. I purchased a temporary disability sticker so that I could park my car outside the gym's entrance. I also made prior arrangements with my long-term trainer, Charles Glass.

Known as the Trainer of Champions, Charles had a more defined role now. He would meet me at the gym's entrance. Subsequently, he followed me up the stairs carrying my gym bag and cane while I used the strength of my upper body to ascend two flights of stairs.

There is no elevator in this gym, so I had to work my way up those stairs. I would repeat the process after taking my post work-out shower, again with Charles's help. I learned that almost anything is possible if you want it bad enough, and I wanted it bad.

With a three-month absence from the gym, I was more than ready. I needed to be back, exercising all my muscles while regaining my strength. My emotional well-being demanded it.

Folks couldn't help but comment as the sight of me walking with a cane seemed a bit odd. Here I am this competitive bodybuilder, whom most people knew as "Doc." But none of that mattered to me. I felt the support of my fellow gym members, and I was indeed home. Even if my walking and coordination were less than optimal, my strength came back rapidly as did my muscle mass.

Always searching for the next challenge, I decided to take a long weekend and travel to San Francisco for a friend's wedding. The trip was noteworthy because I had a new goal in mind.

Nothing was going to stop me from attaining it.

CHAPTER 14

THE TURNING POINT

BY THE SECOND WEEK OF OCTOBER, exactly four months after my back surgery, I was ready to venture outside my comfort zone. A close friend was getting married in San Francisco. A weekend was planned with festivities. Without a specific goal in mind, other than relaxing and walking as much as physically possible, I was stoked.

I was beyond ready to spread my wings.

Deeply challenged, I took buses, subways, and cabs from the airport to Union Square and to City Hall where the brief marriage ceremony took place. Then there was a stop in a restaurant in North Beach for the after-event celebration.

But there was absolutely one stop I had to make on my own: The California Academy of Sciences. The Academy is a mix of a *natural history museum*, a *science museum,* and an *aquarium*...complete with a *"living roof."* This remarkable edifice reopened in Golden Gate Park after a long hiatus of remodeling.

Packed to the gills on a Saturday afternoon, the trip was well worth it. But along with the enjoyment came a plethora of discomfort from having to wait in a long line to gain admission. And there was the hassle obtaining lunch from the various truck vendors. This brought only more lines of hungry museumgoers, not to mention the crowds of folks like myself waiting to gain entry into the various exhibits.

But the most onerous aspect of this day trip was that I had no idea where I was going! Taking a subway from my hotel, and then transferring onto a bus, I was left off at the wrong side of the park. I had to endure a long walk with my trusty cane. I was about to call it a day, but my determination took over.

Thank goodness it did, because the museum was truly a jewel.

See Ya Later, Mr. Cane. By Sunday morning I was pretty exhausted from all the walking. I clearly got the message that it was time to get rid of this cane once and for all. It only added to the burden of traveling solo.

Accustomed to my lifestyle in Southern California, it dawned on me how limited my daily walking had become. After all, we use the automobile for even simple chores like going to the post office or dry cleaners. We literally wait ten minutes in our stalled automobile until there is an available parking space within a hundred feet of the gym.

Then because of my physical infirmities from surgery, I limited myself even more. Imagine, I'd handle ninety percent of my heavy resistance training at Gold's Gym, but *I wouldn't walk two city blocks.*

I had never challenged myself in this arena since my back surgery. But this trip to San Francisco was invaluable in helping me realize my limitations. It was time to expand my limits. Being without an automobile in a pedestrian-oriented city, I was compelled to use my legs every step of the way.

Since my departure was not until late afternoon Sunday, a brilliant idea suddenly entered my mind. Why not fully subject myself to the ultimate test of a *wanna-be-warrior!*

It was time to take the leap.

There was a trolley car leaving Union Square ascending the top of Nob Hill. It was literally outside my hotel door. I proceeded to get in and out of that trolley to the foot of the longest, steepest hill in that vicinity. I took a few deep breaths. Then feeling very grounded, I walked both up and down that hill carrying my cane in both hands above my head.

Admittedly, on the ascent I had to stop a few times. I simply was not conditioned for this particular activity. But the truth of the matter is that I made it both ways, without requiring the cane for assistance.

CHAPTER 14: The Turning Point

Arriving at the airport a few hours later, I simply trashed my cane. It was time. And since I had previously arranged for a wheelchair pick up, negotiating the airport would be a snap!

A true turning point had occurred that weekend in San Francisco. I was far from being cocky or even overly-confident about my skills as a walking man, but I knew it would be *downhill from here.*

I was not going to need a device to assist me with ambulation anytime in the near future.

CHAPTER 15

RENEWING HOPE

Returning to Southern California from my weekend away in San Francisco, I was absolutely certain that it was going to be downhill from this point. I had realized the extent of my limitations. Besides, I was determined to do whatever it took to remedy the situation.

It took a lot.

Walking without a cane meant I had to carefully watch my gait and be mindful of my balance. This slowed me down a bit, but I did master the skill of walking unassisted.

Fortunately, I only suffered a single fall, on the carpeted floor in my office! This happened on a day I was rushing, carrying two large charts in one hand. The take-home message here was that I had to practice mindfulness at all times.

Next, I learned how to ascend the stairway at Gold's Gym, which was no easy feat. I realized how much I had depended on the strength of my upper body to power me.

One day in early November 2008, my trainer asked me to repetitively step up and down on a thick wooden block, one foot at a time. Realizing how difficult this was for me, he observed my lack of muscle coordination and blurted out, "Doc, these muscles aren't contracting."

I later learned that he was referring to my anterior tibialis muscle. Its main function was to dorsiflex my right foot. Then it finally hit me that this wasn't simply about needing more practice walking. I had to accept the fact that I had clearly sustained major nerve damage as a result of my back surgery.

The really tough part? *This damage was essentially permanent.*

This realization was anything but good news. I guess I had been hiding behind my walker and cane for the previous four months. I actually thought that I was the poster child for post-surgical success, in spite of my complication.

Quitting isn't Me. I had to keep searching for answers. Fortunately, my voice teacher gave me the name of a remarkable healer, a Rolfer by the name of Russ Pfeiffer.

Rolfing is a system of soft tissue manipulation and movement education that organizes the whole body in gravity. I call it the Cadillac of deep tissue bodywork.

I had worked with different bodyworkers in the past, most of whom were excellent, but I was still skeptical. How could this guy really make a difference? But I figured, why not give him a try?

What I learned was that Russ was a master of movement, the perfect practitioner to bring me to the next level. We started working together in November 2008, approximately five months after my back surgery.

The amazing thing I learned was that, as a result of accidents, back disability, and aging, many adults adopt unhealthy patterns of ambulation. I was certainly not alone in this regard.

But I made remarkable progress over the next several weeks and by year's end I was walking considerably better, albeit far from perfect. Walking upstairs with my gym bag in hand never really became an easy maneuver for me.

I simply persevered.

Each year has generally brought me hope and promise. 2008 was no exception. I had endured severe pain both before and after my surgery. My post-op convalescence brought major challenges.

Self-Pity is Not My Style. Things could have easily been worse. Despite the nerve damage, I was able to pick myself up and walk again. Without surgery I would have been stuck in a wheelchair. But here I was able to practice medicine full time, as well as return to the gym, doing what I love.

If that wasn't enough, I was eventually able to return to my *weekly singing lesson*. How? Finally, I could carry my huge catalogue of songs across busy Venice Boulevard, and up a flight of concrete steps to my voice coach's studio.

That was quite a lot of accomplishment in a relatively short time. In retrospect, 2008 was a heavy-duty year for me. I had endured emergency back surgery and its attendant neurologic sequelae. This was anything but desirable given my prior active lifestyle.

Nonetheless, I triumphed. 2009 held promise as the year for big change, and indeed it was, but I still had to experience *one huge bump in the road.*

CHAPTER 16

THE UNEXPECTED HAPPENS

A Relapse

2009 STARTED OFF QUITE NICELY. My practice was thriving, my training was going well, and my work with Rolfer Russ Pfeiffer continued. I was feeling very upbeat.

Although I was anxious to try my hand at competing in bodybuilding once again, I made the conscious decision to sit back a year. This made good sense since it generally takes a full eighteen months to heal from back surgery. That decision took a lot of pressure off me at the onset of this new year.

But an event happened mid-January that would forever change the course of events in my life. My office manager of nearly seventeen years came to me on a Wednesday evening announcing that she was going to retire in three weeks. Her plan was to relocate to Texas to be near her family. This seemed incredulous. Carol was indispensable on so many levels.

Truthfully, *I have never dealt well with loss*. Before my back surgery, the majority of my back-pain relapses were precipitated by loss and trauma. I recall sitting there—*motionless*—in my office chair for nearly an hour after hearing the news.

How was I going to proceed? In total shock, I was beyond devastated.

I eventually climbed out of the chair, but upon standing I sensed an intense spasm along the right side of my back. Within seconds I was hunched over in a position I knew all too well.

It was the identical sensation I had experienced in 1996—the onset of my back pain. How can this be? Only seven months had passed since my emergency surgery. This simply couldn't be possible.

Thoroughly disgusted with disbelief, I went home, took 800 mg of Ibuprofen, showered, and prayed. The next morning, I awakened with the same pain, which only intensified over the course of the day. Bed rest was obviously the treatment of choice at this juncture, but I was simply too busy to contemplate that option. Besides, I had missed so much work during the time of my back surgery.

I remember having to go to the hospital that day to visit a patient. I couldn't make the distance from the doctor's parking lot to the entrance. I actually had to stop midway and sit by a concrete wall. The pain was that severe.

In a total state of despair, I phoned my good friend and retired chiropractor Ralph, begging him for advice. I even blurted out, "Hell, take me back to surgery." I never expected to stoop to that level, as I was so against any type of recurrent surgical intervention.

The Power of Pain. As I had learned in the past, pain is an incredible motivator. This felt equal to the pain I had experienced before my surgery seven months prior. Ralph quickly responded, "Never will I allow you to go back under the knife again unless there are simply no options."

I felt instant relief because this time around I knew I had someone on my side. Interestingly enough, it was my back surgery that brought the two of us together as friends. One of my longevity patients, Ralph took an active interest in me, noting how determined I was post-operatively.

He convinced me to take a short course of corticosteroids to help with the inflammation. I complied and by the third day the pain was thankfully manageable.

Within the next three days Ralph encouraged me to return to Cedars-Sinai Medical Center to get an updated MRI. Recurrent pain seven months after a supposedly successful back surgery was anything but expected. It made sense that a reevaluation was in order.

Unnecessary Drama. You'd think that this would be fairly easy

CHAPTER 16: The Unexpected Happens

to obtain. Nope. Don't assume we doctors get preferential treatment.

Being that I am not on staff at Cedars-Sinai, and that my insurance would refuse to pay for an MRI without an ordering physician, I had to contact my neurosurgeon to obtain the necessary order. This took numerous phone calls from both me and my office staff.

After three days he finally phoned the order to the radiology department. Being a bit obsessive-compulsive, I decided to question his order. I learned that *he had ordered the wrong study!*

It is fairly common knowledge that an MRI *with contrast* is necessary after one has had back surgery. After all, the surgery itself and the subsequent scar tissue change the anatomy. My surgeon mistakenly ordered the MRI *without contrast.*

Being that my scan was to take place at 8:00 pm that evening, I placed numerous phone calls to both his office and after-hour's exchange. I literally begged him to correct the order before my actual exam. Never did he grant me, a fellow physician, the courtesy of a phone call.

Assuming I could rectify the situation with the MRI technician, I proceeded to my scheduled appointment. The tech agreed with me; given my history, an exam without contrast was simply inadequate.

However, she was completely unwilling to change the exam to one with contrast. After all, she was simply following protocol; *I was not the ordering physician.* She did attempt to phone my doctor who was actually on-call that evening. But he never returned the call. In the end, I took the exam without contrast.

The results of this expensive study were expectedly *uninterpretable* and therefore, *inconclusive.*

One week later my pain had improved, but I was unable to resume training in the gym. Seeing patients in the office was no problem. However, standing for prolonged periods of time, or any extensive walking was out of the question.

Ralph gave me the names of two reputable neurosurgeons in the area. It was time to obtain a second opinion. The first physician, who shall remain nameless, was clearly someone with whom I could not relate.

Bedside Manner? Bringing my eldest daughter with me with the expressed purpose of not missing any details, I was flabbergasted when he entered the room. He gave neither my daughter nor me any eye contact, or even a simple handshake. Okay, not acknowledging me, a fellow physician, is one thing, but *my daughter is cute as a button.* How could anyone possibly ignore her presence?

His bedside manner was frightful. He entered the room, grabbed the chart, stated his name, and asked why I was there. Obviously, he had never taken the time to read the typed questionnaire that I had faxed to his office three days in advance.

I proceeded to say that I was seven months out from emergency back surgery which resulted in neurologic injury; that I was currently presenting with a painful relapse. I also mentioned that I was recommended by Dr. Ralph Abitbol, a retired chiropractor who had referred him several patients in the past. I expected him to say, "How is Ralph doing?"

Instead, he said nothing.

After reading my operative report he then gave me the most cursory neurologic exam imaginable. Seriously, the exam I performed as a third-year medical student was more complete!

Within five minutes of my visit, he blurted out angrily, "This MRI study is useless! It should have been with contrast."

Saying to myself, "Really? Duh!" I attempted to explain the difficulty I had in reaching my former surgeon, but he had no sympathy.

All he could say was, "This is a waste of time. I need a repeat MRI with contrast, a CT scan of the spine and lumbar-sacral spine films. I'll have my assistant schedule these tests for you after which time we can reconvene." With that he left the room without even saying good-bye.

That was it. I took my daughter by the hand and said, "Honey, we're getting the hell out of here. This environment is toxic and anything but therapeutic."

CHAPTER 16: The Unexpected Happens

I eventually consulted with the second neurosurgeon that Ralph had recommended. This gentleman was beyond kind to both my daughter and I. Taking his time to perform a detailed history and physical, he spent forty-five minutes with us. His impression was that I more than likely would not require additional back surgery.

He did believe, however, that an MRI with contrast as well as lumbar-sacral spine films were in order. Being that we connected easily, I was happy to return to Cedars for a repeat study.

I returned to this physician within a week of my MRI to learn of the results—*which were anything but positive.*

CHAPTER 17

MAKING THE MOST OF A LOUSY SITUATION

I MUST HAVE BEEN IN DREAMLAND. I expected my repeat MRI to show no more than post-surgical changes. Nothing could be farther from the truth. In fact, the results were worse that I could even imagine.

Recall that my surgery was a decompression laminectomy, performed on an emergent basis to treat critical spinal stenosis (or narrowing of the spinal canal). This was at the level of L4-L5.

But after reviewing both the pre-op MRI from 6/2008 *and* the post-op MRI from 2/2009, I learned that in addition to the spinal stenosis, I had another serious problem noted in my pre-op MRI; there was a 3-4 mm disc bulge at the level of L4-L5. This was the exact level of my stenosis.

Imagine my disbelief! Absolutely nothing of the sort was discussed by the neurosurgeon prior to my surgery.

MRI Am Mad! Now, I might have been medicated with plenty of opiates, but I would never forget such vital information. Furthermore, my family and friends who were with me at the time confirmed that there was *never any mention of a 3-4 mm bulge.*

As the patient, I was infuriated. Detailed information from that first MRI was withheld from me. Forget the fact that I was a fellow physician.

It was clear on the first MRI, and on the written report from the radiologist. Yet, this was somehow ignored by the neurosurgeon. It was as if someone said, "Humm, physician and bodybuilder? We're going in and out of this procedure as fast as we can!"

In truth, I have no idea what he was actually thinking, but important anatomical information was ignored. As a patient prostrated in pain, *I suffered as a result.*

The really bad news was that this 3-4 mm bulge was now, seven months later, an 11 mm herniation. If that wasn't enough, I also learned that there remained a fair amount of residual spinal stenosis.

So, here I was with a new problem that could and should have been treated at the time of the surgery with a procedure called a discectomy. This fiasco of a result could have been easily avoided by performing the discectomy simultaneously with the decompression laminectomy. It's a matter of simple physics. The decompression at the time of surgery acted as a vacuum. It more than likely sucked that bulge into a frank herniation.

Sometimes, surgical mishaps do happen, and no physician or surgeon is immune. A laminectomy refers to the cutting away of a portion of the bone, known as the lamina. It is commonly performed to provide more room for the spinal nerves to exit.

Neurologic injury, which is what I experienced, can happen. But to ignore the presence of a bulge—which allows it to be sucked in like a vacuum, creating a huge herniation is *pure negligence.*

This is especially true when the bulge was so clearly visualized on the MRI.

I could have filed a lawsuit against this physician, but putting myself through more stress would do nothing to improve my physical outcome. And the last thing I wanted was another possible heart attack brought on by the lengthy, difficult legal process of a physician suing another physician.

It simply seemed too stressful. And too distasteful.

I decided to accept my reality and embark on a path of rehabilitation. Having my friend and mentor Ralph alongside me, I felt comforted this time around. time around.

Most importantly, I didn't feel alone.

CHAPTER 17: Making the Most of A Lousy Situation

The Creation of my Dream-Team. Ralph, a recently retired and greatly respected chiropractor, orchestrated my therapeutic moves. Ralph became the director of my "Dream-Team," along with my acupuncturist Gale O'Keefe and of course my Rolfer, Russ Pfeiffer.

Fortunately, there was no need for surgery as there were no new neurologic deficits. My only true complaint was pain, which was manageable at this point. Besides, I had made the conscious decision that one back surgery in a lifetime was more than enough for this man to endure.

Ralph researched *spinal decompression* units as an alternative approach. Even though I was left with a large, herniated disc, it is a known fact that discs are not static. They can actually move. I was more than willing to explore this possibility.

Together we visited a couple of facilities. One facility located in Irvine, California, seemed quite sophisticated, replete with several decompression tables. The entire set-up seemed quite impersonal to me.

It looked like an assembly line.

The chiropractic director seemed overly aggressive. He stated emphatically that I would need a minimum of four weekly treatments. Furthermore, at the end of each three-week interval, I would be revaluated by a physical therapist. Their job was to modify my treatment plan accordingly.

This didn't jive well with me. It seemed like an unnecessary, formalized protocol with a copious amount of add-on expenses. Furthermore, given the demands of my medical practice, the hour-plus drive each way was unfathomable.

My Own Medical Advocate. Over the time of my physical struggles, more and more I was claiming the role of Medical Advocate. By now, I had an *intuitive feel for what worked for me,* and I was *willing to go out on a limb* to get it.

Next, we came across a true godsend, Cloud Chiropractic, located one town away in La Habra, California. I immediately sensed

Dr. Glen Cloud to be a kind, hard-working and very positive-minded chiropractor.

He had one decompression table on site, and he was confident that I would experience great relief of my symptoms, and achieve results beyond my expectations. The atmosphere of the office was truly caring and upbeat. I immediately sensed that I had discovered a center conducive to healing.

Don't get the idea that everything was rosy! I still had back pain on a daily basis. Fortunately, it didn't interfere with my duties as a physician. Being both extremely compliant and determined, I attended therapy sessions with Dr. Cloud three evenings per week.

He remarked that I resembled a "human pretzel" when we first met, as I was so twisted, misaligned, and bent over at the waist. The decompression table and subsequent stretching of my spine, along with Dr. Cloud's physical yet subtle adjustments proved to be effective.

Within a month I was completely pain-free, and I was back in the gym in less than six weeks from commencing treatment.

In six weeks, I was able to cut back to two weekly sessions. At the end of the third month, I transitioned to maintenance therapy. At present time, I still do one session per week.

It has served me quite well.

Better Than Money. An additional boost to my healing was an amazingly simple but extremely therapeutic apparatus that Dr. Cloud had acquired. Called an ATM machine, it has nothing to do with obtaining cash! Short for *Active Therapeutic Movement* (www.back-project.com), this machine allowed me to regain what I had lost with back surgery: my *core strength*.

Using the physical resistance of Dr. Cloud and his staff, I was strapped securely in the upright position performing three very basic movements: *flexion* at the waist, *extension* at the waist and *side-bending* to both my right and left sides.

CHAPTER 17: Making the Most of A Lousy Situation

This mere three-minute maneuver brought a feeling of strength and stability that I had lost just prior to my back surgery. This lack of a strong core had continued to plague me post-operatively.

I had done my best to work on my core in physical therapy, but I never achieved sizable results. Given my degree of nerve damage, just *getting on and off the floor was taxing* for me. Forget about manipulating my body using a large medicine ball. I was literally exhausted.

The results had been nil.

I also tried various exercises in the warm therapy pool at the local YMCA. It felt great, but it also did little to strengthen my core. I simply wasn't the average Joe. I was a 220-pound muscular bodybuilder who had sustained a serious injury as a result of surgery. Being weightless in the water simply did not transfer over to being upright and ambulatory on land.

But the ATM machine worked. Words can't express the gains I acquired. Suffice it to say, my training at the gym truly escalated at this time, and by June of 2009, exactly one-year post-surgery, I was feeling my regular self.

I knew intuitively that within another year I would be back on the posing stage for a comeback at the Masters National bodybuilding competition.

Back surgery in itself tends to be extremely debilitating. It often requires a long period of rehabilitation and convalescence. Many people simply relinquish their power to reclaim their health.

But I couldn't follow the path of a defeated individual. With my driven attitude and with the help of my *Dream-Team*, I truly evolved and became my own *Medical Advocate*. This is a position that I maintain to this day, and how I mentor my clients and patients.

My deep belief: *no degree of adversity or recurrent setbacks can alter my quest to achieve optimal health.*

CHAPTER 18

GOOD ISN'T GOOD ENOUGH

From late spring 2009 through the spring of 2010, my goal was to get into the best shape of my life. I was a year out from back surgery, and was finally feeling like my former self. I knew inwardly that I just had to return to the posing stage and compete in the 2010 Masters National bodybuilding contest.

Not Much Agreement. Despite the *consternation of essentially everyone around me,* with the exception of my trainer Charles Glass, I was adamant about proceeding. I believed that it was not only plausible, but absolutely *essential to my physical and emotional well-being.*

I had been forced to bow out of this particular competition six weeks prior to the actual show in June 2008. At that time my focus shifted to *emergency back surgery, subsequent nerve damage* and *a ton of rehabilitation.*

Unfinished Business. If I was going to retire from competition, it would be on my own terms. Emergency surgery was definitely not part of the plan! I owed it to myself to make this comeback. Call it *strong will* and *intense drive.* I simply could not be talked out of this decision.

But it just wasn't about a national-level bodybuilding contest. I had come to believe that I had a much larger goal to accomplish. By late spring 2009 I had made the conscious decision to finally write my book. Additionally, I began my next professional foray, into the world of inspirational/motivational speaking—spotlighting my take on *health and wellness.*

This was not a whimsical decision! I wasn't happy with the practice of medicine in this country, and had planned to write a book as early as 2002.

From Both Sides of the Table: When Dr. Becomes Patient

I envisioned a new paradigm in which patients had both a **bill of rights** *and* **responsibilities** in managing their own health care. Although the term was foreign to me in 2002, I was setting the stage for motivating patients to become their own *Medical Advocates.*

Difficult times. But the time was not ripe. Dealing with an ill ex-wife who eventually passed away, becoming a single working dad, and attempting to nurture two adolescent girls—one with a serious eating disorder—was simply beyond overwhelming for me.

My own medical issues intervened!

Again, there are no accidents. I think I had to become a patient myself and literally experience being hospitalized, before I could fully comprehend the plight of an ill individual.

What I learned was more than I could ever imagine. My experiences as a patient compelled me to get out there and tell my story. My goal was clear: *motivate* others to *navigate* the system and *stay in control* when it comes to their health.

One evening I attended a seminar given by the Independent Writer's Association of Southern California. This was actually a panel discussion on "how to market your book." The last panelist was Jack Barnard, a speaking coach par excellence. In his eight-minute presentation, he mentioned three items that I shall always remember:

1. If you think your *book needs to be published* before you begin your speaking career, you are wrong.
2. If you've had a *hunky-dory life,* no one is interested in hearing your story.
3. If you want to be a *great speaker,* you better be a *great storyteller.*

"Wow," I said to myself, "this guy really speaks my language." I immediately nudged my friend Helen, who attended the seminar with me: "Helen, I need to hire this man."

Jack was speaking to me. I was pretty sure I met his three criteria. I hadn't started writing my book, although I did have quite a few ideas. I certainly wasn't privy to a privileged lifestyle! Having spoken in front of numerous groups in the past, I always felt comfortable. I never suffered from stage fright, and I had always been told I was a good speaker.

But being good isn't good enough. I wanted to become a *great* speaker and storyteller.

Following the program, I introduced myself to Jack. We met within a week. He seemed to like my candid, natural way. He immediately took an interest in my story with all its recent calamities. Most importantly, he was excited by my *mission*: to motivate others to take *control of their health, using myself as a positive role model.*

Within another week he urged me to attend a special forum sponsored by Speakers Services. Jack led a couple of workshops that truly excited me. There was no question that speaking was a way I wanted to proceed.

Jack began to coach me, and in late 2010 I attended an intensive interactive *Speaker's Boot Camp* led by him.

Boot Camp described it quite well! It was serious work. All six of the participants prepared several assignments including *two twenty-minute talks,* a *"niche-pitch"* and an *elevator speech* where we had to describe our purpose in less than thirty seconds.

Most importantly, we learned how to develop a template or basic outline which would serve the speaker regardless of the actual topic of the presentation. What I learned was that the speaker's style never truly varies from one talk to another.

These assignments were taxing, and Jack was a powerful coach who could be quite critical and demanding. But it was an incredible experience.

My Brand: Medical Advocate. I walked away with a renewed confidence, a clearer, more defined purpose, and a branding that I continue to maintain. My hope, my goal is to encourage my patients, my readers, and my audiences to become their own best Medical Advocate by staying in the driver's seat when it comes to their health and well-being.

Truly, this was an exciting, challenging time for me. That painful relapse at the beginning of the year when I learned to explore my options and become my own Medical Advocate impacted me greatly.

It was the impetus to grow myself in every dimension.

Ending the year, I felt confident and ready to return to competitive bodybuilding on the national level. But I had a much bigger quest. I felt the need to truly tell my story and to become an inspirational speaker as the Medical Advocate.

I was driven and determined to expand my horizons in 2010. After all, *being good isn't good enough!*

PART TWO

The Medical: Where Am I?

CHAPTER 19

HEART FACTS: WHY ME?

The Major Players

IT WAS OBVIOUS TO ME, and essentially everyone else around me that I was in complete denial at the time of my cardiac event. (Even today I still prefer to call it an *event*, as opposed to an actual *heart attack*.)

True, I was most fortunate that I did not have a complete blockage in any of my coronary arteries at the time of my presentation. What I experienced were intermittent symptoms, which suggested a "stuttering" heart attack. No sensation lasted greater than twenty minutes.

Subsequent echocardiograms (ultrasounds) performed to check the function of my heart muscle have repeatedly demonstrated normal wall motion. That equates to no objective evidence of heart muscle damage.

Well, that may sound great, but I did have a small, but definite, heart attack-otherwise known as a myocardial infarction. This was evident by a very slight rise of a cardiac enzyme known as Troponin I. Detected by a routine blood test, it was consistent with transient dysfunction of my heart muscle.

After denial comes the next question: WHY ME? I was a patient with none of the usual risk factors, but as we have seen, *no one is immune.*

Maybe you're thinking: *why is it essential to state the pertinent heart facts in yet another book?*

Here's why: Heart disease remains the *leading cause of death* in the western world. Formerly known as a *man's disease,* it has been shown to be an *equal opportunity killer,* crossing all lines of gender, race, education, and economic status.

Cardiovascular disease (CVD) remains the leading cause of death in the United States, responsible for 840,768 deaths in 2016. Approximately *every forty seconds, an American will experience a heart attack.* The average age of first myocardial infarction is 65.6 years old for men and 72.0 years for women. In 2011, about 326,000 people experienced out-of-hospital cardiac arrests in the United States. Of those treated by emergency medical services, only 10.6% survived. That's pretty grim. Most out-of-hospital cardiac arrests are complications of heart attacks. [1]

Being a seasoned cardiologist, I was quite familiar with these facts, but suddenly they took on new meaning for me. I was totally out of touch when I insisted on driving myself to the ER that fateful day in November 2006. My daughter was absolutely correct in telling me to do otherwise.

Know this, I would NEVER recommend that a patient drive himself to the hospital under such circumstances.

So why did this happen to me? Could it have been prevented? To examine this, we must look at the various risk factors that lead to heart disease.

MAJOR RISK FACTORS FOR HEART DISEASE

Risk factors are conditions that predispose a person to more likely develop a disease. The ones listed below have been unequivocally linked to coronary heart disease:

- **High blood pressure (Hypertension)**
- **Smoking**
- **Elevated cholesterol**
- **Physical Inactivity**
- **Obesity**
- **Diabetes**
- **Family history (of early heart disease)**
- **Age...45 or greater for men...55+ for women**

Closer evaluation of these risk factors reveals that *most of the above are either preventable or treatable.* Unfortunately, there is nothing we can do to alter our genetics or advancing age. But with my hand on my (lucky) heart, I can tell you that in my own practice of thirty-five years, I have seen countless patients *beat the odds* by adhering to *a healthy lifestyle,* while not allowing their genetics to run them.

A word about women and heart disease: during my training in the early to mid-1980s, we were still under the guise that this was a *man's disease.*

In fact, essentially all the research to date had been performed on men. This is *like comparing apples to oranges.* We know today that heart disease kills more women than all cancers combined. While the mortality rate for men with coronary artery disease has been declining for the past thirty years, *the number of women who die from it is rising.*

One of the reasons why the concept of women and heart disease has been grossly misunderstood is the age in which women typically present. For women, age becomes a factor at fifty-five and greater. After menopause, women are more apt to acquire heart disease, in part, because their body's production of estrogen drops significantly. Women who have undergone early menopause are twice as likely to develop heart disease when compared to women who continue to menstruate.

MAJOR MODIFIABLE RISK FACTORS FOR HEART DISEASE:

HYPERTENSION (High Blood Pressure)
According to recent statistics from the American Heart Association (AHA) released in January 2018, over one million adults in the United States are hypertensive, most of whom don't even know it. The majority are inadequately treated. This is the *most common risk factor* for not only heart attacks, but also for strokes.

Moreover, it is a major risk factor for advanced kidney disease. In 92% of people afflicted, there is no identifiable cause, hence the commonly used term "essential hypertension." We do know that it tends to run in families and that it increases with age as our arteries stiffen. Unfortunately, there is no cure, but *it is treatable.*

I am often asked what is the optimal blood pressure (Bp) for a given person in their 30s, 40s, 50s, 60s and beyond? My answer is always the same: 120/70. Although this value may not be seen in the average patient, it is still the paragon. In my experience, *folks who maintain normal blood pressure throughout their lives are less likely to suffer heart attacks, strokes and renal (kidney) disease.*

While there is a myriad of treatments available, whenever possible, I prefer to go natural. *Weight loss* and *exercise* remain the mainstay when it comes to a solid reduction in blood pressure. Exercise relaxes the arteries throughout the body, imposing less resistance on the heart to pump. A lower blood pressure will often accompany those who do regular aerobic exercise.

A low sodium diet may help, especially in those who are salt sensitive.

This includes the elderly population, and those with advanced kidney disease. Remember that the majority of the sodium in your diet doesn't come from your saltshaker, but from all the processed and fast foods so readily consumed by our society.

What about supplements? I've had varying success with these. Supplements may help certain individuals, but not others. Not unlike medication, it's trial and error. Certainly, adequate potassium and magnesium are important in maintaining an optimal blood pressure. I'm a strong believer in Co-enzyme Q10 and fish oil as they may also play a role. I created my own product (*Pressurewise*) where the active ingredient, olive leaf extract may help lower blood pressure.

There are some natural therapies as well. Biofeedback may be useful in those with a strong emotional or stress component to their hypertension.

CHAPTER 19: Heart Facts: Why Me?

Having authored a small study on *Earthing*, I was able to see the effects of Earthing (or being grounded) on lowering blood pressure. It can work beautifully in certain individuals. Earthing is a natural blood thinner, and is both anti-inflammatory and anti-aging. It's as simple as walking barefoot on soil or sand, absorbing electrons from the earth's surface. And it's absolutely free! [2]

Now we come to the topic of *medication*—which plays an important role in treating hypertension. Yes, there are potential side effects, not to mention the expense of taking medication—often for a lifetime. Yet, we sometimes have to employ a combination of meds to achieve the requisite drop in blood pressure.

If medication is needed, then I fervently believe that it should be used. Fortunately, patient compliance is better today than in years past, since newer classes of medications have fewer side effects and can often be administered on a once-daily basis.

How low do we need to go in order to achieve survival benefits? In my practice I attempt to use as few medications as possible to get the blood pressure below 140 for the top or systolic value and below 85 for the diastolic or bottom value. I am more aggressive with my younger patients, where I am often able to get the systolic blood pressure down to 130 or even lower.

Adequate blood pressure control requires patience for both patient and physician. One size clearly does not fit all. It's more of a trial-and-error phenomenon.

Looking at published data, however, only 50% of the general population in the United States can boast a blood pressure less than 140/90. This underscores the difficulty in obtaining adequate blood pressure control.

SPRINT...Recently, an important trial published in late 2015 brought this very topic to the forefront. Known as the *SPRINT study*, the investigators found that deaths were reduced by nearly one-quarter when systolic blood pressure was lowered to a target value of 120 rather than 140 mmHg. Furthermore, there was a 30% reduction in cardiovascular events and stroke. [3]

This was a large multi-site trial that enrolled more than 9,300 subjects. The participants were all over the age of 50, and diabetics were excluded.

These findings shocked many cardiologists. Keep in mind that the design of the study was complex. Following such a stringent protocol is *simply not practical in the real world.*

Even the authors of this study concluded that attempting to achieve these new goals would be demanding and time-consuming for both providers and patients, with increased medication costs and more frequent office visits.

I raise this question: *Do the risks outweigh the benefits?* More than likely a practice like this would require a minimum of three drugs taken daily. Potential adverse effects—due to sudden dangerous drops in blood pressure—include dizziness and fainting. Then there are possible electrolyte abnormalities and worsening kidney function.

A recent meta-analysis (a statistical procedure for combining data from multiple studies), concluded that a systolic Bp target of less than 130 mmHg provided optimal balance between efficacy and safety [4]

What's my bottom line? As a practicing cardiologist I attempt to do whatever I can to improve both longevity and quality of life in my patients. I've always assumed that lower was best in treating hypertension, but achieving lofty goals like this is simply *unrealistic for most.*

A word of caution. Regarding the elderly population, a study published in the Archives of Internal Medicine in late 2012, reported that *older hypertensive patients are at risk of falling and sustaining subsequent hip fractures* after initiation of blood pressure-lowering therapy. This is most commonly seen during the first forty-five days of beginning treatment. [5]

We need to be especially cognizant of this fact in treating this population. Any sudden drop in blood pressure could lead to dizziness and falls.

CHAPTER 19: Heart Facts: Why Me?

The actual strategy employed will surely differ among cardiologists. I, for one, always adhere to the philosophy I learned in medical school: "primum non nocere." This is an old Latin phrase which translates to "first, do no harm."

Hypertension remains the number one risk factor for heart disease and stroke. Even with no definitive cure in sight, it is treatable for the majority of people. There simply is no reason why anyone today should be walking around with poorly controlled blood pressure.

SMOKING

What can I possibly say about the perils of smoking that have not been previously addressed? Yet, it is a truly a pet peeve of mine since it took the life of my father at the age of sixty-three.

But I understand it fully. It is not simply a matter of will power. I don't believe the majority of smokers love it.

It is a serious addiction, and *smokers carry more than twice the risk of heart attack than nonsmokers.* It is also the leading cause of lung cancer which claimed my dad's life, not to mention Chronic Obstructive Pulmonary Disease (COPD), the third most common cause of death in the United States.

There is absolutely no saving grace when it comes to smoking. *Smoking is also the most preventable risk factor.* Like most physicians, I echo these words: **"If you smoke, quit."**

But I don't stop there. Some patients can quit at will. Certainly, being hit with a heart attack or stroke is a good enough reason to quit. However, let us not forget that we are dealing with an *addiction*.

As far as a pharmacologic approach is concerned, there are nicotine patches or chewing gum, which I call a temporary fix, since they still contain the parent drug, NICOTINE. Then there is Zyban (Bupropion Hydrochloride) which has been studied as a non-nicotine aid for smoking cessation. Initially developed and marketed as an antidepressant (Wellbutrin), it has subsequently been shown to help in smoking cessation.

Then the pharmaceutical giant Pfizer came out with a medication of a completely different class. Named Chantix (Varenicline), this is a non-nicotine pill, which targets nicotine receptors in the brain, attaches to them, and blocks nicotine from reaching them.

A 2006 JAMA study demonstrated that Chantix was effective in smoking cessation in 44% of users, versus 30 % of those taking Zyban and 18% of those taking placebo (sugar pill). This studied contained over 1,000 patients and took place over a twelve-week period. [6]

But know this, *Chantix is no panacea,* and the relapse rate is significant. Furthermore, it can pose some serious *psychiatric side effects,* including *depression and suicidal ideation.* A 2011 on-line review by Dr. Curt Furberg, professor of Public Health Sciences at Wake Forest Baptist Medical Center referenced the fact that Chantix was eight times more likely to be linked with a risk of suicide. [7]

An updated review by the FDA in 2011 reported that Chantix may increase the risk of cardiovascular events. A meta-analysis ordered by the governmental agency and conducted by drug maker Pfizer found a higher occurrence of major adverse cardiovascular events with this drug than with placebo—including death, heart attack and stroke. The FDA noted, however, that such events were uncommon in both groups, and the increased risk was not statistically significant. [8]

No question, *smoking* carries significant health risks. It is responsible for *one in five deaths in the United States* each year, and adds $139 billion to health care costs annually. Quitting is exceedingly difficult. 36 % of the nation's smokers try to quit each year, but *less than 5% succeed* for six months or longer.

There have been reports of varying success with alternative modalities such as *hypnosis* and *acupuncture.* Fascinating to me is a form of neurofeedback known as *LENS* (Low Energy Neurofeedback Systems). This is a passive non-pharmacologic approach which involves communicating with your native brainwaves to make alterations in brain "gridlock"—allowing for *healthier behavior,* such as allaying generalized anxiety and the anxiety associated with addictions. [9][10]

CHAPTER 19: Heart Facts: Why Me?

Here's the bottom line: *simply saying "don't smoke" may not be terribly effective* for those suffering from true addiction. Physicians must encourage their patients to quit smoking, but what is needed is *close follow-up and ongoing encouragement.*

Being open to various options is also important. In my opinion, optimal success can be achieved when there is a solid patient-physician relationship, and a willingness from the patient to change behavior.

ELEVATED CHOLESTEROL

Opinions vary regarding the significance of elevated cholesterol and the risk for heart disease, but most agree that the risk increases as your total amount of cholesterol rises. In general, your total *cholesterol goal should be less than 200 mg/dl.*

HDL, the good cholesterol—I call it the *healthy cholesterol*—acts to transport cholesterol back to the liver for disposal. This value should ideally be greater than 40 mg/dl in men and 50 mg/dl in women. Elevated HDL is generally thought to be advantageous. It helps to *prevent plaque formation in our arteries.*

LDL, known as the "bad cholesterol"—the *lousy cholesterol*—is one of the many components of arterial plaque. This value should be less than 130 mg/dl.

Do I try to achieve such values in every patient? My answer is an emphatic NO! This is when *risk stratification* comes into play. Due to media promulgation and the availability of statins, I'm concerned that *many people are being over-treated* by a list that includes *lovastatin, pravastatin, simvastatin, Lipitor* (atorvastatin), and *Crestor* (rosuvastatin).

Presently we are even treating children with statins, not knowing the long-term risks.

To avoid further events, anyone with *confirmed coronary disease* or a *previous event* or *intervention* such as balloon angioplasty/stent or bypass graft surgery *should be treated aggressively.* Other high-risk groups are those with *carotid artery disease* and/or *peripheral artery disease.*

We also tend to be aggressive with the diabetic population, as up to 70% of diabetics will experience a heart attack or stroke in their lifetime.

With these high-risk groups, the aim is to lower the LDL to the 70 range, if possible, without causing untoward side events. I completely agree with the need to use statins in these high-risk groups.

A new class of meds has entered the scene which reduces LDL cholesterol to very low levels. There seems to be this push among many cardiologists practicing today that "lower is better." We are talking as low as 50-60, or even lower. I'm not so sure about that. We need LDL cholesterol for the brain.

These new drugs are biologics, and are known as PCSK9 inhibitors. Injected subcutaneously twice a month, they are relatively new and long-term studies on safety are unavailable. There may well be a place for these drugs in a select number of cases (and I have used them on several of my patients). Their exact role, however, has yet to be defined.

Still, I see folks coming into my office on a weekly basis on statin therapy with mild-to-moderate elevations in their cholesterol levels, and *no history of coronary disease or stroke.*

This is overkill and all it benefits is the pharmaceutical industry!

Cholesterol is not some major villain within our body. It is essential for life. It is a precursor for all sex hormones, vitamin D, and bile acids. Furthermore, it is a vital component of cell membranes within our brain.

We can't live without it!

Run-of-the-mill *cholesterol isn't the culprit* in causing arterial plaque, but *oxidized cholesterol is.* Oxidation is a chemical reaction that occurs within our body. Think of a nail that rusts when exposed to water, or a freshly- cut apple that turns brown when exposed to air. Oxidation is defined as the interaction between oxygen molecules and the many substances with which they contact, from metal to living tissue.

CHAPTER 19: Heart Facts: Why Me?

Oxidized LDL can promote inflammation within our arteries that supply blood to our heart and major organs. We now know that inflammation sets the stage for plaque. This is what increases our risk of a heart attack or stroke. The oxidation of LDL occurs when the LDL cholesterol particles within our bodies react with free radicals. The oxidized LDL itself then becomes more reactive with the surrounding tissues, which can produce tissue damage.

We know that consuming a diet high in *trans fats* can increase the oxidation of LDL. Other factors that can contribute to LDL oxidation are *smoking*, poorly controlled *diabetes or metabolic syndrome*.

Once LDL becomes oxidized, it can damage the inner lining (endothelium) of our blood vessels setting the stage for arterial plaque.

So, it isn't merely LDL cholesterol that causes plaque, but *oxidized LDL.*

LDL is not some homogenous deadly substance. Sophisticated laboratory testing can further break down LDL cholesterol into the size of the actual particle. This is to distinguish large buoyant or fluffy LDL particles from small dense LDL particles.

Small dense LDL particles are readily oxidized and enter arterial walls more readily than large buoyant particles by 40%. *Why is this important? The therapy is completely different.* Statins are by far the most widely used medications today, which lower both total and LDL cholesterol. In fact, they lower LDL cholesterol quite nicely. However, they do nothing to alter the *size* of the LDL particle. Only *niacin* has been successful in this regard.

The only way to measure LDL particle size is to ask your physician to order the test. There are a number of specialty labs that perform this test. One is the *VAP cholesterol test*. Another excellent option is available at *Quest Diagnostics*. They have adopted the testing methodology from the now defunct Berkeley Heart Lab. Quest has also recently purchased Cleveland Heart Lab. This lab can actually measure oxidized LDL. Additionally, Boston Heart

Diagnostics, one of my very favorite labs, performs advanced cardiac testing as well.

Don't be surprised if your physician is unaware of this test. Many cardiologists fail to order it. Here's a clue that might prompt you to ask for this testing: if *your triglyceride level is high and/or your HDL level is low,* there is a good chance that you may have a preponderance of *small dense LDL particles.*

But again, getting actually tested is the only valid way to assess your individual risk.

Anyone can be at risk of developing small, dense LDL cholesterol, but there seems to be a large inherited predisposition with incidence among 35-45% of the population. And lifestyle can play a role. People at risk of developing small, dense LDL cholesterol include those who fall into the following categories [11] [12]

High carbohydrate intake
High trans fat intake
Uncontrolled diabetes
High triglycerides, low HDL
Metabolic syndrome

LIFESTYLE

When approaching the topic of lowering cholesterol, more specifically oxidized LDL, I first employ and even exhaust *lifestyle measures.* Going straight to medication goes against my grain, unless we're talking about astronomically high levels, or in patients who have experienced a cardiac event or stroke.

First, this process did not happen overnight, so there is *no immediate need to urgently lower the levels.* Furthermore, when we go straight to meds, physicians are not engaging the patients in lifestyle modification. *Empowering patients* might well benefit them by not only *preventing heart disease,* but also *cancer* and other diseases of *aging.*

It's as if we're saying, "Well, I know you won't be able to do this on your own, so we might as well go straight to meds." I am completely against this philosophy of medical practice. *Patients need to feel* **empowered, not belittled.**

CHAPTER 19: Heart Facts: Why Me?

To prevent the oxidation of LDL cholesterol the following are mandatory:

- *Stop smoking.* Period!
- *Exclude trans fats* from your diet, such as pastries, deep-fried foods, potato chips, and foods cooked with lard. This basically includes all processed foods and anything edible found in a box, a bag, and in many cases, cans.
- *Add plenty of fruits and vegetables.* Besides packing in a lineup of nutrients, they possess antioxidants with anti-inflammatory properties that may help reduce LDL oxidation.
- *Control diabetes and/or metabolic syndrome,* since these entities are inflammatory in nature and set the stage for LDL oxidation.

Although small, dense LDL particle size is most likely genetic in the majority of cases, there are some measures one can take to help mitigate the formation of this LDL subclass. These include:

- *Lower carbohydrate and trans-fat intake*
- Optimally *control diabetes or metabolic syndrome*
- *Manage obesity* (by weight loss and regular exercise)
- Use the *appropriate medications* if needed (i.e. medications that alter the LDL particle size). Niacin can often accomplish this task. **Statins will do NOTHING to increase the LDL particle size.**

Quite a lot has been published on the effect of *elevated cholesterol and heart disease,* but I personally believe it has been *overemphasized.* Certainly, it is a major risk factor for heart disease—especially in the oxidized state and for folks with small LDL particle size.

However, *a normal cholesterol level doesn't mean that one is off the hook.* Know this: **50% of those who experience a heart attack have normal cholesterol levels.**

I was one of them!

PHYSICAL INACTIVITY

Over the past four decades, numerous scientific reports have examined the relationship between *physical activity, physical fitness,* and *heart disease.* Expert panels, convened by such prestigious organizations as the Centers for Disease Control and Prevention (CDC), the American College of Sports Medicine (ACSM), and the American Heart Association (AHA), along with the 1996 US Surgeon General's Report on Physical Activity and Health, reinforced scientific evidence linking regular physical activity to cardiovascular health.

The bottom line is clear: *the more active or fit individuals are at any age, the less the incidence of coronary heart disease* (CHD). [13]

The scientific data noted above, which was apparent by the mid 1990's, led to the decision by the AHA to add *physical inactivity* to the list of major risk factors for heart disease, joining *hypertension, smoking* and *elevated cholesterol.*

With the information we have today, **failing to exercise on a regular basis is as much as a mistake as continuing to smoke.** It's as if one is asking for a premature death and/or morbidity. This is not wellness!

Research shows that physically inactive people are *twice as likely* to develop heart disease as people who engage in regular exercise. As many as 250,000 deaths per year in the United States are attributable to a lack of regular physical activity.

These benefits hold true *not only for prevention of heart disease,* but for a number of non-cardiovascular diseases, such as *adult* (type 2) *diabetes, hypertension, osteoporosis,* and various *cancers.*

The truth of the matter is that most Americans lead sedentary lives, exercising infrequently or not at all. In fact, less than a one-third of Americans meet the minimum recommendations for activity as outlined by the CDC, ACSM, and AHA. [14] People who don't exercise have higher rates of death and heart disease compared to those who perform even mild-to-moderate amounts of physical activity. Even leisure-time activities like gardening can lower one's risk of heart disease.

My recommendations are essentially the same as outlined by the AHA. The average healthy adult should exercise *thirty minutes a day, five days a week at moderate intensity.* To benefit the heart and cardiovascular system, exercise should be *aerobic*, involving the large muscle groups. Such activities include brisk walking, cycling, jumping rope, rowing, or swimming.

OBESITY
Obesity has become a major epidemic in the United States, with as much 42% of adults affected. In all, more than two-thirds of adults in the United States are *overweight or obese.* What is even more troublesome is that these figures appear to grow each decade with no sign of let up. Fatness is associated with a number of comorbidities, including several forms of heart disease.

Although heredity explains 30-70% of cases of obesity, *environmental* contributions seem to be increasingly more common since the gene pool has remained stable since the mid-1970s. [15]

Diets high in fat and calories are a major factor. But there has been a reduction in fat consumption in this country from 40% of calories in 1965 to 34% of calories since the 1990s. Still, a decrease in obesity has not taken place. In fact, it continued to increase during this time period.

The major villain? SUGAR!

In the 1990s there was much attention to reducing fat from the diet. Enter the advent of *fat-free cookies, cakes,* and *cereals*, all packed with sugar. Thinking they could reduce weight, *Americans kept eating.* The converse actually occurred. The country got fatter!

Prior to the 1990s the relationship between obesity and coronary heart disease was viewed as indirect. We cardiologists knew the association between obesity and other risk factors, including hypertension, elevated cholesterol, decreased HDL or good cholesterol, and Type 2 diabetes. But more recent long-term studies have definitely targeted obesity as an independent risk factor for coronary artery disease.

This ultimately led to the decision of the AHA to "upgrade" obesity to the status of a major risk factor, joining those discussed in the preceding paragraphs. This correlation appears to exist for both men and women. [15]

With regards to treatment, weight reduction is obviously necessary. Again, this goes back to my personal preference, *lifestyle*. *Weight loss* and *a regular exercise program* are keys to optimal health.

I generally do not subscribe to fad diets—or any particular diet in general. I have never had much faith in weight-reduction drugs due to their side effects, especially with regard to the cardiovascular system.

There are currently more weight reduction drugs in the pipeline, in the process of being scrutinized by the FDA. I don't place too much hope in these medications. (And it certainly adds burden to our ailing medical economy, as such drugs will not be inexpensive!)

Know this; *drugs do nothing to encourage a change in lifestyle. NOTHING!* They can even act as excuses to condone poor behavior.

Side note: *Bariatric surgery* is rather drastic, and is certainly not devoid of major side-effects, but it *may prove lifesaving for the morbidly obese*. Several studies have suggested that gastrointestinal surgery for obesity does reduce cardiovascular mortality and in those with Type II diabetes, both cardiovascular and overall mortality. [16]

DIABETES

The 1989 U.S. National Health Interview Study showed a much higher prevalence of coronary disease in people with diabetes. In the *Multiple Risk Factor Intervention Trial*, the age-adjusted incidence of coronary disease was *four times greater* in people with diabetes. [17]

Here are some more grim statistics: *For diabetics, coronary disease causes at least 60% of their deaths.* (Many feel that number today is closer to 70%.) Heart disease remains the number one cause of death in diabetics. Diabetics have a threefold increased risk of coronary disease and are two-to-four times more likely to die from heart disease. [17] [18]

CHAPTER 19: Heart Facts: Why Me?

Due to recent studies, the AHA has added diabetes to the five major controllable risk factors for heart disease described in the preceding paragraphs. [19]

Type 2 diabetes is the cause of 90% of diabetes in the United States. Formerly known as *adult-onset diabetes,* it is different from juvenile-onset diabetes which is characterized by a complete lack of insulin. Today the juvenile disease is thought to be an autoimmune disorder in which the body attacks and ultimately destroys the beta cells of the pancreas, the site of insulin production.

Type 2 diabetes is acquired later, and develops as a result of *insulin resistance.* The body fails to recognize or correctly utilize its own insulin, and as a result, *it tries to compensate by producing even more insulin,* a state known as *hyperinsulinemia.*

This is harmful since excessive insulin leads to weight gain and is deleterious to the heart. If this cascade is not broken, the pancreas eventually burns itself out, and ultimately those afflicted may well go on to require insulin.

Poorly controlled diabetes spells disaster. Besides heart disease, it is also associated with an increase in *cancer* and *Alzheimer's disease.* It's also the number one cause of end-stage *kidney disease,* necessitating the use of a kidney machine (dialysis) to sustain life.

Diabetes has become a *major epidemic* in both the United States and the Western World. It has risen sharply in this country since 1995—and the trend seems to be increasing with no end in sight. Those at highest risks include African Americans and folks residing in the South. [20]

Over twenty-five million children and adults in the United States have confirmed diabetes, with approximately 7 million not even diagnosed. [20] A very sad fact is the growing incidence of Type 2 diabetes in children, hence the name switch from adult-onset diabetes to Type 2 diabetes.

In my entire training, I can't recall seeing a child with this devastating morbid disease. But with the *increase in obesity* among our youth along with *more sedentary lifestyles,* I can only foresee a future where such young people succumb to heart attack and stroke at earlier ages.

Then there is a whole new problem of *pre-diabetes*—and those with metabolic syndrome, formerly named Syndrome X. These folks present with truncal obesity, hypertension, elevated triglycerides, and low HDL (or good) cholesterol. So often these younger patients will go on to develop full-blown diabetes. I see at least three such new cases a week in my solo practice.

Surely the reader is appreciating the enormity of this ever-growing population. So, what can we do about it? I am frequently asked what, in my opinion, is the best treatment for diabetes.

My answer is always the same: PREVENTION.

PREVENTION

I am scrupulous about diagnosing new cases of metabolic syndrome and diabetes. *Weight reduction* with both *exercise* and *dietary change* is an absolute must. I also encourage my patients to *read all that they can* so that they can be well-versed about their disease.

This is how I motivate patients to be their own best Medical Advocates—the overriding theme of this book.

I strongly encourage patients to attend the diabetic teaching classes held at our local hospital (Presbyterian Intercommunity Hospital in Whittier, California). Most community hospitals have similar programs. These classes provide a great source of information, and participants can obtain valuable reference materials.

My practice is fortunate as I have a clinical nutritionist on staff to assist patients with their dietary choices. But as their physician, I feel inclined to make a few recommendations. I favor cutting back on not only *sweets*, but on all *starchy carbohydrates*.

My words are, "avoid anything that is white."

I find that patients almost always do best on a *moderate protein, healthy fat diet* that includes *avocado, nuts, natural peanut butter, olive oil, eggs,* and *fish*.

CHAPTER 19: Heart Facts: Why Me?

A discussion of the various medications used to treat diabetes is beyond the scope of this book. Some of these medications can lead to weight gain and hypoglycemia, or sudden drops in blood sugar. Some are potentially toxic to the liver and others are associated with adverse cardiac events as well—such as heart failure.

So many of these drugs themselves are replete with problems.

Still, it is crucial to obtain good control of diabetes to avoid many of the long-term complications inherent in the disease. We often have to employ *medication* to achieve this goal. Fortunately, some of the newer classes of medications are well-tolerated and pose less danger than the ones used in the past.

I stick closely to my dictum: PREVENTION IS THE REAL KEY TO THE TREATMENT OF DIABETES. I frequently follow my patient's HgbA1C, a simple blood test used to monitor patient's control of their diabetes. I prefer to get the number as low as possible, in many cases in the non-diabetic range.

It's not easy, but it is certainly doable. *A close relationship between patient and physician is the key to success* as far as I am concerned. My thirty-five years in practice have taught me that this really works!!

∽

I've discussed the six major, preventable risk factors for coronary heart disease. Here's the clincher: *not one of these applied to me!!* Furthermore, *my family history did not include heart problems.*

I'll never forget the faces of the doctors at Cedars-Sinai Medical Center in Los Angeles when I presented. "But you don't match the profile of someone having a heart attack."

Later, I came **to my own conclusion—which you will soon learn.**

CHAPTER 20

WHERE DO I FIT IN?

The Minor Players

PERHAPS I SHOULD LABEL THESE as the *less traditional risk factors*. Their association with heart disease is certainly not controversial, but their *individual importance is not as well defined* when compared to the major risk factors discussed in the previous chapter.

In my particular case, I lacked all the major risk factors. So again, I asked the question: where do I fit in?

The search continued.

MINOR RISK FACTORS FOR HEART DISEASE:

- **Elevated Triglyceride Levels**
- **Elevated Lp(a)**
- **Elevated Homocysteine Levels**
- **Persistant Elevation in C-Reactive Protein**
- **Periodontal Disease**
- **Inflammatory Markers**
- **New Genetic Markers**
- **Elevated Fibrinoge Levels**
- **Environmental Pollution**
- **Stress/Depression**

ELEVATED TRIGLYCERIDE LEVELS
Triglycerides are blood fats like cholesterol. However, their exact role in the causation of coronary artery disease is not well understood.

But make no mistake about it, *elevated levels are not associated with good health.*

In fact, elevated triglycerides are an important barometer of poor metabolic health and *often accompany coronary heart disease, diabetes, metabolic syndrome, obesity, and fatty liver.* Mexican Americans have the highest rate of triglycerides (33.2%), followed by non-Hispanic whites (33.2%), and African Americans (15.9%). [1]

People with elevated triglycerides—greater than 150 mg/dl by most standards—should *limit their intake of fructose* that is mainly found in soda and fruits. *Adopt a healthier diet.* Increase your consumption of vegetables, low fructose fruits, and healthy fats—such as what's found in fish, olive oil, avocado and nuts. Avoid alcohol, simple sugars and refined grains.

Triglycerides over 1,000 mg/dl are especially dangerous and can lead to acute pancreatitis, a painful disorder that can be fatal. Folks with pancreatitis often have some underlying genetic disorder or a serious acquired problem such as uncontrolled diabetes, gallstones, or alcoholism.

Remember, we have data demonstrating that *lowering LDL cholesterol* brings a subsequent *reduction in heart disease.* Still, it has yet to be determined that lowering triglycerides to a certain level actually decreases one's cardiac risk.

Elevated triglycerides are markers of poor metabolic health in general, so they should be lowered to goal. Fortunately, adopting and maintaining healthy lifestyle measures through diet and exercise are very effective and can lower triglyceride levels by up to 50% [1]

ELEVATED LIPOPROTEIN (a)

Lipoprotein(a), also known as Lp(a), is another *blood fat* that consists of a *protein* and a fragment of *LDL cholesterol.* Numerous studies have identified it as a risk factor for coronary artery disease and stroke. [2] [3] [4]

One of the ways it leads to adverse events is by stimulating release of a chemical substance that promotes blood clots. Lp(a) also *carries cholesterol,* and thus contributes to *plaque formation. Moreover, it attracts inflammatory mediators to the site of plaque,* leading to unstable plaque which may be more *prone to rupture.* [5]

Unfortunately, Lp(a) levels are essentially unaffected by diet, exercise, and other environmental factors. Most of the commonly prescribed lipid-lowering drugs, such as *statins are ineffective* in lowering Lp(a).

However, *niacin* can be useful. Some studies have shown reduced levels of Lp(a) by 20-30% with the use of niacin. In my practice, the results have been a mixed bag. But because of its relatively low expense and favorable safety profile, I still think niacin is a worthwhile consideration in the hands of a qualified cardiologist. Often large doses of 2000 mg/day are needed to lower Lp(a).

Some studies have shown some benefit from using *fish oil* supplements, while other studies have shown that regular consumption of moderate amounts of *alcohol* may be useful. These are small observational studies, however, and more research is warranted. [6] [7]

The effect of *estrogen* on Lp(a) levels is *controversial.* Estrogen-replacement therapy in post-menopausal women appears to be associated with lower levels of Lp(a), but the overall effect on heart disease risk is less clear. [8] Additional studies of greater magnitude will be necessary in establishing a beneficial role for these agents.

ELEVATED HOMOCYSTEINE LEVELS
Although not yet classified as a major risk factor for heart disease by the AHA, we *preventative cardiologists* screen our patients for *elevated homocysteine levels,* since we believe there is an association that is not trivial.

Homocysteine is an *amino acid* in the blood, a breakdown product of protein. An excess of it can lead to a higher incidence of *coronary disease, stroke, and peripheral artery disease.* [9]

Homocysteine levels are not affected by diet or exercise. We now know that elevated levels are the result of a gene variant, which is merely a change in a DNA sequence that is different from the expected DNA sequence. The MTHFR gene provides instructions for making an enzyme called methylenetetrahydrofolate reductase. This is the enzyme responsible in breaking down homocysteine.

Elevated levels of homocysteine appear to damage the inside lining of arteries, promoting *inflammation and blood clots.* [10]

The good news is that it is *relatively easy to treat* without the use of pharmaceuticals, but with the combination of certain *B vitamins.* The three B vitamins that break down homocysteine into amino acids less toxic to the arterial wall include *B9* or folate, *B6* and *B12.*

Although evidence for the benefit of lowering homocysteine levels is lacking in the form of large, randomized placebo-controlled studies, there are studies linking high levels of homocysteine to heart disease. [11] [12]

I personally favor treating this abnormality in my patients. It is inexpensive and generally effective in most individuals with elevated levels. Treatment has no known adverse effects.

ELEVATED C-REACTIVE PROTEIN (CRP)
C-reactive protein is produced by the liver. There is a simple laboratory test that determines the level of CRP in the blood. This level is merely a *non-specific marker for inflammation.* In the process of fighting a cold, flu or any infection, one would expect to have an elevated CRP, for that indicates that the body is actively trying to defend itself.

Most of the time, inflammation is a lifesaver that enables our bodies to fend off various disease-causing bacteria, viruses, and parasites. *The trouble occurs when inflammation gets turned on and doesn't get turned off.* This is what is known as *chronic inflammation* and it does real damage to the body.

Walking around with a persistently elevated CRP is not good, as it indicates the presence of chronic inflammation. We know today that the chronicity of this condition is a *risk factor for developing heart disease,* as well as other diseases of aging, such as *cancer, autoimmune disorders,* and *Alzheimer's disease.*

A level less than 1.0 mg/L is ideal, as normally there is no active inflammation. Unfortunately, the test is non-specific. An elevated level reveals that inflammation is present somewhere in the body, but it cannot pinpoint the exact location.

According to the American Heart Association: [13]

√ **You are at low risk** of developing heart disease if your level is lower than *1.0 mg/L*

√ **You are at average risk** of developing heart disease if your level is *between 1.0 and 3.0 mg/L*

√ **You are at high risk** of developing heart disease if your level is *higher than 3.0 mg/L*

When I was a fellow studying cardiology at Northwestern University in the early 1980s, we never associated the term inflammation with coronary artery disease. Today we know that *inflammation plays a major role in the development of arteriosclerotic plaques.*

The picture is far more complex than merely speaking about the ill effects of hypertension and elevated cholesterol levels. Even today the entire cascade of events is not completely clear, but as stated previously in the last chapter, LDL-cholesterol gets oxidized and burrows into the inner lining of the arteries. This sets the stage for inflammation and subsequent plaque.

People who have a *higher degree of inflammation* in their bodies are at greater risk for not only *heart disease,* but also *Alzheimer's disease, cancer, autoimmune disorders,* and a host of other illnesses. [13] [14] [15]

PERIODONTAL DISEASE
Gum health helps define one's *smile* and *general appearance.* In most cases it also reflects *social status.* We see unfortunates with missing teeth and decayed mouths—but how many celebrities or politicians are walking around with missing teeth and poor oral hygiene?

We tend to think of gum health based on how it helps preserve the integrity of our teeth as we age.

Today we know a lot more about the oral cavity, and more specifically about gum health. We must be concerned about periodontal, or gum disease not merely to retain our teeth and overall appearance, but to preserve our general health.

This fact is important. I was never taught this in medical school, or in any of my formal medical training. But we know today that periodontal disease is essentially inflammation of the gums and oral cavity.

Reflecting on what I wrote in the section above on C-reactive protein, chronic inflammation of any cause is a risk factor for developing not only heart disease, but also cancer and other diseases of aging.

This fact is so relevant that I ask every one of my patients who has persistent elevations of C-reactive protein about the health of their gums.

How healthy are your gums?

How often do you see a dentist and undergo *prophylactic oral cavity exams?* Are you having *regular cleaning* by a qualified dental hygienist? This may be twice a year for many, but as much as four times a year for others. How often are you being screened for *deep pockets?* These are the areas which harbor bacteria, and which are major sources of chronic inflammation. Do you *floss* and *brush regularly?* Do you note any *bleeding* between dental exams?

If there is any question, I do not hesitate to refer patients to a qualified periodontist.

It may seem strange to you that a cardiologist routinely asks his patients these questions, but it's all about *prevention*. I'm not merely talking about heart disease, but cancer and essentially all diseases of aging.

There is no doubt about it: *chronic inflammation from any cause,* and we are talking about periodontal disease in this instance, *bodes poorly for wellness and longevity.*

The gums, also known as the gingiva, surround the teeth and protect them from the bacteria and other insults in your mouth.

CHAPTER 20: Where Do I Fit In?

Unfortunately, the gums are the site of a battle between bacteria and your immune system. The mouth is full of bacteria and studies indicate that *there are somewhere between 400 and 500 different types of organisms.* [16]

Because of three basic elements (warmth, moisture, and food), our mouths serve as the perfect *incubators for bacterial growth.* Simple sugars from our diets are the major culprits. To make matters more complicated, there is both good and bad bacteria in the mouth. As long as a balance between the two is maintained, the patient remains relatively healthy.

The mouth fortunately is not defenseless against the bacteria. The good bacteria can help keep the population of bad bacteria in check. But this balance can become disrupted depending on *what you eat*, how *stressed* you are, what *disease(s)* you may have, and other factors such as *smoking* and *drug use*. Good dental hygiene must be maintained. [16]

Periodontal disease is the term used for diseases where the bacteria irritate the gum enough to cause irritation and inflammation. Afflicted patients often have no symptoms, but symptoms that raise red flags are the following:

- *Redness, pain* in the gums
- *Gums that bleed* while brushing or flossing
- *Bad breath*
- *Bad taste* in your mouth
- *Loose teeth*

Your chances of **developing periodontal disease** are greater if you:

- Have *a disease that impairs your immune system (leukemia, HIV, or Addison's)*
- Have *problems with blood sugar control such as diabetes or metabolic syndrome*
- Have *hormonal fluctuations such as pregnancy or puberty*
- *Take certain medications such as calcium channel block*ers

for blood pressure, steroids, anti-epilepsy drugs, oral contraceptives or immunosuppressive agents
- *Smoke or chew tobacco*

There is no doubt that periodontal disease can cause a rise in the amount of whole-body inflammation. The chemicals within the body that indicate inflammation, such as C-reactive protein, are higher in people with periodontal infection. [17] Treating people successfully who have periodontitis will cause a fall in the amount of C-reactive protein. [18]

There are **three mechanisms** that explain how the bacteria in the pockets of your gums can affect the rest of your body. [16]

The *first* is the simplest to explain and suggests that *bacteria in your mouth become dislodged* from their primary location and *move through the blood stream and set up shop elsewhere in the body*. A simple example is pneumonia. Here bacteria enter the lungs from the mouth. Another example is gastric (stomach) ulcers, where the bacteria leave the mouth and enter the stomach.

A **second** theory is that the *bacteria in your mouth turn on the inflammatory system.* It is this *rise in inflammation* that causes the damage. The tissues in your brain, your heart, your lungs and elsewhere are more susceptible to damage when the whole body is under attack with inflammation. So, the inflammation may not only be the cause of heart disease, but also diabetes and Alzheimer's disease. [19]

A **third** theory is that the *body may attack the bacteria appropriately,* but then *mistake a cell of the body for the bacteria.* This is the theory behind autoimmune disease. As long as the original bacteria remain, the body will continue to attack. [20]

All three mechanisms (bacterial infection, general inflammation, and autoimmunity) *have been tied to atherosclerotic plaque development in the heart.*

Why am I making such a big deal out of this? First, 50% of those who show up in the emergency room with a heart attack have normal cholesterol levels. Moreover, many have no history of hypertension. Again, I was one of those.

There is a part of this mystery called HEART DISEASE. We now know that a big player here is *inflammation*, which is prevalent in all diseases of aging. And *it has not received the attention it deserves!*

Many of us now think that the inflammation/periodontal disease connection may be the strongest link in the chain.

Remember that periodontal disease is often a silent, painless disorder. Most people have no idea that they have it. In fact, *over one-half of the people reading this book have periodontal infection and don't even know it! [16]*

At the time of my ER presentation in November 2006 I had no known periodontal disease. I was seeing a qualified dentist and had quarterly dental cleanings. But I did have a family history of periodontal disease, and within three years I did begin to experience some periodontal problems. Presently, I see a periodontist at regular intervals and endeavor to maintain meticulous oral hygiene.

OTHER INFLAMMATORY MARKERS

1. Lp-PLA2 (Lipoprotein-associated Phospholipase A2)

Lp-PLA2 is a *vascular specific inflammatory enzyme* involved in the formation of *rapture-prone plaque*. This has important implications, because we now know that it isn't the degree of stenosis (blockage) that counts. Instead, it is the *vulnerable plaque*, which can lead to rupture, and ultimately a life-threatening blood clot or thrombosis. [21] [22] [23]

For example: my case. When the blood clot in my coronary artery was successfully removed by a thrombectomy catheter, I was left with what appeared to be less than 50% blockage. Yet this plaque must have been vulnerable enough to have ruptured and cause a subsequent thrombosis.

Conversely, I have seen many patients in my practice with documented tight blockages of 90% or greater in one or more of their coronary arteries. Yet, these same individuals have never had a coronary event. They were obviously blessed to have stable plaque that never progressed to rupture.

Lp-PLA2 is responsible for generating potent pro-inflammatory mediators from oxidized LDL cholesterol. Inflammation then sets in, and the plaque becomes vulnerable. Studies have shown Lp-PLA2 to be independently associated with cardiovascular disease and stroke in over twenty-five prospective epidemiological studies. [24]

A Lp-PLA2 value less than 200 ng/mL is optimal. Values greater than 235 ng/mL may double one's risk of a heart attack or stroke in the subsequent four to six years.

Fortunately, Lp-PLA2 levels can be reduced with appropriate weight loss, exercise, and proper diet. Cholesterol reduction and blood pressure control are also important. This may be a very good reason to be taking a statin. Niacin and omega 3 fatty acids (fish oils) may also reduce LpPLA2 levels.

I employ these tests carefully. My intention is to obtain the greatest amount of useful information in assessing an individual patient's cardiac risk.

2. MPO (Myeloperoxidase)

MPO is another *enzyme activated by inflammation* which also portends an *increased risk of cardiac events.* It is important in defending us against bacteria and other invaders that threaten our health. The source of MPO in the blood is *activated white blood cells.*

A considerable number of studies have demonstrated an association between elevated levels of MPO and cardiovascular disease. It is also felt that this enzyme is important in LDL oxidation which we know leads to plaque in the coronary arteries. [25] [26]

MPO values in the 400-500pmol/L range are of particular concern.

In summary, the two enzymes described above, Lp-PLA2 and MPO, are not considered cardiac risk factors in themselves, but when elevated, they may increase the risk of coronary events and strokes.

GENETIC MARKERS

This is the newest trend in stratifying cardiac patients, and is an area I find most exciting. These three markers are currently in vogue, but there will likely be even more discoveries in the field of human genetics.

1. ApoE (Apolipoprotein E)

The ApoE genotype test *helps predict lipid abnormalities and responsiveness to different dietary fat intake.*

As with all genetic markers, *we receive one member of a genetic pair (allele) from one parent and one from the other.* The presence of one E4 allele indicates a strong predisposition for enhanced cholesterol absorption from the gut. [27] [28]

These patients do quite well with medications or supplements that affect cholesterol absorption. The presence of a single E4 allele has been reported to be associated with 26-53% increased risk for coronary disease in men and an even higher risk for coronary disease in women. [29] [30] [31]

Compared to the general population, a single E4 allele is also associated with a 2.2-4.4 times increase in the risk of developing *Alzheimer's disease.* This association appears to be more prevalent in diabetics and in African Americans. [32] [33]

Lacking the Apo E4 allele, however, does not exclude the presence of Alzheimer's disease. In fact, the majority of those afflicted do not have this genetic defect. We are just scratching the surface in understanding the genetic basis of this disease.

2. KIF-6 Genotype Test

In 2008, a group of researchers discovered that a common variation in this particular gene seemed to increase a person's chance for developing coronary disease. *We have two copies of the KIF6 gene in each cell, one inherited from each parent.*

Genes are complex structures, but suffice it to say *a slight variation as to what amino acid goes into a specific location on this gene can make a difference in cardiac risk.*

The cardiac event rate can be up to 55% higher in some populations, but research has shown that *statin drugs* may be of benefit in decreasing one's risk. [34]

More recent studies have underplayed the significance of this particular genotype and have not found a major benefit in statin therapy in lowering an individual's risk. [35] [36]

This research is relatively new, and large-scale studies are lacking. I am mentioning it for sake of introduction and awareness. I do inform my younger patients with a positive family history, as they should be aware of cutting-edge technologies.

More research is in progress.

3) 9p-21 Early MI Genotype test

New evidence points to an *abnormality on chromosome 9* that predicts *increased risk* for early *onset myocardial infarction* (heart attack), *coronary artery disease* in general, and *abdominal aortic aneurysm* (AAA). [37]

Identifying these carriers allows clinicians to aggressively treat the various risk factors in such patients, and to carefully screen those at risk for developing AAA as they age.

∼

I might add that most cardiologists do not screen their high-risk patients for these genetic variants. The research is new, not universally accepted, and generally the testing is not reimbursable by third party carriers.

But make no mistake about it, you will be hearing more about these and other genetic markers in the very near future.

Knowledge is powerful, and I have found that identifying these genetic variants is important, especially in my younger patients with a significant family history. I believe that they should be aggressively counseled regarding lifestyle measures and risk-factor reduction.

FIBRINOGEN LEVELS

Fibrinogen is a *protein synthesized in the liver*. It is an essential component of our blood-clotting cascade. Without it we could easily bleed to death when severely injured.

It transforms into a clot in response to injury. The combination of elevated fibrinogen with other inflammatory markers can substantially increase disease potential. Values in excess of 277 mg/dl have been associated with a 2.4-fold increase in cardiac events. [38]

AIR POLLUTION

When discussing causes of heart disease, air pollution is a potential risk factor that rarely crosses one's mind. But I find it not only interesting, but also timely. It has been demonstrated that *long-term exposure to air pollution*—especially fine particulate matter—may play an important role in *hardening of the arteries* (atherosclerosis). [39] [40]

Studies are out there showing that there is an association between air pollution and damage to the endothelium of our blood vessels. The endothelium is a one-cell-thick inner lining that serves as a barrier to plaque formation.

Once the endothelium has been disrupted, a term we call endothelial dysfunction, the stage is set for LDL cholesterol to be oxidized, which can then burrow into the walls of our blood vessels. This initiates the inflammation cascade that I have mentioned frequently in this chapter.

It is akin to what happens with prolonged hypertension and smoking. *Air pollution adds injury to an already compromised system.*

All of us need to be activists in preserving our precious environment. Our hearts, lungs and immune systems are dependent on it.

Of all the various risk factors for heart disease, surely, this is one we could well do without!

∽

So, there you have a description of all the many *risk factors known to play a role in the development of coronary heart disease*—which remains our nation's biggest killer. Additional ones will surface from time-to-time. My intention here is to focus on the ones that affect us most frequently, and for which research is aplenty.

Going back to my story, the genetic markers just mentioned were not readily available in November 2006. But I can tell you that I have been studied since, and all of these tests/markers came back negative. Again, *there appears to be no genetic basis for my event!*

I have also had my blood tested for clotting abnormalities. These panned out negative as well.

With me, was it simply a situation of bad luck? I think not. In the next chapter you will learn what I believe was most valid in my particular case.

It's the *risk factor most poorly understood*...**STRESS!!**

CHAPTER 21

THE REAL QUESTION: WHY *NOT* ME?

AFTER READING THE PREVIOUS TWO CHAPTERS you can see why I was a true enigma when I presented to Cedars-Sinai Medical Center in November 2006. Not only did I not fit the usual profile of a cardiac patient having a heart attack, I—of all people—was in total disbelief and denial.

My actions seem frighteningly comical today. *I am a board-certified cardiologist!* You would think that I would have known better and been more circumspect. In reality, I was not unlike so many men out there who are completely out of touch with their bodies.

Being a doctor seemed to have played no role when it came to saving *me*. Instead of asking myself "why me," I should have asked, "why *not* me?" After deep reflection, it became more and more obvious: I was an extremely stressed individual.

And I was not handling my stress well.

I was one of those guys who felt he could carry the whole world on his shoulders. My life was teeming with stress, but I never stopped or slowed down long enough to recognize that I was not Superman.

Unhappily ever after. My troubles started to climb rapidly when I was battling a difficult marriage. At the request of our marriage counselor in February 1999, my wife and I finally decided on a "trial separation."

Because of extreme loneliness coupled with what is commonly known as "Parent Alienation Syndrome," I was a total mess. This syndrome describes a parent, usually the father, who is separated from his children both physically and emotionally. I would spend

Saturday mornings alone in a studio motel for transient business executives, crying myself to oblivion.

The separation was critical for me, but I was fortunate to meet influential people who guided me along a new path. Eventually, I was able to find some solace and independence. Within a few months it became obvious that we really could not remain husband and wife, so I filed for divorce later that year.

Divorce, as too many of you know, is not simple. It is extremely costly, time consuming and more divisive than anything I could ever imagine.

It became increasingly difficult to focus on my practice—which did suffer as I struggled to pay both a mortgage payment and an apartment rental. There was also spousal and child support.

But that was just the financial. Worse was the stress of going to court numerous times to be granted the usual parental visitation rights. The drain—emotionally, energetically, and financially—was enormous.

But a victim I am not. Divorce, unfortunately, is all too commonplace in today's world.

Seemingly out of nowhere, my wife became severely ill. She was diagnosed with Stage 4 breast cancer in October 2002.

The entire family was greatly affected. Per her wishes, I did not discuss any remote possibility of her death. This information was withheld from our children, which was especially difficult for my youngest daughter, who was only thirteen at the time.

The cancer put a temporary hold on the hostility between us. I withdrew my divorce plea. However, our marriage eventually ended in divorce six months before her death.

The Protocol. Following my ex-wife's prognosis, I took the lead in orchestrating her care. I learned about a scientist in Phoenix, Arizona, who had experience working with advanced cancer patients, in conjunction with a gynecologist in Texas. They had established non-FDA treatment protocols for extremely ill cancer

CHAPTER 21: The Real Question: Why Not Me?

patients. Because she had so few options, she agreed to proceed. She was simply too weak to undergo chemotherapy and was given only a few weeks to live.

Nanci received a special intravenous line that was surgically inserted into one of her great veins. I was then able to teach this rather complicated protocol to both my eldest daughter and a family friend.

My wife received daily intravenous mega doses of vitamin C along with B vitamins. Then there were coffee enemas, horrible tasting mushroom shakes to help build her immune system, and a complete vegan diet that anyone would find challenging.

Cancer patients have poor appetites as it is. Imagine filling up on bland, tasteless food every day for weeks on end. In addition, an hour was spent daily in a hyperthermia tank to elevate her core body temperature to 105 degrees. Since cancer does not thrive in heat, this was an essential component of her treatment.

Her sense of well-being as well as her immune system did improve, but unfortunately the cancer progressed. After three months on this protocol, Nanci reluctantly agreed to undergo radiation treatment. This seemed essential as the bone pain was simply overwhelming. The pain was the result of extensive cancer spread (metastasis) to much of her skeletal system.

She subsequently received an intravenous treatment called Herceptin, an agent which allowed her cancerous bones to heal. It proved effective for a while, as she was able walk again without mechanical assistance.

Other than the radiation and the Herceptin, the remaining protocol was considered experimental, and was, therefore, not covered by insurance. Although the financial drain was huge, these measures to bring her comfort and prolong her life afforded my children the opportunity to spend a full twenty months with their ailing mother.

Initially she had been given a mere few weeks to live.

Eventually she succumbed to liver failure as the cancer continued to spread. Despite the horrific pain and suffering, Nanci was an ideal patient, a trouper who never once complained.

There was one positive aspect: her illness brought the family back together amid a divisive divorce.

But problems and stress just continued to mount after her death. I moved in with my children. This was the home where Nanci and I had raised them.

Although the house was anything but a safe place for me due to all the sad memories, I had to assume the role of grown-up and single, working dad. The children were distraught after their mother's death. They were simply not able to fathom living anywhere else.

Life was chaotic. I had not lived in this house for over five years. There was discord, and terrible arguments between both children and I. Fortunately, we immediately proceeded into family therapy.

My eldest daughter soon developed bulimia, which she was somehow able to eventually control. Nine months following her mother's death, she decided to leave home.

This allowed me an opportunity to bond with my youngest daughter, which was a blessing. I was finally able to get truly close with this child.

But the fairy tale soon ended. Over the next two years she became increasingly more withdrawn. She maintained excellent grades, but it was becoming apparent that she was suffering from depression.

Stress, stress, more stress. Around the same time, I was dealing with a breakup of my own, which left me heartbroken. Within three months of the demise of that relationship, while still in mourning, I developed a horrific case of Herpes Zoster.

Commonly known as Shingles, this infection involved my left eye. Shingles is the Chicken Pox virus which returns to haunt its victims at times of severe stress.

I am generally an upbeat person, but stress seemed almost the norm for me by late 2005.

I have never been burdened by headaches, but I suffered a severe

CHAPTER 21: The Real Question: Why Not Me?

unremitting one on my left side. If that wasn't bad enough, I also experienced severe eye pain which lasted long after the rash had come and gone. Known as post-herpetic neuralgia, the pain was incessant for an entire month.

Imagine being unable to work for a week and unable to drive. Plus, I needed the lights in my office dimmed, so that I could function and see patients while wearing sunshades!

I couldn't be outside. I had such severe photosensitivity that I could only look down at the ground while going from car-to-office or from car-to-home. Then, there was the extreme eye fatigue that allowed me to see only three patients consecutively before having to retire to my office chair. I literally had to shut my eyes for fifteen minutes.

To top it off, I developed a progressive visual disturbance which left me with a permanent astigmatism in that eye. Nothing seemed to resolve the pain. The usual medications, which included opiates and gabapentin, only gave me horrendous side effects, most notably severe fatigue, constipation, and tremors.

Not satisfied with the suggestions of more than one neurologist, I started looking outside the box. I learned of an acupuncturist on the west side of Los Angeles. After one treatment, along with the use of Chinese herbs, the pain was completely resolved within 24 hours.

Thankfully, it has never returned, though the visual defect in the left eye has persisted. NOW THAT WAS STRESS!...severe pain, loss of income, and a permanent defect in vision

I did bounce back after that ordeal in the fall of 2005. But 2006 was the clincher for me. I noted that my youngest daughter was eating very little, was exercising excessively, and was losing weight, lots of it.

She developed full blown anorexia nervosa. Initially she denied it, but it became fairly obvious by the spring of 2006. A couple of Emergency Room visits were prompted by her literally passing out in front of me due to dehydration and electrolyte abnormalities.

We immediately entered outpatient therapy.

I located a facility in West Los Angeles that specialized in eating disorders, but it proved to be of no avail. She was blessed with having a wonderful therapist, but there was nothing we could do to convince her to eat.

Like all people immersed in addictive behavior, she was able to manipulate her way out of every possible therapeutic maneuver. Indeed, all our efforts to help her gain weight as an outpatient proved abortive. I eventually concluded that I could not serve as *father* and the *food police*—as well as a *physician* in private practice.

Entering her senior year at high school, she looked like a human skeleton. She weighed 75 pounds. This was a weight loss of nearly 40 pounds in less than one year.

Thankfully, I had one advantage on my hands; she was still a minor. After conferring with her guidance counselor and school principal, I decided to take the bull by the horns and admit her to an inpatient residential facility. It was close to home, a terrific facility that served adolescents with severe eating disorders.

She entered against her will mid-September 2006, a mere two weeks after starting her final year of high school. It proved to be a life-saving decision.

My daughter spent a total of three months at this facility where the children were randomly searched for food that could conceivably be stashed in their underwear. They were also escorted to the bathroom on a regular basis.

The rules were severe, and for good reason; this is a serious disease that has a 10% mortality rate, as well as an extremely high rate of recidivism. I was involved with her therapy, meeting with her therapist and the staff psychiatrist, as well as participating in regular family therapy sessions and weekend visitations.

Eventually she thrived and became an exemplary inpatient. Through all the work she did in therapy, it became apparent that her issue was one of *control*. The discovery was that she *had no control* over her mother's illness or death, but that she *did have control* over what she ingested. She completed her entire first semester of

CHAPTER 21: The Real Question: Why Not Me?

her senior year at this facility with no outside tutoring, scoring 4 As and one B!

My daughter was in her third month of treatment when I had my heart attack in November 2006. I was seemingly fine one day and dealing with a potentially life-threatening medical illness the next. In retrospect, it was no wonder that stress had taken its toll on me.

Metaphorically speaking, I had been a human pressure cooker for well over a six-year period. It was just a matter of time before I exploded. It was simply too much for me to handle, yet I never admitted that to myself. I simply figured *I could do it all.*

Nothing could be farther from the truth.

In my work, I struggled to honor all my patients' needs—both in the hospital performing interventional procedures, and in the outpatient setting in my office. Plus, I was often forced to leave the office suddenly and tend to my pre-terminally ill former wife, as well as bring my daughter to school and to therapy sessions.

Then there were the missed days from my practice due to my severe case of Shingles. *Availability* is a vital component in the life of a successful physician. But there were several instances in which optimal attendance from me was simply not possible. This only added more stress to my already full plate.

More important than all that was the negative impact this stress had on my health. I was wearing too many hats. I never stopped long enough to see how I was feeling.

I knew about meditation and ways to deflect stress. Actually, I had been mentoring my patients for years about this. But I was so immersed with everyone else's needs around me, *I forgot who I was.*

This circus had to end. Fortunately, I was given my wake-up call —which I also consider my second chance—on November 16, 2006.

In truth, this was a life-altering event that would forever change me.

CHAPTER 22

STRESS: THE MISUNDERSTOOD RISK FACTOR

IN THE LAST CHAPTER you read about the stress leading up to my heart attack. Given my lack of the usual risk factors for heart disease, I was an enigma to the medical staff at Cedars-Sinai Medical Center.

However, I believe that the enormous amount of stress in my life at the time—coupled with my inability to handle it effectively—is what *triggered* my event.

This prompted a fair amount of soul-searching. Where is the *research linking stress and heart disease?* What about *dis-EASE in general?*

The Facts of Stress. First, stress means different things to different people. My stress may be gratifying to you. Furthermore, it's not so easy to correlate stress with the extent of disease. In other words, we cannot say that this amount of stress can lead to that degree of heart disease. Therein lies the difficulty in fully recognizing stress as a major risk factor.

Stress is a normal part of life. But if left unmanaged, it can lead to *emotional, psychological,* and even *physical* problems, including heart disease, chest pain and irregular heartbeats.

In my cardiology practice of thirty-five years, I have seen numerous patients presenting with chest pain and palpitations. The work-up on most of these individuals is negative, meaning *no demonstrable heart disease.* I then question these patients about the stress in their lives. Subsequently, I often give advice as how best to manage it.

The body responds to physical, mental, or emotional pressure by releasing stress hormones such as epinephrine, norepinephrine, and cortisol. These hormones subsequently raise blood pressure, speed heart rate, and raise blood sugar levels. These changes help a person act with greater speed and strength to escape a perceived threat, such as being chased by a saber-toothed tiger! **Or a jilted girlfriend!! Fight or flight!**

But make no mistake about it. *If left unchecked, chronic stress is harmful and can lead to true disease.*

As a holistic body-mind physician, I never tell my patients that they have to live with chest pain, shortness of breath or palpitations. Instead, I instruct them to journal their symptoms. I want them to learn to *identify triggers for their stress.*

But I don't stop there. I also teach them how to *breathe* and how to incorporate *mindfulness training* into their daily routines. These are the same practices that I have learned, and that I continue to employ every day of my life.

Stress can be a risk factor for heart disease. Additionally, high levels of stress may worsen other risk factors, such as blood pressure or cholesterol. For example, while under stress, an individual may overeat, exercise less, smoke and drink—subsequently experiencing an increase in blood pressure.

Know this: *chronic stress exposes your body to unhealthy, persistently elevated levels of stress hormones such as* **adrenaline** *and* **cortisol**.

Some of the more **common stressors** include the following:
- *Illness* (either personal or a family member or close friend)
- *Death of a friend or loved one*
- *Personal relationship problems*
- *Work overload*
- *Unemployment*
- *A new job*
- *Unhappiness at a present job*

- *Retirement*
- *Relocation*
- *Legal issues*
- *Financial challenges*
- *Pregnancy*
- *Perfectionism*

Voila! At the time of my heart attack, I can personally attest to at least eight of the thirteen stressors listed above. Being stressed is one thing; Not knowing how to manage it is by far more dangerous.

In 1988 the National Heart Foundation of Australia published a report, *"Stress and Cardiovascular Disease,"* which posited that although acute catastrophic events might trigger a heart attack or sudden death, there was insufficient evidence that any form of "stress" consistently predicted the development of coronary heart disease (CHD). The report concluded that psychosocial stress had effects on conventional risk factors but had no independent influence for heart disease. [1]

Depression. In an updated review published fifteen years later, the authors concluded that there was strong and consistent evidence that *depression is indeed a risk factor* for CHD and its prognosis. The association exists for both men and women, subjects living in different countries, and various age groups.

Furthermore, *the risk of CHD is causally related to the severity of depression:* a one-to-twofold increase in CHD for minor depression and a three-to-fivefold increase for major depression. The authors stated that the strength of this association is of similar magnitude to that of standard risk factors such as smoking or elevated cholesterol. [2] [3]

Also reported was strong and consistent evidence that *social isolation* and *lack of quality social support are independent risk factors* for CHD onset and prognosis. [4]

Acute life event stressors can trigger CHD events, although it is extremely difficult to quantify their magnitude. Examples of acute stressors include *bereavement*, as well as catastrophic events such as *earthquakes* and *terrorist attacks*. [2]

You may be wondering about the association between *behavior patterns and risk* for CHD?

Type A Personalities: I always knew I exhibited several features of the typical *Type A behavior*—which I'm sure you can easily deduce. You have undoubtedly dealt with folks like me. You may even be one of us! We're the ones with certain personality trait characteristics such as being *rushed, ambitious and competitive*...along with *impatient*. [5]

That's me all right!

Fortunately, there are two Type A traits that I generally lack: *hostility* and *intolerance*. The good news is that early positive studies have now been displaced by many studies concluding that *Type A behavior pattern has no direct association with CHD.* [6]

In terms of their contribution to heart attacks, according to the *Harvard Heart Letter p*ublished in June 2005, psychosocial factors are on par with smoking, high blood pressure, obesity, and elevated cholesterol. [7] No one knows for sure how emotions, behaviors or social situations promote heart disease or make it worse, but there are plenty of theories.

MANY STUDIES

Stress hormones top the list. They constrict blood vessels, speed up the heartbeat, and make the heart and blood vessels especially reactive to further stress. Psychosocial factors have also been linked to increased inflammation, which as we know from Chapter 2 in this section plays an important role in the artery-clogging process. The result is an increased risk of heart disease.

According to a report published in December 2012, people with a persistent elevation in C-reactive protein (CRP) have a two-to-three-fold risk of depression. This study was based on data collected on more than 73,000 adults in Copenhagen, Denmark.

CHAPTER 22: Stress: The Misunderstood Risk Factor

It is suggested that *elevated CRP* levels probably indicate an increase in chemicals in the blood called *cytokines* that can increase feelings of *stress*. Whether increased CRP is a cause of the depression, or only a manifestation of it is not known. (In other words, we don't know at this point what is the chicken and what is the egg.) We also don't know whether lowering the CRP will help relieve the depression. [8]

A recent study evaluated how hair analysis in elderly people can reveal potential heart disease risk. This study conducted in The Netherlands examined scalp hair to identify patients with elevated cortisol levels (a stress hormone). Those with *elevated cortisol levels* over time were more likely to be at risk for coronary heart disease. These patients were also more likely to have a history of stroke and diabetes. [9]

Still other studies link *psychosocial* factors to coronary heart disease (CHD) and survival among patients with CHD. [10]

There is an incredibly positive causative role for *depression and anxiety* (11 of 11 studies), psychosocial *work stress or job strain* (6 of 10 studies), and *social support versus social isolation* (5of 8 studies). [11] [12] [13]

Also noteworthy is the negative effect stress has on *prognosis* and *survival* in those with CHD. [14] [15]

Smile...make your heart happy. A recent study from John Hopkins published in the American Journal of Cardiology found that people with *cheerful temperaments* are significantly less likely to suffer a coronary event—such as a heart attack or sudden cardiac death.

I think it is noteworthy that previous research has centered on *negative psychosocial states* such as *depression* and *anxiety* and how these states are associated with *poorer outcomes.* Thankfully, *current research* shows that a *general sense of well-being,* such as feeling cheerful, relaxed, energetic, and satisfied with life, actually *reduces the chances of a heart attack!* [16]

This is just a sampling of the research on stress, anxiety, and depression, and how it relates to heart disease. Regrettably, *stress is still not accepted as a major risk factor* by the American Heart Association (AHA).

To be clear, here in the 21st century, those of us practicing integrative cardiology have little doubt that the *risk is greatly underestimated* and *misunderstood.*

Speaking as an overly stressed cardiologist who lacked all the usual risk factors, but who still sustained a minor heart attack, I believe that stress played a significant role in my case.

Stress & other health conditions. The deleterious effects of stress on our health aren't restricted to heart disease. What about the effects on *cancer*? A fact sheet published by the National Cancer Institute at the National Institute of Health made these key points:

1. Psychological stress alone has not been found to cause cancer, but stress that lasts a long time may affect a person's overall health and ability to cope with cancer. [17]
2. People who are better able to cope with stress have a better quality of life while they are being treated for cancer, even though they might not necessarily live longer. [17]

Research has shown that people who experience intense and long-term (i.e. chronic) stress can have *digestive, fertility* and *urinary* problems, and a *weakened immune system.* They are also more prone to *viral infections*, such as the flu or the common cold, as well as chronic *headaches, sleep difficulties, depression,* and *anxiety.*

Stress & cancer. Although stress can cause several physical health problems, the evidence that it actually causes cancer varies from study to study. In other words, the evidence is not conclusive.

Apparent links between stress and cancer could arise in several ways. For example, people under stress may develop certain behaviors such as smoking, overeating, or drinking alcohol, all of which may increase a person's risk for cancer.

Although there is no conclusive evidence that successful management of stress improves cancer survival, there is evidence from experimental studies suggesting that stress can affect a *tumor's ability to grow and spread* (metastasize). [18] [19]

Another study supports evidence for a link between psychological factors such as stress, depression, and social isolation and *progression* of cancer. Contributors to disease progression appear to be *stress hormones and ongoing inflammation.* [20]

Other voices. Even though there is no consensus of opinion on the exact role of psychosocial stress on cancer, there are plenty of studies in the medical literature that suggest an important association.

One review was a meta-analysis, a statistical method used by combining data from several studies to develop a single conclusion. The authors published the results of 165 studies which indicated that stress-related psychosocial factors are indeed *associated with* higher cancer incidence in initially healthy populations.

In addition, there was a *correlation between stress and poorer survival in those diagnosed with cancer* (330 studies), and higher cancer mortality seen in those who were highly stressed (53 studies). Site-specific analysis indicates that psychosocial factors are associated with a greater incidence of lung cancer and poorer survival in patients with breast, lung, head and neck, and blood borne cancers (leukemias). [21]

An interesting book that challenges many of the published data on risk factors was written by the controversial psychologist Dr. Hans Eysenck. He stated that *personality* and *reactions to stress* are significantly more *predictive of cancer and heart disease* than smoking, cholesterol level, blood pressure and other physical factors.

As one can imagine, his views have been widely disputed. However, it is stimulating reading for those interested in the psychosocial factors affecting health and illness. [22]

Your immune system. Although we still lack knowledge about the full effect of the correlation between psychosocial stress and cancer, we do know that *a weakened immune system can lead to cancer.* There have been numerous reports in the medical literature addressing the roles of stress and depression on the immune system relative to cancer.

A lengthy discussion on this timely topic is beyond the scope of this book, but an interesting review was published in 2004 in the British journal, *The Lancet.* It looked at the interactions of stress hormones, neurotransmitters (or chemical messengers in the brain such as serotonin and dopamine) and inflammatory cells.

The persistent activation of all these chemicals in the human body on the chronic stress response and depression more than likely impairs the immune system and contributes to the development and progression of some cancers. [23]

Some conclusions:

- It has been said that anywhere from *60-90% of office visits to health care providers are stress related.*
- Recent studies of human well-being have shown that *the US population is "mildly happy" only 54% of the time.*

Without doubt, psychosocial stress takes a significant toll on human happiness and well-being.

∽

As you can see, there are conflicting views on the role of stress and depression regarding both heart disease and cancer. I have shared with you the overwhelming amount of stress I experienced during the time of my heart attack. I personally know the effect that stress had on *my* experience.

Still, it may take years until this is fully appreciated and elucidated. But there are few holistic-minded physicians practicing medicine today who would discount *the important role that stress plays on both the contraction of dis-EASE and its progression.*

PART THREE

Becoming a Medical Advocate

CHAPTER 23

STAY IN THE DRIVER'S SEAT

ONE OF THE MANY LESSONS that I have learned as I go through life is that *nothing is free* along the way. Remaining complacent and letting the world pass you by doesn't generally bode well when it comes to your health and well-being. Furthermore, *no one is immune from illness or "bad luck."*

Over a nineteen-month period, I had two emergency admissions to the hospital for unrelated reasons. I learned firsthand that *being in prime physical condition wasn't enough.*

And despite a *negative family history of heart disease* and a lack of all the usual risk factors, I went on to have a small, but *definite, heart attack.*

My life was *teeming with stress* at that time—which I was not handling well.

Having a *known back problem*, thought to be congenital in nature, which simply means I was born with it, was a defect I carried throughout my years of intense physical exercise. It finally caught up with me in late May 2008 and within a couple of weeks, I was under the knife.

The surgery was partially successful in so much as I was able to eventually walk again, but it was far from complete and I was left with nerve damage affecting my right foot and ankle.

So, I was a physician in prime shape…but this did not prevent me from experiencing medical complications. Nonetheless, I was able to *identify with the plight of ill, hospitalized patients.* This gave me great purpose in using my voice—as well as my medical background—to *motivate others to take charge of their health.*

The biggest learning experience for me was pulling in the reins and truly taking control of my health. It was no longer about resting on my laurels. It didn't matter that I was in great physical shape, and that I ate healthily, never smoked, and exercised way beyond the norm.

Take my first hospitalization, for example. When my attending interventional cardiologist discharged me, I was astounded by these words: "Dr. Elkin, everything is going to be fine. You've got a new stent and everything is fixed now."

My response to myself was, "Really? If things are so fine, why did this happen in the first place, and how am I going to prevent a recurrence?"

This experience prompted me to look deep within. I was compelled to develop my own personal cardiac rehab program for a guy in prime physical condition.

Even more importantly, I had to truly examine my life from inside out. I had to *acknowledge my stress.* I implemented new methods such as a regular meditation practice.

Making tangible changes and *relinquishing the notion that I could do it all* was the start of a new journey for me.

My point is that it takes much more than swallowing a daily aspirin and a statin. Yes, I realize that this is the current medical post-cardiac event recommendation.

You can't just stop there!

For the long term, I really don't believe that medication alone would have served me well. Being a Medical Advocate goes way beyond the traditional medical model. Yes, taking medication, as directed, is important, but it is not the end-all-be-all for optimal health and longevity.

What is most essential here is truly assessing your individual situation and taking control of your health.

Flash forward nineteen months later when years of back disability finally caught up with me. This time around I had no option. It boiled down to surgery or a wheelchair. I chose emergency surgery.

CHAPTER 23: Stay in the Driver's Seat

Post-operatively, I quickly learned that I was left with a severe neurologic deficit. This was anything but positive news, but I went back to my practice of being my own best Medical Advocate.

While in the physical rehab unit, I only concentrated on my recovery. I refused to watch television or read the newspaper. Instead, I concentrated on my task at hand. I worked through the horrific post-op pain. I chose to journal my progress and seek assistance from the staff psychologist on how to relax and breathe.

It was as if I had to relearn all that I had forgotten, because the pain and trauma of emergency back surgery was simply more than I could handle alone. I needed the help of others.

I didn't just grasp it, I embraced it.

But it didn't stop there. It took months of recovery while I developed my personal Dream-Team of allied health professionals who would help support my goal of becoming the healthiest me possible.

It's not over! I continue on this path and mission to this very day.

You don't have to be a physician or even have a medical background to be your own best Medical Advocate. In the next chapter you will read about those who went above and beyond in order to take control of their health.

Let me be clear here. *Being a Medical Advocate isn't about pitting you against the medical profession.* Being a traditionally trained physician who chooses to look outside the box, I believe that taking control of your health works to everyone's advantage. It's about *partnering with your physician.* This enhances communication between the two of you.

Hopefully, this will result in better medical outcomes.

Medical Advocacy. These are a few simple suggestions that essentially all of us can practice:

1. **Embrace the power within.** No one knows your body better than you do. A physician relies on the information that you give him/her. *Trust yourself.* If you feel that your doctor is disinterested or judgmental, then perhaps it's time to find

someone who will listen to you. If you have bad vibes about your interaction with your doctor, you might need to make a change.

My bottom line here is that as a patient *you should always be heard. This is your birthright.*

2. **Don't feel compelled to make a hasty or immediate decision.** When your doctor recommends a specific diagnostic test and/or treatment, take a deep breath. *Learn about your options.* Although my two hospitalizations were bona fide emergencies, most medical problems are not of an urgent nature. This gives you time to do your research and seek a second opinion if that speaks to you.

3. **Know your body.** This was obviously the lesson I had to learn. Recall that I denied my symptoms for nearly fifteen hours before finally seeking medical attention. I knew inwardly that something was not right. Yet, I simply could not face the fact that I was up against a serious life-threatening situation. You don't need to make my mistake, which could have cost me my life.

If you feel that something is truly wrong, seek medical attention.

4. **Trust your instincts.** This really sums up the three points mentioned above. I believe in patients' smarts for the most part. Why shouldn't you?

~

None of us can control what is outside our individual realm. It doesn't matter if it's about health reform or dealing with bureaucratic insurance companies who have us all paying more for less medical benefits. There seems to be no end to this external frustration.

No one is immune to disease and illness. Calamities happen. But we can all do our best to embrace healthy lifestyles and remain in charge.

After all, whose body is it? It's your body!

So please be your own best Medical Advocate, and stay in the driver's seat when it comes to your health.

CHAPTER 24

MY HEROES

Aka Medical Advocates

Now I know what some of you are saying to yourselves: "Well of course he figured it out, he's a doctor." But I'm here to tell you that you don't need to be a doctor, a nurse, or even a medical professional to become your own Medical Advocate.

In fact, doctors and nurses are often the worst patients imaginable because they know too much. Furthermore, they often live in a kind of fear that breeds denial.

Look at me. I was completely clueless about my status. Yet I was walking around with a stuttering heart attack. Foolishly, I did my own thing for fourteen hours, before I was essentially taken by the hand by my best friend to seek medical attention.

Yes, it's ridiculous and hopefully you are laughing with me, not at me. I was anything but in touch with my body. But an amazing transformation took place. I quickly learned that it was going to take more than just a stent, a beta blocker, an aspirin, and a statin to sustain me. Realizing the shortcomings of the traditional western medical model, I knew I had my work cut out for me.

I became my own Medical Advocate! My new role took me through my post heart attack recovery as well as my second hospitalization nineteen months later when I needed emergency back surgery.

Most important of all: I found my true calling.

It became time to branch out and motivate others to be their own Medical Advocate. That has become my mission, whether it be my individual *patients, my audiences, or my readers.*

Fortunately, I have had the pleasure to meet and interview people who were not medical professionals, but who went beyond the norm to seek answers. They, in turn, became their own Medical Advocate. I call them my heroes, and I am going to share their stories with you.

SH

SH was an amazingly brilliant woman whom I knew from high school. We renewed our friendship many years later on Facebook.

She fought a valiant, several year battle with breast cancer. I had the good fortune of interviewing her while she was visiting Southern California.

At the age of forty-nine she was diagnosed with advanced breast cancer. From the onset of her diagnosis, she displayed an extraordinarily strong will. "I wasn't content to just have a death sentence, or to live life in a mediocre fashion, going in and out of doctors' offices for the rest of my life."

She said to her oncologist, "I might not be able to live on my own terms, but if I can't have a good quality of life, then I really don't want to live. Sometimes you have no other life course available to you. But if there is any way in my power that I can do it, then I'm going to. That's just the way I've made up my mind."

That is the determination she displayed throughout her battle with cancer. She underwent extensive treatment, including radical mastectomy, opting to forgo reconstruction surgery, followed by an extremely potent chemotherapeutic protocol.

She spent her down time reading voraciously about cancer survivors and complementary medicine. "I learned that cancer is a failure of the immune system. The root question for me was whether I could repair my immune system."

As her own Medical Advocate, she developed her Dream-Team, selecting the best breast cancer specialists available. Despite her super aggressive chemotherapeutic regimen, it was determined that there was residual cancer.

CHAPTER 24: My Heroes

She underwent radiation therapy. "It was at this time that I realized that I really had to take matters into my own hands. It wasn't that I didn't respect the medical profession. Many of them spent hours with me, and they gave me their best knowledge. I just realized that their knowledge had its own limitations. In effect, I had to be my own physician."

She decided she needed to get back to her former passion, "running and working out." Three weeks post-radiation she ran a 5-K, a *Race for the Cure*. "It was tough," she said, "but paramount to my sense of well-being."

Three months following radiation her tumor blood markers spiked. Considering all she had endured; she was admittedly discouraged. However, she concluded that her immune system was truly depleted after "all this chemo and radiation."

Her doctors had little to say, and she felt "alone in the dark. All I wanted to hear was that the chemo destroyed my immune system," but they offered no real answers.

As a model Medical Advocate, she started seeking holistic practitioners. She found a naturopathic practice affiliated with George Washington University Medical Center. They recommended a myriad of supplements but, "I didn't stop there. I started doing my own research and came up with my own blend of supplements."

She added supplements to combat the inflammation associated with the cancer, as well as ones that helped strengthen her immune system. To the surprise of her cancer physicians, her tumor markers came down.

Next, SH began a regular practice of *visualizations*. She had this notion that she had to have "perfect blood." She wasn't told that by her physicians, but she simply felt this way inwardly. She literally visualized the lab printout with her blood being perfect, with nothing out of range. "Then I would automatically eat the right foods. For example, I researched basil. Basil helps improve your red blood cell count. So, I'd eat more foods with basil."

She did the same with her white blood cells. "The visualization helps you make a goal, and you automatically find ways to fulfill it."

SH described this phenomenon as the "drive theory of motivation."

I interrupted her for a second to ask, "So if you believe it, it can happen?"

She agreed, but carefully pointed out that this is not the same as wishing. "The whole idea is that if you visualize it, it becomes concrete. We may not know what reality is. We only know what we can see. And so, when you begin to see something with your mind's eyes, it then becomes concrete."

I believe SH was a paragon of what I call the true Medical Advocate. She never let go of the reins with regard to her health.

She did all this despite the grave nature of her illness. She employed the best knowledge that Western medicine had to offer at the time. Moreover, she looked outside the box to maintain an active lifestyle on many fronts.

Sadly, SH eventually lost her battle to cancer. In the fall of 2010, we saw one another at our 40th high school reunion.

She took me aside and notified me that the cancer had spread to her lungs. She looked absolutely fabulous that evening and her spirits were high. We kept in touch remotely as she went through an even more potent chemotherapeutic schedule than the first time around.

I chuckled seeing photos of her on Facebook donning her Lady Gaga wigs. She never once lost her sense of humor, or her will to live.

SH left this world in early 2014, more than three years after the cancer had spread to her lungs, and thirteen years after learning her initial diagnosis.

Not only was she the ideal Medical Advocate, but she remained a strong symbol of hope and determination.

I'll never forget these words: "I hear people talking about the word 'fight', but I don't really want to fight. It's not that I want to give up. I'm not a person who gives up. But for whatever reason, I've always felt that fight connoted something negative. If a faulty immune system coupled with poor genetics is the root of my cancer,

CHAPTER 24: My Heroes

I need to heal. To fight seems counter to me. It never made sense to me to think of fighting. I choose to think about gratitude and healing."

∼

DC

DC was a busy professional in his mid-fifties who was completely caught off guard when he was suddenly taken off the treadmill during a routine stress test. "I think you have a blocked artery," said his physician.

Those words seemed most uncanny. After all, he had been *working out regularly* since his late twenties and appeared to be in great shape. Furthermore, *he lacked any symptoms.* There was no chest pain, shortness of breath, nor any ill feelings whatsoever.

Within a week he saw a cardiologist who performed a cardiac catheterization. A tight 90% blockage was noted in one of his three major coronary arteries. To his chagrin DC was also told that there were several other blockages in his remaining two arteries, but they were less severe.

The blockage was successfully ballooned and stented. Unfortunately, the procedure was complicated by a hemorrhage into his lower abdomen. This resulted in a large blood clot that required emergency surgical evacuation.

Despite the complication, DC was discharged the following day and he subsequently healed beautifully. This entire event impacted him tremendously, as he was determined "never to return to that or any other hospital again." Still, he clearly knew that he was at risk for future cardiac events and procedures due to the presence of disease in his other coronary arteries.

He immediately grabbed the bull by the horns and made lifestyle changes. Prior to his event, DC worked out regularly with weights. What he learned was that his exercise program was not balanced. Therefore, he added 30-40 minutes of cardio to his daily routine.

It was also obvious that he needed a diet overhaul. He opted to add more fish along with chicken and turkey breasts. He cut way back on his consumption of red meat. He drastically reduced his sugar intake.

Before long he noticed a "big change in my weight, blood pressure, and overall fitness." He has maintained a healthy weight in the ensuing years. Additionally, he has noted a major improvement in his cholesterol and triglyceride levels.

He delved further into instituting a healthy life plan for himself. He added supplements such as fish oil, flaxseed and psyllium husk, along with various other vitamins and minerals. "At the age of 64, I look better and am more fit than when I was in my 20s and 30s. I can feel it and I can see it."

DC takes very little in the way of medications. All he has required is 81 mg of aspirin daily and the lowest possible dose of a statin. "I truly believe that my exercise and diet has made the most difference in my overall heart health and fitness level."

But DC went even further to deal with his daily stress. He accomplishes this "through meditation and walking along the beach, enjoying nature, and getting together with friends for lunches and dinners."

His cardiac event, which caught him by complete surprise, was truly a wake-up call. "My ordeal made me much more aware of my own mortality, so I choose to spend more time enjoying life and less time worrying about making money and surrounding myself with material possessions."

DC also speaks freely about what he believes is a *pitfall in the current medical model.* "I do believe that most doctors are truly interested in helping their patients improve their various health issues. Unfortunately, they are too busy and overworked to take the necessary time to advise us on how to get back on that path to wellness."

He states emphatically that, "the American medical system is extremely ineffective and relies on *too many tests and procedures.* It is too *reactionary, instead of being proactive.* We get prescribed far too many pharmaceuticals in this country and not enough counseling from our doctors."

CHAPTER 24: My Heroes

Another prime example of a true Medical Advocate, DC continues to fare well both from the standpoint of his heart health, and his health in general. It has been greater than ten years since his initial event.

Despite the fact that he has significant blockages in his other coronary arteries, he has not required additional procedures. His Medical Advocacy, while taking his health into his own hands, has clearly paid off.

I have practiced invasive cardiology for thirty -five years, and I'm here to tell you that *DC is unfortunately not the norm.* Most cardiac patients earnestly attempt to get on the path of wellness post-event. However, the situation often looks a bit dismal a year or two down the line.

Many patients fall off the wagon and revert to their former lifestyle habits. This culminates in repeated cardiac events including heart attacks, sudden death, or multiple ongoing procedures such as bypass graft/open heart surgery and multiple balloon angioplasties and stents.

But as we have seen from DC's choices, it doesn't have to be this way.

DC sums up his success story with these words: "Only *you* can make a difference in improving your health. That means adhering to a healthy diet and doing lots of exercise. Relying on doctors to improve your health status is futile if you are not willing to take charge of your body and do what is necessary to give it the tools needed to heal its wounds."

Spoken like a true Medical Advocate!

YW

YW was a remarkably spry woman who had been her own Medical Advocate for as long as she could remember. Born and raised in Brooklyn, New York from Italian parents, she knew well the benefits of the Mediterranean diet way before it became fashionable.

Remaining active and healthy for most of her life, she came to my attention at age eighty-five when she was seeking an "integrative cardiologist."

I'll never forget my initial meeting with this bigger-than-life woman—all of five feet, weighing no more than one hundred and five pounds. "I'm not sure I even knew what an integrative cardiologist was all about, but I did know that I didn't like who I had for my doctor, and that I was willing to travel over seventy-five miles each way to find you."

Walking two plus miles daily for years, YW was taken by surprise when she suddenly became ill at the age of eighty. What she noticed was sudden shortness of breath with minimal exertion.

The events at that time rapidly evolved. She ended up requiring emergency open-heart bypass graft surgery. Being in the prime shape that she was, she went through this ordeal in flying colors. It's what happened in the next five years, and the manner in which she pulled in the reins is what makes her story so remarkable.

Once she was discharged from the hospital after her successful heart surgery, she was followed by a cardiologist who recommended that she obtain a primary care doctor. She located such a physician, with whom she was not happy.

One day she found herself at the local bookstore because, "I am convinced that God hangs out at Barnes and Noble." There she came across a book entitled *Supplement Your Prescriptions*.

This book, written by a physician, spoke about the adverse effects one can experience by taking prescription medications. This book really appealed to YW because, "I've always been interested in alternative medicine, even though I never even knew it had a name."

She learned through her reading that those who take statins, a commonly used drug to lower cholesterol, should also take Coenzyme Q10. This supplement can help ameliorate some of the commonly seen side effects of statins.

By this time, she had shunned her primary care physician, as "we weren't on the same page." To everyone's consternation she retained

CHAPTER 24: My Heroes

the services of a family-practice nurse practitioner who espoused *functional medicine.*

When she brought up Coenzyme Q10 to her cardiologist he simply, "put his eyes down and shrugged his shoulders. I hated his expression, because I sensed that he disapproved of my seeking answers outside the norm."

But her nurse practitioner did offer her answers and they retained a very close relationship. "The more I went to Bonni the more, I thought, I needed to find a heart doctor who practices the kind of medicine I want."

She went back to Barnes & Noble and "God put this book in my hand, *Reversing Heart Disease*," by Stephen Sinatra MD. There she learned that there was a name for what she sought, an *integrative cardiologist.*

At the end of the book, there was a list of physicians whom Dr. Sinatra recognized as like-minded practitioners. That's where she located me several years ago, and she made the long seventy-five-mile trek each way to see me on a repeated basis.

Her friends often referred to her as being "weird because I ask a lot of questions, take a bunch of supplements, and listen to that voice that's inside of me."

As a true Medical Advocate, YW researched everything she put into her mouth. For example, she was having joint pain in her knee which put a damper on her daily walks.

She knew about the negative effects of the commonly prescribed NSAIDS (non-steroidal anti-inflammatory agents). But she learned through her reading about a supplement that I had never heard about, by the name of *Wobenzyme.*

It's purported to reduce swelling and inflammation in the joints. "There was an 800 number on the bottle, so I called them up and spoke to them."

Satisfied by what she learned, she started to take the supplement, and in two weeks her symptoms greatly diminished. Since that initial episode she has had to take it only on rare occasions.

Her next venture into wellness and fitness was Chi Quong, an ancient traditional Chinese practice that cultivates and balances qi (chi) or what has been translated as *life energy*. "I have become strongly interested in this practice. I have to drive from Camarillo to Santa Barbara which is about forty minutes each way, but it's worth it. I would do it every day if I could."

It matters not that YW is by far the oldest in the class. She says it has helped both her posture and balance, not to mention her self-confidence. "I'm one of the few ladies in my age group who can walk unassisted and without leaning over."

YW was indeed a prime example of not only a Medical Advocate, but a symbol of determination. She clearly took an active role when it came to her health and well-being.

Unfortunately, we lost this gem of a woman in the late spring of 2016. Her demise was related to a rapidly growing cancer.

YW was an active octogenarian whose memory will remain indelibly within me. Her sound advice would make folks a fraction of her age applaud her actions.

∼

SL

Originally from the East Coast, SL moved to Los Angeles at the age of twenty-one to pursue a career in show business, as a dancer, singer, and actress.

While still in her teens, she was diagnosed with severe endometriosis. This is a chronic condition in which tissue that normally lines the inside of the uterus, known medically as the endometrium, grows outside this organ. Most commonly this abnormal tissue grows in and around the ovaries, bowel or the tissue lining the pelvis. The displaced tissue becomes trapped and leads to adhesions and an array of problems.

SL suffered for years with heavy menstrual periods that were extremely painful. Her first surgery was at age seventeen, and "I had four surgeries before the age of twenty-five."

CHAPTER 24: My Heroes

She was told that she could never bear children, which was unacceptable to her. She sought medical help and alternative help. "I went to chiropractors, homeopathic specialists, and naturopaths. Unfortunately, there wasn't much out there forty years ago, which is when I eventually found the tools to heal myself."

This quest, which led to an intense search for answers, was eventually the impetus for SL to make a career change from the world of show business to the healing arts. She was introduced to *kinesiology*, otherwise known as *muscle-testing*.

Some of the chiropractors she met along the way had performed it on her, but she found it to be a "very incomplete system." But through her tenacity she found a chiropractor from Oregon who taught her a very advanced system, incorporating acupuncture meridian systems and chiropractic kinesiology. She subsequently spent three years studying with a Chinese Taoist master, where "I actually performed acupuncture before it was even legal in this country."

"Somewhere along the line, I put it all together. I figured out through the muscle-testing, how to test every substance that went into my body. Even foods that are supposed to be healthy, such as wheatgrass, raw milk and whole wheat were very toxic to my system." Through her testing and intuition, she began eliminating everything from her diet that "was disturbing me, while taking into my body only those vitamins or herbs that were right for me."

Some events happen that can't be explained by science alone. SL witnessed such a miracle.

She eventually became "radiantly healthy," and by the age of twenty-eight she had the first of four healthy daughters. The result was both elating, if not miraculous, but it also led her to examine the patterns of the body and how "we store emotions."

With two emergency surgeries in two years and with everyone from her physicians to her family pleading with her to sign a consent form allowing them to remove her uterus if it was deemed necessary, she simply refused to relinquish her ground.

Through her journey, SL learned to trust her intuition. "By applying the muscle testing, it helped put me in touch with the truth within myself and also within other people."

This work on herself led to her life's work as a *medical intuitive* and *herbalist*. Over the course of her career, she has assisted in the care of those with disabling conditions such as AIDS.

She has always had a strong sense of intuition, but the muscle-testing "gave me a tool" which allowed her intuition to function better.

She didn't stop there. By studying alternative medicine to heal herself, SL developed a passion for *perfumes, flowers* and *herbs*. She began incorporating nature into her life and into the lives of those she treated.

SL is another prime example of what I call a true Medical Advocate. Her situation is a bit different, as her quest to heal herself led to a career change. She found her true calling in treating others afflicted with complex medical problems. These are individuals who seek alternative and/or integrative treatment.

But it was the ability to *look deep within herself, trust her intuition,* and *take complete control* of her health that makes her story so compelling.

∽

EE

EE is an amazing example of a true Medical Advocate. He not only remains in the driver's seat when it comes to his health, but he also toots his own horn and makes his own decisions. This has been the case even if it goes against the grain of the western medical model.

At age fifty-two he presented with a heart attack and underwent an emergency balloon angioplasty. The event took him by surprise as he had lacked symptoms prior to his hospital admission. Furthermore, he was in top shape, "or so I thought."

He was discharged on nitrates, a form of nitroglycerine, and a statin. From the onset he rejected the notion of taking statins because of potential "serious side effects."

CHAPTER 24: My Heroes

Six months following his heart attack, EE was referred to me. We have enjoyed a long-term relationship for over thirty years. "You have allowed me to direct my treatment while being a role model for a healthy lifestyle," are his exact words.

EE continues to refuse medications generally recommended for a cardiac patient. However, he follows a strict program that most patients could or would never be able to sustain. "I eat only whole foods, exercise six times a week, keep stress to a minimum, and I take forty-two supplements every day."

When his angina, or chest pain recurred a few years ago, he underwent a series of EECP treatments in my office. (Enhanced External Counter Pulsation). This is an FDA-approved noninvasive treatment modality for those with coronary disease who suffer from angina. This significantly ameliorated his symptoms.

For years EE was relatively symptom free, while living a very active life. However, in 2019, and again in 2020, his symptoms rapidly progressed, and he went on to require revascularization with balloon angioplasty and stenting.

Despite the need for these interventions in his 80s, EE remains active, energetic, and incredibly positive. He clearly intends to live past the age of one hundred!

Like many Medical Advocates, EE sees a common problem with the traditional medical model. "The entire medical profession has a very serious fault. They focus on treating the symptoms and not addressing the actual cause. If physicians focused more on prevention and correcting the actual cause of an ailment, we would have a healthier society."

EE directs his own wellness plan by *eliminating as much stress in his life as possible*. He feels that the average American diet is not merely incredibly unhealthy, but that it contributes to the top six causes of death. He says, "you must divorce the 5 whites in the diet: sugar, white flour, white rice, milk and salt."

Furthermore, he believes that a "regular exercise program is a must."

Knowing that his heart has sustained a fair amount of damage and that his cholesterol remains elevated does not put a damper on his attitude. "Despite my cardiac history, I have been able to thrive due to my total commitment to a healthy lifestyle."

EE's zest for life is abundant, as he is a public speaker at various service organizations where he espouses a vibrant lifestyle. "Although I am not a medical professional, I have extensively studied good health and longevity. My talks are all about improving your health and extending your life. My latest talk is entitled *"How to Survive to 105."*

∼

PD

PD has been an amazingly successful businesswoman, entrepreneur, and philanthropist. Married at age eighteen, she had her first child within a year and a second child by the age of twenty. She started a staffing business in her twenties and eventually built an executive search firm.

In the 80's and 90's she helped build over 250,000 careers for people, many of whom were executives at prestigious organizations. Her business continued to grow as she supervised projects for major corporations and governments across the country and around the world.

Having sold her business in 2006, she expanded her coaching practice. Although this career change was originally intended to slow her pace a bit, it grew like all her other business venues. Today she's as busy as ever.

Weight Issues. Although PD has been fortunate to enjoy good health, her weight has plagued her for years. Describing herself as a *big girl*, she weighed 140 pounds by the time she graduated high school. Standing five feet ten inches tall, she "always hid it well."

Two children later and after many successful business ventures and mergers over a span of 30 plus years, she maxed out at 250 lbs. That was her weight at our first meeting.

Commuting for years from a new home in Santa Barbara to her

CHAPTER 24: My Heroes

executive search firm in downtown Los Angeles was tough and ultra-time consuming. "I really let my physical needs go to the bottom of my *To-Do List*." By that time "my arthritis was killing me, my knees were bothering me, my feet were sore. I knew I was in trouble. I was coming to a point when I had to have a real awakening. That was about the time I met you."

What was surprising to me was that her medical doctors rarely questioned her about her weight. No true weight loss or lifestyle suggestions were given the attention needed.

Our relationship was not doctor-patient. Oddly enough, it was I who approached the topic gingerly after being a guest speaker in an organization she led.

Like many overweight people, she had tried several diets in the past. She went as far as attending one of those medical weight loss clinics at the age of thirty.

She received B12 injections and followed a very strict diet of "green beans, beef consommé and not much else. It was a very strict diet." Her weight went from 176 to 146 within a couple of months. She kept that weight off for over a year, but then she went through a divorce and a new marriage and within five years she had gained back all the weight she had lost, plus an additional 25 pounds.

Over the ensuing years she tried Weight Watchers, "and I certainly tried my own diets at home, but I didn't understand the power of the Paleolithic diet or the importance of being my own Medical Advocate."

The day of reckoning. Mother's Day 2008. She was visiting family in Alabama and failed to pack a bathing suit. Rushing to the local Target was a demoralizing experience. She was obliged to gaze at herself in the mirror, wearing a size 24 bathing suit. "That size alone was enough to cement what I needed to do."

At this point she realized she needed a bit of comfort, as eating as a source of self-medication was no longer an option. She settled for a little shopping.

While browsing she came across a book entitled *Skinny Bitch*, billed as "the tough girl's guide to looking good." The first point was, "How do you expect to look good if you keep putting all that crap in your mouth?" "Reading that was like a splash of cold water," she said.

This was the point of no return. "Enough was enough." She decided to grab the bull by the horns. What also helped to motivate her was the fact that she was doing a lot more "one-on-one personal coaching" now that her business had been sold. PD truly believed that her physical appearance would adversely affect her relationships with her clients.

In any event, the time was ripe for her to make cogent changes.

She enlisted the services of a no-nonsense fitness coach in Santa Barbara where she began a tough program. She finally learned that "exercise can be fun." The diet was rigorous, but very doable. It centered on the Paleolithic theme which basically says if it doesn't run in the wild or grow naturally, it probably has no place on your plate. She came to realize that she had a true addiction to carbs—one of her major pitfalls when it came to losing weight.

Her program was based entirely on lifestyle changes with no drugs, surgery, special supplements, or pre-packaged foods. She attributes a lot of her success to developing a Dream-Team of her own. "I think it's really important that people have coaches and mentors and a support network to help them attain a goal and to break an addiction. In my case it was an addiction to sugar and carbs."

Her relationship with her trainer was paramount to her success. "My goals were pretty simple in the beginning: to get in better shape and to lose fifty pounds." She truly felt that was achievable.

Whenever we would meet for lunch, I noticed how mindful she was. It's not easy to shun bread and pasta at an Italian restaurant, but she passed on anything sweet, starchy or white.

Exercise was not something with which she had familiarity. Fortunately, with the aid of her trainer, she came to enjoy it. It evolved to the point where she felt lousy whenever she had to miss a workout.

One of the keys to PD's success was implementing an exercise program that she could embrace. "I happen to like walking. I'm a big animal lover so doing trail hiking with my dogs was enjoyable to me." Over the ensuing months as she got fit, she started climbing hills, and eventually "I'd look for even more difficult hills."

After reaching a minor plateau in her weight loss, her trainer brought on yet another challenge. Her new fitness quest was running up the 84 steps at the Santa Barbara City College stadium.

This was no easy feat, and it took months before her coach was actually able to convince her to tackle this goal. She eventually found great joy in running up those stairs. This became part of her weekly routine.

She would literally start her Saturday morning by running up the stairs. After twenty minutes of this intense exercise, she was joined by a power-walking group that she assembled. She was combining exercise with networking. "I'd get exercise, sunshine and an opportunity to talk with people about their business or career issues."

The take-home message here is that one is more likely to stick with exercise when it's a group effort. Combining it with business adds an entirely new twist!

Being so well known in her community and throughout Southern California, it was hard for people not to take notice of the change in her appearance. She walked with a special glow while saying, "I'm in the best shape than I have been in my entire life."

It seemed that just about anyone who knew her stopped her long enough to ask, "How did you do it?" Enlightened by all the attention she was receiving, she decided to write it all down in a book entitled, *How I Lost It.*

Visualization. To stay on track PD will occasionally play little games with herself. "Sometimes I sort of hypnotize myself and pretend like I've had this surgery and that I've had a miracle cure and that my job now is to maintain it."

What she is doing here is visualizing a given situation where she is the winner. This keeps her on track. There is no doubt in her mind that she can do it without surgery.

Most of us are aware of the grim statistics regarding weight loss and inability to keep the weight off. Over 90% of those who lose weight with dieting eventually regain their weight plus more. PD did lose over ninety pounds naturally in a span of eighteen months, which is truly monumental.

What advice does one of the most successful business coaches of our time have for others embarking on a similar path of weight loss and lifestyle changes?

"Don't think you have to do this alone. Get yourself a coach, a nutritionist, and a medical team, as well as a few training buddies to keep you accountable. Don't try to change everything overnight. Set a big goal as well as smaller goals that are doable. Addiction to sugar is truly serious. Take it seriously as you learn about your addiction and how to control it."

PD is truly a leader. Not simply content with her many business accolades, she seriously took on her health as a goal in itself. She continues to hone in on her quest to "stay in the driver's seat" as it relates to her health and wellness.

I am thrilled to be involved as her medical coach and indeed a member of her Dream-Team.

∼

JC

JC was 27, a graduate student at MIT, as well as a lifelong athlete training for his black belt in Tae Kwon Do when his left arm and leg suddenly gave out while on the basketball court.

After limping around campus for the next two weeks with little relief, he saw his doctor, who was quite concerned. JC had developed an eye problem the year before, known as optic neuritis.

With this second neurologic problem within a short time span, he was referred to a neurologist. After an MRI and a second opinion by a renowned neurologist at Brigham and Women's Hospital in Boston, the diagnosis was clear: Multiple Sclerosis.

Being hit with this diagnosis at such a vital time in his life was simply not acceptable. Within three months from the onset of his

CHAPTER 24: My Heroes

MS symptoms, his body returned to normal.

His neurologist wanted him to go on Betaseron, the new block buster MS drug at that time, But JC refused. "I was a young guy with no sense of my mortality. I didn't internalize the diagnosis; I denied it. I made a deal with myself to deny the diagnoses and push the accelerator button on life until I was forced to make changes."

Going on medication to him was internalizing the diagnosis. He simply could not go there. He decided to move to Southern California. He plunged forward with vigor and never looked back.

Denial worked for six years. JC ran marathons, a triathlon, and climbed four of the fourteen thousand-foot peaks in California, including Mt. Whitney and Mt. Shasta. He rode the most difficult mountain bike trails in the Santa Monica and San Gabriel mountains. He worked long hours at home managing software teams who implement software applications. He also built enterprise applications for Fortune 500 companies.

"I was determined to beat the diagnosis. It wasn't going to slow me down. I was in denial and denial worked for me. I went seven years without a relapse."

Eventually he went into a decline. "My body steadily weakened. I was falling and shuffling my feet like an elderly man." His muscles weakened to the point where he could not sit up in bed. Furthermore, his speech was slurred and delayed.

The progression of his disease marked the turning point for JC. Initially he tried all the major therapies for MS, none of which seemed to have a significant impact. At that time drugs were the only option offered to him by the medical community.

Still, he remained positive as he proceeded to look outside the box and become his own Medical Advocate. "I could no longer continue to deny my disease, and I started taking greater responsibility for my health and stopped looking for external answers for my well-being."

He searched for other like-minded individuals who appeared to be thriving. He concluded that a diet and lifestyle change was the key. He learned of a retreat center in San Diego named the Optimum Health Institute where people went to improve their health through diet, detox, and reworked thinking. Visiting this center for a week, he came to the conclusion that it was right for him.

He asked his employer for a medical leave of absence for three months, which actually turned into four. This began his true journey into wellness. It also became the impetus for a book he authored, *Shadow Summit*. Jon also began speaking to appreciative audiences about his exceptional journey. In fact, I met Jon because we have the same Presentation Coach.

When JC's illness took off seven years after the initial diagnosis, there was essentially no talk about nutrition. But through his residence at the OHI, he acquired the tools to launch his healthy nutritional plan.

"I track my vitamin D level and I take fish oil daily. I recently added magnesium to deal with muscle spasms." He is now learning about the importance of healthy gut bacteria in maintaining one's immune system, and how those afflicted with MS tend to lack such beneficial bacteria.

JC constantly challenges himself physically. He employs the services of a trainer who assists him in his quest to lessen any muscle imbalances.

"I walk daily, stretch and do a martial art called Nei Gung to stimulate my chi energy." Next on his list is to add a weekly kick-boxing class to his regimen. He hopes to put on ten pounds as a means of boosting his strength. Suffering from fatigue, he has found that 8-9 hours of sleep nightly is essential for him.

Today there are a handful of primary MS therapies that help slow progression of the disease. JC takes one of these. But he doesn't rely on medications to carry him through. "I prefer something very basic and natural. It's called exercise."

∽

CHAPTER 24: My Heroes

The folks profiled above are a mere sample of those who have taken the bull by the horns. These individuals have done their utmost to remain in the driver's seat as it relates to their health.

It doesn't take a medical degree or any specialized medical training. What it takes is tenacity, guts, and determination to thrive even in the face of adversity. These people are indeed heroes in my mind, and I salute each and every one of them who made a conscious choice in their lives.

CHAPTER 25

MY DREAM-TEAM

It Takes at Least a Village!

As you can see from my personal experiences, I didn't become my own Medical Advocate overnight.

And I certainly didn't do it alone.

Sure, I had the mindset and determination to do whatever it took to attain optimal health and wellness. (My presentation coach says I have a Type A+ personality.) But engaging the right mix of health care professionals is what propelled me to reach my goals.

Enter my Dream-Team. Although in some situations one prime medical professional might suffice, it often requires several practitioners. Personally, I believe it really does take a village.

Hopefully, you will easily appreciate the importance of my Dream-Team. They are invaluable in my never-ending quest for total wellness.

The Director of Your Team. In most cases this role would be fulfilled by your primary care physician, internist, cardiologist—or whatever specialist best tackles your specific problem.

Post heart attack, I was under the care of both a cardiologist and my internist, who also served as my primary physician. Because I was a cardiologist, I was eventually able to be weaned from the specialist, while continuing to be closely followed by my internist.

Even though I amazed myself with the degree of denial I demonstrated at the time of my presentation, I came to my senses, and subsequently became the ideal cardiac patient.

Fortunately, I have been able to maintain that position.

The situation with my back was much different and definitely more complicated. Initially, given the nerve damage I had sustained from the surgery, I was completely unable to walk and care for myself. However, I received excellent care from the staff rehab physicians and nurses at Cedars-Sinai, as well as from the physical therapists and occupational therapists.

The rehabilitation unit proved to be invaluable.

Once discharged, physical therapy three times weekly became as much a part of my regular routine as the hours spent in my office caring for patients. I followed this regimen for three solid months until I was able to self-care and return to the gym.

Pandemonium. It was late January 2009 when my relapse took place, a mere seven months following the surgery. I felt terribly betrayed by my neurosurgeon who ordered the incorrect MRI at the time, necessitating a second trip to the MRI suite. This cost me both time and money. To make matters worse, he neglected to answer any of my phone calls prior to the actual study.

I chose not to place any blame on his surgical skill when the nerve damage became obvious. After all, surgical mishaps do happen. But feeling completely abandoned after suffering a major relapse of back pain was unacceptable to me. I had lost both confidence and respect for this physician. It became apparent to me that he was no longer a member of my Dream-Team.

Enter Dr. Ralph Abitbol, a retired chiropractor who became my dear friend and mentor. Dr. Abitbol is a keenly intelligent man whose major interest is spine health. He possessed the caring and confidence that I clearly needed. As a result, he became the leader of my Dream-Team.

At the time of my relapse seven months post back surgery, I was in so much pain that I could barely walk a block without stopping. I remember phoning Ralph one day pleading with him to support me while I underwent a second surgery. Hell, I was willing to do essentially anything to rid myself of that pain. He said, "I refuse to let you endure a second back surgery."

CHAPTER 25: My Dream-Team

From that moment on, I simply surrendered and followed his direction.

The first step was obtaining a second opinion by a qualified neurosurgeon with whom I felt comfortable. Dr. Abitbol believed that getting two separate opinions would suit me best, given the serious nature of this relapse.

All of us have heard horror stories of unsuccessful back surgeries, but a major relapse seven months post-surgery is certainly not the norm.

As you recall, the first neurosurgeon was anything but helpful. He had no place on my Dream-Team. But the second surgeon was quite sympathetic and caring. He ordered both the correct MRI with contrast, as well as a CT scan of my spine. Both tests revealed a huge disc herniation at L4-L5, the site of my actual laminectomy.

By the time of my follow-up with this physician, my pain had ameliorated somewhat. He felt that repeat surgery was not warranted. This was clearly what I needed to hear.

He endorsed an aggressive course of rehabilitation. (Perfect for me, I might add.)

Dr. Abitbol did the research and after a couple of trials at various centers, we came upon Dr. Glen Cloud in La Habra, California. Fortunately, his office was a mere fifteen minutes from mine. Dr. Abitbol actually took me by the hand on these visits until we both felt a sense of comfort.

I made a remarkable improvement over the ensuing three months.

It hasn't always been a bowl of cherries. There have been a few pitfalls along the way. But as the director of my medical team, Dr. Abitbol has been there for me time and time again. I am forever grateful for his presence in my life.

He viewed me as a victim of the medical system: "What I saw was someone who basically was standing there alone, wanting to take care of himself. As I viewed it, your doctors seemed clueless about your case. They had no experience with someone with your background in bodybuilding, your sheer mass."

I rarely use the word "victim" as I believe it should be reserved for those who are either emotionally or physically handicapped. But, at that time, I was incredibly physically handicapped!

I am a physician. Keep this is mind. Can you imagine the possible scenario for a lay person in such a circumstance? For this one reason I admonish all my patients and readers to select their own Dream-Team of health care practitioners with whom they can develop trust.

Those who truly know me realize that I do my best to be a physician role model. I consider myself a regular guy who happens to be interested in attaining and maintaining vibrant health.

Other than my medical training, is there some special quality I possess that might separate me from the average?

MAC. Let Dr. Abitbol sum it up: "Frankly, you're one in a million. What separates you from the rest is what I call *MAC*. I'm talking about someone who has a sense of Memory, meaning you know where you've been, someone who takes Action on that, and someone who has a level of Confidence. Once that level of confidence is established, you move forward. It's about going beyond that extra yard. You decided that you were going to take the bull by the horns and that nothing was going to stop you. In my twenty-six years of practice, I've met maybe two or three patients like you."

No short cut. The above may seem quite flattering, but the take-home message is that there is no free lunch. If your desire is to shoot for the stars, then you better be prepared to work for it. I'm not so special, but I am as tenacious as they come.

Absolutely nothing can interfere with my quest for optimal health and wellness.

This was the gift I received when I became a patient. Now my aim is to share my experience so that you can, in turn, do whatever it takes to achieve your health goals. Subsequently, you will become your own Medical-Advocate. It all starts from within.

Take my lead; you don't have to do this alone.

Forming your own Dream-Team is one of your basic steps. Dr.

CHAPTER 25: My Dream-Team

Abitbol gave me the direction and hope that I needed to proceed.

The human pretzel. When I first entered Dr. Glen Cloud's office shortly after that infamous relapse in early 2009, I was bent over at the waist and leaning to the left.

At this vulnerable time, I was searching for a non-surgical way to manage my pain. I was dealing with a 2-4-millimeter bulge pre-surgery at L4-L5—which became a frank 11-millimeter herniated disc seven months later.

This was no small matter. Something had to be done.

Dr. Cloud and his staff gave me a warm reception that impressed both me and Dr. Abitbol. Dr. Cloud felt that his decompression unit could help me greatly and he recommended three treatments a week for the first two months.

Spiritual Support. What I remember most about that first meeting with Dr. Cloud was his sense of positivism which matched my own belief system. That is an essential quality as one builds a Dream-Team. There was also a spiritual side and an interest in the supernatural which appealed to me.

Dr. Cloud: "I don't function merely in the natural. My general philosophy is that the power that *made* the body *heals* the body. I believe that given the correct tools and direction, God's great creation can heal itself."

We are not talking about religion here, although religion could very well play a role. Instead, I believe that this entire concept is about faith, which leads to hope.

To endure an obstacle of this nature...I needed hope! And I continue to exercise both faith and hope to this very day.

Self-healing. It's important that members of your Dream-Team have a certain commonality with you. I've always believed that we humans do have an innate ability to heal. But this mandates taking appropriate measures to ensure good health.

And we must actually believe that we can tap into that power of self-healing.

From Both Sides of the Table: When Dr. Becomes Patient

In essence, I knew inwardly that I was in good hands with Dr. Cloud. His office became an extension of my home.

Dr. Cloud had his work cut out for him. My mere presence forced his positive nature to further expand. "To be honest with you, you literally looked like the letter Z. You were bent over and twisted, and I thought to myself, 'Oh man, this is going to be a challenge.' Those were my exact thoughts."

As far as my initial presentation was concerned, on a one-to-ten scale, Dr. Cloud ranked me "pushing close to ten," with ten being the most severely impaired. Dr. Cloud: "Seriously I did not know how he was functioning. It was absolutely amazing. He probably needed a wheelchair to be rolled into my office. He was that bad."

But he never openly displayed any doubt in my presence. We proceeded with three decompression treatments weekly for the first two months. Within just a few weeks my back pain from the spasm subsided as we stretched my spine and nourished my discs.

We then proceeded to work on my core strength which was necessary to take stress off my spine. Through a device called Active Therapeutic Movement (www.backproject.com), my core strength soared by using three simple movements. By bending from the waist while being carefully strapped and supported in the upright position, I worked on flexion, extension, and side bending.

My response over the course of two months was legendary. By the third month I was able to cut back to twice monthly for another two months before embarking on a maintenance program of once weekly.

We were all elated with my progress. When asked about the key to my success, Dr. Cloud replied, "Coming from an athletic background, there was this perseverance that was quite apparent from the start. His attitude, his willingness and his consistency—his total compliance with therapy gave him that edge."

My chief interest is for all of you to become your own Medical Advocates, so I asked Dr. Cloud to render his opinion. "At the end of the day we are all responsible for our health. Our big thing is to

CHAPTER 25: My Dream-Team

encourage people to take care of themselves BEFORE they have health issues. Eat well, drink plenty of water, exercise, keep the spine and nervous system working optimally, get your heart checked, and see your doctors regularly."

These recommendations mirror mine. Sadly, most Americans choose not to adhere to them. The advice is simple and common sense, yet not adopted by the majority.

Use it or Lose it. Dr. Cloud: "People don't really value their health until they lose it. Our job as health practitioners is to encourage people to value it while they still have it."

You can see why Dr. Cloud remains to this day an integral part of my Dream-Team. It's that commonality that binds us and which gives me continued faith and hope.

∼

Western and Eastern. Gale O'Keefe is an acupuncturist licensed in California for several years. Most recently, she earned her doctorate degree in acupuncture and traditional Oriental medicine.

Gale believes that this career move greatly helps her bridge the gap between Western and Oriental medicine.

An active member of my Dream-Team from the beginning, Gale practices with a passion that I find refreshing.

Gale: "I love what I do and am thrilled that you have embraced my work and have encouraged so many of your patients to seek out this type of treatment. I think it's opened a whole new world for them as far as what possibilities there are in healing themselves."

Energy medicine is an unfamiliar term for many of us. It's an essential component of the therapy Gale utilizes to obtain a sense of comfort and wellness in her patients.

I asked Gale about the many skeptics in the Western world, including some of the physicians who have treated me and who downplay this whole concept.

This is her response: "Do these doctors believe in the electrocardiogram (EKG), the electroencephalogram (EEG)? Do they insert pacemakers into selected patients? Doesn't that explain it somehow? We are electrical beings. We are energy beings."

Her many patients can attest to the effectiveness of her treatment. "It really doesn't matter if I'm dealing with a patient who is well-acquainted with my style of work, or someone who is a complete newbie with a skeptical mind. Energy is energy. I can move the majority of them. They seldom deny the shift in energy that occurs during a particular session."

Gale shares a unique quality with all my Dream-Team members, a sense of positivity which I believe is essential for all aspects of healing. I sought her help early in my post-operative stage, as I wanted my laminectomy scar to heal optimally both on the surface and internally.

Within a week of my discharge Gale noted a small stitch abscess which was handled with traditional antibiotics. But the healing was enhanced by her special touch. In a relatively short time, the scar was barely noticeable.

In addition, she used her acupuncture needles on both sides of my invaded spine and placed her hands on my bare feet to transfer positive energy from her to me.

I felt a sense of healthy balance that remains with me to this day.

Treating me within a couple of weeks post discharge, Gale remarked, "My initial approach was to reduce the inflammation surrounding the incision, to help calm the subcutaneous tissue—including the muscles on both sides of your spinal column. And I wanted to do whatever was possible to innervate the nerve fiber that went down into your leg, to deal with the dropped foot."

This included acupuncture needles with added electrical stimulation to to assist the nerve fibers in augmenting muscle contraction .

Fortunately, we achieved favorable results.

Gale: "You healed much quicker than my average post-op patient. Your back relaxed and we were able to keep your muscles out of spasm. And when you consider the size and depth of it, the incision healed beautifully. We then worked on an energetic level, making

CHAPTER 25: My Dream-Team

sure that you were balanced completely and that there was no residual blockage in the area of the low back."

Gale and I worked together for several weeks, and she witnessed my progression from walker to cane to an ambulatory being requiring no assistance. Unfortunately, the nerve damage from the surgery was permanent, but that didn't stop us from making great strides in my convalescence.

Since then, Gale has treated me for a myriad of problems, all with success. This includes a couple of bouts of TMJ (temporomandibular joint pain) and shoulder pain from a torn rotator cuff muscle. Also, there were ongoing relapses regarding my back, as well as treatment of blocked sinuses.

Gale remains a vital part of my Dream-Team.

"What I do with my process of acupuncture and energy medicine is hone in one one's ability to heal," she said. As a result, Gale has seen miraculous results in countless patients suffering from chronic pain related to orthopedic problems, as well as the post-operative state, be it post-open heart surgery, laminectomy, major abdominal surgery or post-mastectomy.

Even though it can be healing and lifesaving, let's not forget that surgery is an invasion of the body. Optimal healing is what we all strive for, and Gale has certainly provided that platform for me.

∼

I've been extremely fortunate to attract positive folks who have served me well. It was my singing coach who introduced me to Russ Pfeiffer, a certified Rolfer who practices in Venice, California.

I met Russ in late 2008, when it became apparent that the nerve damage sustained post-back surgery was permanent, and that I was going to need something extra special to drive me to the next level. Even though I wasn't quite sure what that next step was, Russ assessed my situation quite rapidly, and we proceeded to work together.

Rolfing is a sophisticated form of bodywork developed by Ida Rolf who was actually a biochemist. She initially formulated a static style of bodywork that incorporated deep tissue manipulation with "whole body dynamics." Ida Rolf was certainly not the first bodyworker who helped numerous patients recover from injury, but her technique was different. It eventually integrated deep tissue work with movement such as yoga and early forms of craniosacral therapy.

Traditional Rolfing is based on a protocol of ten steps or sessions, after which the focus shifts to whatever needs emphasis. The training is rigorous and to become certified, one must attend a special institute or school over a two-year period.

But Russ is not a typical Rolfer. He has a rich background, emanating from childhood sports, followed by early adulthood experience with Tai Chi and yoga. He also has a strong spiritual sense of self, stemming from a Christian Scientist childhood.

As a result, he started growing from the inside out. "I acquired more a sense of allowing, rather than controlling and doing." He transitioned from massage to Rolfing, and even after he became certified, he proceeded to study other forms of bodywork with an emphasis on "coordinative movement."

His vast experiences and quest for the spiritual made him an ideal member of my Dream-Team. I am forever grateful for his many contributions.

What makes Russ's work so special and uniquely appealing to me is not only the value of his deep tissue manipulation, but his work with movement/motion. I'll never forget what he said at our first meeting. "There are over six hundred muscles in the body, most of which come into play when we walk."

That statement opened up new doors for me. I was this muscular, 220 lb. competitive bodybuilder who could clearly use the deep tissue work. But given the neurologic deficits that affected my everyday walking, I seriously needed the attention to movement.

Russ was determined to do more than simply break down scar tissue from my back surgery. He was deeply concerned with my restrictive movement.

We commenced work together just a month prior to my fateful

relapse in January 2009, a mere seven months post surgery. His emphasis was on my central nervous system, which needed re-education on how to walk normally. We were just getting down to brass tacks when I suffered my relapse.

Placing bodywork and Rolfing on hold, my attention was pain relief and decompression under the direction of Dr. Cloud. Within two months of thrice-weekly decompression sessions, I was able to walk well enough to return to Russ's therapeutic hands.

The work done with Russ was like none other. Starting from a firm foundation, we attacked the fasciae and the scar tissue. This was truly deep-tissue work.

Eventually we gravitated to the nervous system. This part of my healing was crucial, as I truly had limitations based on fear.

I had suffered a degree of post traumatic stress disorder (PTSD) prior to my hospitalization in June 2008. Recall that when I fell to the floor that fateful Saturday night, I was unable to get back up on my feet. I literally crawled until 7:00 a.m. the next morning when my friend Barry came to rescue me.

My new reality. I am a former gymnast, fearless for the most part, but I realized through working with Russ that my life had clearly changed. Prior to our sessions I simply ignored my limitations and fears, choosing to focus on bodybuilding and gaining more muscle mass.

This program was no longer working for me. I had lost my former coordination and the ability to recognize stimuli.

This resulted in a major loss of confidence.

I was literally afraid to jump into a swimming pool because I feared I might slip, fall and be unable to pick myself up. This actually happened a couple of years after my surgery when I was about to jump into the shallow end of the pool at the Bellagio Hotel in Las Vegas. I totally freaked out and just couldn't do it. It was shocking. Here I was able to dive into the deep end without difficulty, but simply freaked when it came to jumping feet first into the shallow end.

Russ brilliantly took my fears into consideration as we worked on both coordination and timing. "We're not going to make you Baryshnikov in two sessions, but we can teach you how to yield to the ground."

Well, it took more than a session or two, but by getting on and off the floor a few dozen times, I learned to accept ground, as opposed to fighting it. It's a process that I'm still trying to master.

My work with Russ has been incredibly helpful…and comforting. It's one thing to rest on your laurels and marvel about the past. But what really counts in the end is the ability to deal with your current deck of cards. Subsequent success in performance stems from this acceptance, along with a lot of hard work.

Russ sums up the experience of working with me with these words: "The biggest challenge was the trauma that affected your nervous system. You had a dropped foot, and your back was still organizing itself, so there was some stability that had to happen there. We had to work in a way where you felt safe, because the biggest trauma—being a mover like you are in a body like yours—is to lose all that you've worked so hard to attain. For a non-high-performance athlete that might not have been such a big deal. But for you, that was huge."

In essence, the work we do together goes way beyond deep tissue bodywork and Rolfing. It even goes beyond functional movement. He uses intuitive reasoning in dealing with me, as we work on both the physical and emotional components of the nervous system.

What is so amazing is that the gains are cumulative. I'm not taking one step forward and then two steps backward.

Russ: "It's truly about building that rock-solid confidence. All the work we've done on the back and the right lower extremity—along with learning new skills in how to ambulate—is what makes my work with you a success."

"You never give up. You never say, 'I'm not going to get better.' Every time I see you there's this deeply held belief that you are going to get better, and that you are going to make yourself better."

CHAPTER 25: My Dream-Team

In January 2015, I began working with Michele Cazares, DPT, OCS. DPT stands for Doctor of Physical Therapy, and I felt this was the missing piece of my therapeutic regimen.

Prior to 2015, I had inwardly felt that I was losing strength in my right foot and ankle. I had not experienced any recent trauma or setback, but I slowly, insidiously, found it more difficult to ascend stairs.

I started working with Michele, who was the perfect allied health professional to join my Dream-Team. She possessed the necessary anatomical knowledge and intuition to help better my situation.

We started working on my unstable spine and the residual, seemingly permanent nerve damage from my back surgery. Michele had her work cut out for her, but she kept that glimmer of hope and positivity that was the common link in all my Dream-Team members.

What impressed Michele was my ability to ambulate with confidence and determination, but I expended a tremendous amount of energy with every step. I was only able to overcome the effects of the foot drop by using power and strength in other areas.

What resulted was a lack of symmetry in my pelvis and a shift in my trunk to the left side. I had to hike my right hip in order to fully bring my right foot forward.

Picture me earnestly trying to get through each step, dragging my right foot, and then hiking my right hip during the swing phase. Add to this a lack of initial contact and a limited push off at the completion of each step.

I take nearly 10,000 steps daily, so this degree of energy expenditure was huge.

Once Michele broke it down for me, I finally got it.

Michele immediately took notice of all the compensation I had developed to keep upright and ambulatory. Unfortunately, not all that compensation was healthy or even constructive to my well-being.

Our work together. Our ultimate goal was to learn new ways of compensation that would serve me well for the long term, while reducing energy expenditure, and avoid stressing other parts of my skeleton and supporting structures.

Hands-on therapy was performed to reduce contractures or permanent shortening of my foot and toe muscles as a result of the nerve damage previously sustained.

We focused on improving the imbalances in my hip strength, my proprioception (ability to receive stimuli), as well as correcting standing foot placement. Furthermore, we worked on calming the sympathetic nervous system, allowing me to trust my foot on the ground.

I had been dealing with some of these issues with my Rolfer Russ Pfeiffer, but Michele brought a renewed perspective to the table. The two communicated with one another as they interacted with me—independently but synergistically—in a way where I clearly benefitted.

Goals change with time. My case was no exception. Next, we worked on ascending and descending stairs, getting on and off the ground, and walking on uneven surfaces. We were dealing with a true neurologic deficit which could conceivably result in a fall, so we actually needed to trick the nervous system so that I could easily recover and indeed avoid a fall.

I continue to see Michele for maintenance on a regular basis. Her skill, intuitive thinking, and compassion stand out. I appreciate each and every session.

"Howard has an inner strength that radiates from within his soul. His presence and positive energy allows me to be creative and think outside the box during our treatment and time together. He enjoys a challenge and will fight to overcome the fear that comes with pushing his body to new limits. He uses great tools such as self-talk, meditation, breathing and repetition to perfect a task."

∽

As you can see, I have been most fortunate in having an extensive network of practitioners and support persons who comprise my Dream-Team. Using myself as an example, my hope is for you to realize and embrace all your available resources.

It might be one or two members that constitute your team, or there may be a half dozen or more. You don't have to ride this journey alone.

Yes, it takes work, time, effort, and money, since not everything beneficial or even medically necessary is covered by insurance. As a patient you have the same options that I have had. Please realize that this journey is never-ending.

That said, my recommendation it to make the most of it, and do whatever it takes to assemble the best members of your Dream-Team.

I definitely see myself as a role model with a compelling voice. My experiences as a patient have shaped me into being the best physician and Medical Advocate possible.

I have indeed been on both sides of the table.

As a physician and patient, I trust that the body can heal. I believe that my higher power is the ultimate healer, but I can't rest on that premise. I yield to those whom I feel can help me, but in the long run I have to rely on myself to do the necessary work. I'm in control, and that alone keeps me feeling constantly empowered to improve my lot.

And it's not all about me.

Achieving optimal health is your birthright. Make sure you assemble the right Dream-Team for you. If a given physician or allied health practitioner gives you bad vibes, leave! Seek another! I don't care how many degrees they have on the wall.

After all, whose body is it?

It's your body! Make the most of it now and for always.

PART FOUR

The Medical Advocate's Guide to Wellness

CHAPTER 26

THE KEY TO VIBRANT HEALTH

YOU'VE BEEN READING ABOUT MY STORY—my personal journey —which is truly a work in progress.

But please know this: I'm putting myself on the line, *not because I have any special qualities,* or that I'm *better or smarter* than anyone else. I share my experience to demonstrate what is humanly possible when one assumes the role of Medical Advocate.

I may be a doctor, but I've also been a patient, and I've clearly learned along the way that *my wellness* **depends on me** *taking control of my own health.*

So, my aim is to spread the message so that everyone can attain a vibrant sense of health by "staying in the driver's seat."

As a practicing physician, I take my role very seriously. I fervently believe that *doctors should be role models.*

I am glad that in the modern age, views towards us have changed. We are not infallible. We're human. We make mistakes. We just happen to have *spent years training and treating the infirm.*

And thankfully, *folks of all ages are increasingly interested in learning how to remain healthy.*

We physicians need to embrace this broader concept and keep our minds open. Surveys indicate that the number one complaint patients have with their doctors is that *they don't feel heard.* Patients feel rushed and intimated by medical jargon.

Poor communication results, and patient care suffers.

The practice of medicine is based on scientific evidence and reasoning. We should all be grateful for the amazing research over the decades that has led to countless lifesaving breakthroughs.

The Art of Medicine. This is an important and often forgotten aspect. Outside of life-threatening situations, there are *options* that can be considered. Examples include selecting a blood pressure medication, deciding how to treat a patient's elevated cholesterol, and choosing surgery, stem cell therapy, or intensive rehabilitation for an orthopedic problem. There are options.

In the world of medicine, there really is no cookie-cutter approach. This is despite the pressure from commercial insurance companies, the government, and various other third-party payers.

Clinical pathway. I've too often been asked by the discharge nurse, "Dr. Elkin, aren't you going to prescribe a beta blocker and/or an ACE inhibitor for Mr. Jones?"

Knowing well which meds I should prescribe at the time of discharge, I will often reply with a simple, "No."

The nurse may well come back at me and say, "But Doctor, the patient's discharge will *fall out of compliance.*"

This can really be unnerving, but I also realize that the nurse is merely doing her job. For whatever reason, if I believe prescribing a particular medication is not truly in the patient's best interest, I simply will not prescribe it. But then I must be prepared to be questioned in an ongoing fashion about not adhering to a set protocol or "clinical pathway."

We need to truly listen to our patients and take their individual needs into account. And it's definitely not cool for me to say, "Do what I say, not what I do." This is what I mean about being a role model as a physician. It would be ludicrous for me to preach about weight loss, exercise, or stress management if I didn't adhere to my own recommendations.

With this section of the book, I address the salient aspects of a wellness program: *nutrition, supplements, exercise, stress management,* and *longevity, with an emphasis on hormone replacement therapy.* My aim is that you will discover suggestions that you can utilize for your personal program of vibrant health.

These chapters are preceded by a discussion on the 5 DIMENSIONS OF WELLNESS.

This is how you become your own best Medical Advocate.

∽

As you peruse this section, keep in mind that you, as the patient, are entitled to what I call a *Bill of Rights*. It's a birthright.

But it doesn't end there. To ensure optimal communication with your Dream-Team, you also need to assume certain *responsibilities*. The end result: *better outcomes.*

PATIENT BILL OF RIGHTS

RIGHT OF INDIVIDUALITY: Constructing a unique treatment plan for the individual patient. You CAN question the cookie-cutter or "clinical pathways" approach. More than merely treating the disease or medical problem...it's about *treating the individual patient.*

RIGHT OF CHOICE: Choosing a physician and allied health professional who exhibits more than *knowledge* and *experience*. They should also demonstrate *empathy, listening skills,* and *intuition.*

RIGHT OF ENCOURAGEMENT: Selecting a physician who is able to clearly maintain a connection with the medical establishment, while keeping abreast of ongoing research. Also, vitally important, being *open to alternative or integrative treatment modalities.*

RIGHT TO BE HEARD: Having someone on your team to whom you can say, "Doctor, listen to me. I don't doubt your knowledge, but I know my body."

PATIENT RESPONSIBILITIES

PERSISTENCE: Dealing with the medical establishment can be challenging, so persistence is paramount. At times you may even have to educate the physician about what you've read, and what option you might wish to explore—and why. A patient-driven society is what is needed to dictate necessary changes. Therefore, it is incumbent upon the patient to set the stage.

SELF EDUCATION: Thankfully, there is a plethora of literature available in books, periodicals, and the Internet. Warning: information may be everywhere, but it can be overwhelming. Exercise discretion. This is especially true coming across sites that want to sell you a "cure" in the form of a supplement or magic bullet. Get all the information you can, and beware of scams. If it sounds too good to be true, it most likely is!

Also make use of support groups and second opinions. I often end my presentations with this simple question: "Whose body is it? It's your body, so do your homework and learn all than you can."

ASSUMPTION OF FINANCIAL RESPONSIBILITY: We are presently paying more for our health care premiums than ever before, yet we are receiving fewer benefits. This is the obvious trend and it's doubtful that things will get better for the health consumer regardless of who is in the White House or what party controls Congress. The truth of the matter is that we all must pay for certain services that are just minimally covered...or aren't covered at all.

I dislike saying "You get what you pay for," especially when it comes to health care, but it boils down to a conscious choice. What is one's priority here? I continue to say this simple phrase repeatedly: "Without our health, we *have nothing.*"

CHAPTER 26: The Key to Vibrant Health

We are witnessing a challenging time in health care, but it is also a very exciting period in history when we have *so many incredible resources available to us*. By assuming the role of *Medical Advocate* and seeking your *Bill of Rights* as a patient, I truthfully believe that optimal care is available.

This is how I have been practicing medicine for several years and I have been both humbled and amazed by my patients' outcomes.

CHAPTER 27

THE 5 DIMENSIONS OF WELLNESS

H*EALTH* is a state of being; **Wellness** is the state of *living a healthy lifestyle*. **Health** *refers to physical, mental, and social well-being;* **Wellness** *aims to enhance well-being.* Merriam-Webster

Wellness. Long before I became the Medical Advocate, I was keenly interested in a relatively new concept in medicine, one that promoted wellness. By 1990 I began to see the writing on the wall. Health care in this country, as often dictated by the government in the form of Medicare—as well as commercial insurance carriers—was quickly *shifting to managed care.*

Now managed care—in the form of HMO's—does not necessarily equate to bad medicine. But with regards to accessing physicians, and more specifically specialists, *it can severely limit the health consumer's ability to choose:*

- Various *treatments* may be limited, thus affecting patients' role in managing their medical care.

- Often, large powerful *organizations* in charge follow *strict guidelines*, like what I mentioned in the last chapter regarding "clinical pathways."

- Typically, *office visits* can be brief, therefore limiting communication between patient and physician.

A *natural progression.* By 1992 I had developed a new arm of my practice that promoted wellness. I changed the name to *HeartWise Fitness Institute.* This shift made sense, as I was always holistic-minded with an interest in nutrition and exercise.

As a young cardiologist, my practice had been fairly traditional in scope. Patients were referred to me because of either a documented or suspected heart problem.

Prevention. As I explored the realm of health, my practice shifted. When you came to me, we talked about *prevention*. It was no longer necessary to wait and see me for heart dis-EASE. I became the doctor you visited to **prevent illness.**

To me this all made perfect sense, but it was clearly a change from the traditional medical model. For years we have all been encouraged to see the dentist at least twice a year to help *prevent* cavities and periodontal disease.

Why should seeing a physician—even a specialist—be any different?

Interestingly enough, a key businessman in my community was pivotal in getting the word out about my work at HeartWise. Although he had no significant heart problem, he did have a couple of risk factors, and he decided to seek my services.

His friends would say, "Why are you seeing a cardiologist if you don't have a heart problem"?

He would reply, "Because I want to **prevent** a heart problem."

He continues to practice prevention to this day, and at age eighty plus he remains robustly healthy.

In the 90s, I developed my first promotional brochure for HeartWise Fitness Institute. Needing a catchy phrase, I developed an original quote that resonates with me as much today as it did then:

"*WELLNESS IS MORE THAN THE ABSENCE OF DISEASE. IT'S THE ATTAINMENT OF VIBRANT HEALTH.*"

As we approached 2000, I thought the time was ripe to go out on a limb and hold my first weekend retreat. The program was entitled *THE POWER OF HEALING: Tools for Healthy Living in the New Millennium.*

It was a huge undertaking, but it was a goal that I felt was necessary to reach. I wanted the changing time to reflect a more

CHAPTER 27: The 5 Dimensions of Wellness

integrative approach to health care. Therefore, I introduced an *alternative, body-mind* approach to wellness.

These topics were not exactly new, but in 2000 they had yet to be embraced by the masses. This integration of both Western and Eastern medical practices, as well as my fellowship in anti-aging medicine opened up new doors for me as a practicing physician.

Over the course of the next several years I would expand my cardiology practice, while incorporating challenges inherent to aging. Just to name a few, these include the following: *hormone replacement, supplementation, autoimmune disorders, inflammation,* functional *gut health, neurotransmitter imbalances* and *adrenal dysfunction*.

To mark my board certification in anti-aging medicine, I once again made a minor name change to *HeartWise Fitness and Longevity Center*.

∼

About this time, I introduced the *5 DIMENSIONS OF WELLNESS* which, in my opinion, is the basis for any solid wellness program.

PHYSICAL WELL-BEING

This is the typical dimension we normally think of when we seek a physician or allied health care provider. Some examples of the questions I typically ask include, but are not limited to the following:

- How do you assess the current states of your *physical health*?
- Most women know that by a certain age they should have **annual mammograms and pap smears**, but *did you know* that you should also be screened for **diabetes**, which is more than a fasting blood sugar? You should know your level of **Hemoglobin A1C** which is a marker on the red blood cell which gives a good idea as to how well your blood sugar has been managed over the previous three months.

- In obese and overweight individuals, it might be useful to know one's fasting **insulin level**, since metabolic syndrome and Type 2 diabetes is becoming rampant in our society. Insulin resistance is often the problem and one needs to measure this value in order to detect its presence.
- By your mid-thirties you should be screened for **hypothyroidism**, otherwise known as an underactive thyroid. I might screen for this even earlier depending on family history.
- Another very important test is the **C-reactive protein** which was previously discussed. A level greater than one is clearly abnormal and indicates the presence of *inflammation* somewhere in the body.
- By age 50 a woman should be screened for **osteoporosis.**
- Men, are you getting screened by age 50 for prostate cancer with a **PSA** level? I highly recommend screening younger individuals in light of a positive family history of prostate cancer, or if one is African American.
- How about **colon cancer screening** for both men and women by the age of 50? Again, I might suggest screening earlier depending on family history. Please keep in mind that colon cancer is one of the most preventable cancers. The role of screening colonoscopies isn't to prevent colon cancer per se, but to help prevent **death** by colon cancer. It accomplishes this quite nicely. So please allow yourself to be inconvenienced long enough to have this important study performed. It may well save your life.
- What about the status of your **hormones**? I realize that this is a personal choice, but let's face the truth. It doesn't get better with age! Most physicians don't even measure hormones, including most gynecologists. If you have the desire to have this evaluated, I suggest searching for a physician who is board-certified in anti-aging medicine.

- What role does **nutrition** play in your life? (The next chapter will discuss this in detail.)
- Where does **exercise** fit in? Is it sporadic, or actually scheduled?
- How are you doing with the **aging process**? Does the maintenance increase with each passing year?

These are just a few of the questions you might want answered regarding your physical well-being.

MENTAL **WELL-BEING**

This aspect of your health basically addresses your memory. *What value do you place on the clarity of your thought processes?* Have you had bouts of forgetfulness lately?

Senior moments —we all have them. Have you forgotten where you left your keys? Have you been confused regarding names, places, or dates? Do you have to follow a trail of breadcrumbs to locate your parked car?!

The aging process can definitely affect your ability to process information and to focus. But trust me; ***you don't have to wait passively for this to happen.***

You can proactively face the aging process head on. Otherwise, you'll eventually be placed on medications such as Aricept and Namenda. At best, these give temporary relief of symptoms. Warning: There are *numerous side effects* associated with these meds.

Presently there is no apparent cure for Alzheimer's disease, the most common cause of dementia in the elderly population. Most importantly, these medications do not really alter the course of the disease.

Diet and exercise. A sensible *diet* and *exercise* regimen is what being proactive looks like. Increasing blood flow to the brain with exercise is one inexpensive way to help boost memory. Also, along with the appropriate diet, there are numerous brain-healthy *supplements* that can aid with memory.

Keep in mind, there are some exciting *new modalities* to consider such as hyperbaric oxygen, and in certain instances, a ketogenic diet.

The future looks bright for maintenance of our mental well-being.

EMOTIONAL **WELL-BEING**

What role do emotions play in maintaining your state of wellness? Have you or anyone you know become ill after an emotionally grueling experience? Have you ever grieved the loss of a loved one and come down with the flu?

I'll give you a personal example. After a particularly difficult breakup several years ago, I developed a horrific case of Herpes Zoster, commonly known as shingles, which involved my left eye.

It is a known fact that stress often precipitates the outbreak of the herpes virus. Shingles or the Varicella Zoster virus is rather unusual, as it is the same as the chicken pox virus which remains dormant for many years, only to reappear with accompanying stress.

Nearly everyone has an Achilles heel of some sort. Mine is clearly my back. So many of my relapses took place after experiencing some sort of loss: a failed marriage, death of a loved one, the loss of a key employee. These emotional events triggered something within me —which centered on my weak link: my ailing back.

Emotions need to be expressed...not suppressed. Although not conclusively proven, it is believed by many that the "cancer prone personality" is seen in folks who tend to withhold their emotions. They can appear calm and collected, but are teeming with negative emotions—such as grief and hopelessness.

Denial of your feelings can contribute to heart disease! An emotional blockage can lead to a physical blockage within your arteries.

This is certainly not a healthy way to live!

We have learned over the years that *prolonged anger and stress depress the immune system.* This sets the stage for a myriad of health problems commonly known as dis-EASE.

What can we do about the rampant stress in our society? Since

9/11, we are living in an increasingly hostile and complicated world. The important thing is for all of us to *be in touch with our feelings, whether positive or negative.*

There is no room for denial!

Denial is an extremely primitive defense mechanism which often leads to fear. Fear can keep us from affirmative action.

Here's an example: My ex-wife had an unfounded fear about contracting breast cancer since her mother had succumbed to the disease at a young age. Nanci was so afraid of the C word that she stopped having yearly mammograms as soon as we separated. When the symptoms eventually surfaced, she denied their presence. When finally diagnosed, the cancer had spread to almost every bone in her body. With the diagnosis of stage 4 cancer, she was dead within a year-and-a-half.

Emotions are meant to be expressed. It doesn't matter if you employ professional help—a therapist or clergy member—or join a support group or a twelve-step program. You can even write about it. I'm a firm believer in keeping a journal for this expressed purpose. (I've been journaling sporadically throughout the years since my early twenties. It can be quite therapeutic to review what you've written years before...just to confirm your personal growth.)

The available tools are numerous. *Emotional release work* can be quite useful, especially if you're a physical person such as myself. A treatment modality that I especially like is **LENS** or *Low Energy Neurofeedback System.* This is a great methodology for treating *chronic anxiety, obsessive compulsive disorder* and *panic attacks.* With LENS your brain waves communicate with a software system so that your brain can delete patterns of behavior that no longer serve you, or that have become dysfunctional with age. It's like the recycle bin on your desktop. This, in turn, allows you to assume *new patterns* that might be beneficial to your mental hygiene.

There are many available tools to deal with stress and anxiety. The bottom line: You don't need to live with stress and/or unresolved feelings. Harboring fear and denial can lead to toxic lifestyles and physical illness. *Your emotional well-being is crucial to your overall state of wellness.*

There are safe ways to express our various realities. We all need to search for them and experiment to see what works best for us.

SPIRITUAL WELL-BEING

By this time, it's likely evident that these aspects of wellness are *inextricably intertwined.* The overlap between them is fundamental to the whole concept of wellness.

Higher Power. The one dimension that is vital to life itself is spiritual well-being. I'm not necessarily talking about religion, though that might play a role here.

I'm talking about *living life from the inside-out*, rather than from the outside-in. The very success of all twelve-step programs rests on spiritually based STEPS. When we acknowledge a higher power, we become free from all the stuff that is outside our control.

Formerly a control freak, I would be obsessive about my needs and wants. I just had to be right. But so often I was left with frustration, anger, anxiety, and disappointment. Today I willingly give to my higher power that which I cannot control.

As a result, I'm not only happier, but I'm a lot nicer!

Anyone who knows me will attest to the fact that *I am as tenacious as they come.* I never give up. (If you've been reading this book from the beginning, I'm sure you've already figured that out!) But through my own journey I have learned to yield when appropriate.

Prayer and meditation are as paramount to me as showering and shaving every morning. It frees my head and grounds me for the coming day. I view each day as part of a continuum. Becoming spiritually enriched is what allows me to get out of myself and attain a keener sense of humanness.

It's no longer all about me.

All You Need is Love. Wellness and healing are first and foremost about LOVE. Love of family, friends, community, and most important love of oneself. I invite all of you to consider this spiritual side as the truest core of wellness and wholeness.

SOCIAL **WELL-BEING**

When I first developed the dimensions of wellness, there were only four. I named these the FOUR QUADRANTS OF WELLNESS. However, my eldest daughter convinced me that I had left out an important component: social well-being. She was right. As you can see, by following these guidelines, you can become your own Medical Advocate. But let's face it, we don't live in a bubble. *We need one another to truly thrive.*

We (really) Are the World. I believe that this holds true today more than ever before, especially considering the mass shootings, violence, and overall divisiveness seen in the United States and around the globe. We all have a part to contribute for the common welfare of our communities.

It's about embracing the interdependence with others and with nature. Look at the world today. We are compelled to deal with global warming, polluted water and air, along with soil that has been so over-farmed that we can no longer depend on obtaining essential vitamins and minerals.

In these troubled times, hate crimes are constant…and we can't deny reality. The war on terror affects all of us.

Within our own country, we can all see how divisive, self-centered, and hostile politicians—and people in general—can be. The 2016 and 2020 campaigns are prime examples. It shouldn't be just about red states or blue states, or defaming one party or person against another.

The country truly needs to come together.

This fifth dimension begs you to become more aware of your importance in society. We all have a role here. It's overwhelming in this day and age to think that as individuals we can make a difference. But I truly believe that by working together we can.

I'm not a dreamer, but a realist, and I believe all of us can make the world a better place.

It's empowering to realize your impact on nature and in your community. This awareness frees obsessive insular thinking about all the *stuff you don't have*. More importantly, by sharing with others you broaden your mind.

And it gives your life purpose.

∼

The five dimensions of wellness are for all of us to adopt.

Refuse to rest on your laurels, strive constantly for vibrant health, and you will lead a more balanced existence during this short journey we all have called LIFE.

CHAPTER 28

YOU ARE WHAT YOU EAT

"Let food be thy medicine and let medicine be thy food."

THESE ARE THE WORDS of the Father of Modern Medicine—Hippocrates—from the ancient Greek age of Pericles. They are as meaningful today as they were 2,300 years ago when first written.

These days, there are way too many books written about healthy diets. It can be pretty confusing. My approach to vibrant living and healthy aging is practical, and can be followed by most.

Everyone is unique. First of all, let it be known that I personally do not believe that there is one diet that fits all. That's like saying one shoe fits all, or one hat fits all.

There are simply too many variables to consider when choosing a particular diet plan:

- *Genetics*
- *Individual goals* (performance, weight loss, enhanced energy, etc.)
- *Age*
- *Food allergies/sensitivities*
- *Lifestyle* (career, exercise, travel)
- *Medical history* (heart disease, hypertension, cancer, diabetes, obesity, autoimmunity, dementia, etc.)
- *Lipid profile* (cholesterol, LDL particle size, triglycerides)
- *Metabolic profile* (diabetes, prediabetes, metabolic syndrome, non-alcoholic fatty liver disease, polycystic ovarian syndrome)

- *Gut function* (leaky gut, irritable bowel disease, inflammatory bowel disease such as ulcerative colitis or Crohn's disease, SIBO—small intestinal bowel overgrowth)

So, whether we're talking about straight vegan, Mediterranean, paleo, ketogenic or something in between, all the variables listed above play critical roles in formulating specific diet plans.

Say NO to fad diets. Personally, I tend to shun most of the fad diets that have populated the media over the last several years.

Why?

It's simple. Most don't work for the long term. Multiple studies demonstrate that they may succeed initially with weight loss, but *they ultimately fail.* Within a year of discontinuing the diet, the majority of folks gain back the weight they've lost.

Plus a few extra pounds.

That's a pretty lousy success rate as far as I am concerned.

You might then wonder why most diets flop. Think about it; something about the diet process itself simply sabotages our best efforts to lose weight. (The word *diet* doesn't help. *D-I-E-T*...remove the T and what do you have?!)

Diets don't work. I don't believe that dieting per se—with its attendant self-deprivation—is the way to proceed. It's overly restrictive, self-defeating and leads to a major ego blow. Most dieters eventually relinquish all hopes of success, and subsequently return to former unhealthy lifestyles.

Don't say No to all forbidden foods. I don't believe in that. (Excluding the really bad stuff—fried foods, most fast food, hot dogs, luncheon/cured meats and processed foods.) Even then, I may make an occasional exception. Like you...I'm human! For example, my favorite junk food is potato chips. Even though I know they are anything but healthy, I will indulge from time to time. (Stupid, I'm not. You won't ever find potato chips in my home!)

When you become too restrictive, food cravings can be overpowering. Then you feel deprived and you subsequently rebel. *Before*

CHAPTER 28: You Are What You Eat

you know it, you're a diet-disaster!

Food is food! There are healthy foods and unhealthy foods, and everything in between. The trick is to find *balance* while favoring as many healthy foods as possible.

You might ask, "What does he know about dieting? He's a bodybuilder, an athlete. He doesn't have to diet."

Not quite true. In all the years of competitive bodybuilding, oftentimes I had to diet—which gave me a taste for something antithetical to vibrant health. Yes, it was what I had to do to compete and win contests. And yes, I would probably do it all over again because it was a major part of my life for quite some time.

But my priorities have clearly changed.

Know your purpose. Whether you're talking about weight loss, cholesterol lowering, heart health, cancer prevention, healthy aging or nutrition for peak performance, you need to *clarify your goals* and *choose an individualized program* that can be followed for *long-term success.*

Before discussing some of the various options, let's dispel a few **diet myths and misconceptions:**

MYTH #1: **EGGS** (ESPECIALLY THE YOLKS) **SHOULD BE AVOIDED** BECAUSE THEY RAISE CHOLESTEROL LEVELS

Wrong! It's been shown that cholesterol in the diet (and each egg is comprised of about 270 mg. of cholesterol) does not raise our blood cholesterol level. *Eating eggs does not increase our risk of heart disease.* In fact, a major U.S. government's agency, the Dietary Guidelines Advisory Committee, withdrew its longstanding warning about cholesterol in 2015. This move undid almost 40 years of government warnings about egg consumption. [1]

MYTH #2: SATURATED FAT IS BAD FOR YOU

Since the 1950s, people have been led to believe that saturated fat is bad for your health. This was originally based on observational studies showing that countries that consumed a lot of saturated fat had higher rates of death from heart disease.

The diet-heart hypotheses states that saturated fat raises LDL cholesterol in the blood which supposedly lodges in the arteries and causes heart disease.

Even though this hypothesis has never been proven, most dietary guidelines are sadly based on it.

Interestingly, numerous recent studies have debunked this link between saturated fat consumption and heart disease.

For example, the Cochrane collaboration (based on fifteen randomized controlled trials with over 59,000 participants) found no statistically significant link of saturated fat consumption to heart attacks, strokes, or all-cause deaths. [2]

Still other reviews have shown similar results. Saturated fat intake was not linked to heart disease, stroke, Type 2 diabetes, or death from any cause. [3] [4] [5] [6]

Some studies have demonstrated that saturated fats may actually have *beneficial effects*. They can raise HDL (good cholesterol) and increase the size of the LDL particle. [7] The latter action renders the "lousy" or bad cholesterol less likely to form plaque in our arteries.

In essence, saturated fats in small-to-moderate amounts can be part of a healthy diet.

MYTH #3: GRAINS ARE GOOD FOR YOU

This was the thinking in the 1990s when the American Heart Association Diet was in vogue. Grains were placed at the bottom of the food pyramid, the foundation of a healthy diet. Fats were placed at the very top and were supposed to be eaten sparingly.

This diet failed miserably! The country got fatter, and diabetes became an epidemic. In the 21st century we are currently dealing with an extremely unhealthy population with a condition known as *diabesity*. Consider this a result of *SAD, the Standard American Diet.*

Looking back in history, our prehistoric ancestors did fairly well without grains. Interestingly enough, the human genome hasn't

CHAPTER 28: You Are What You Eat

changed all that much. The agricultural revolution introduced grains to the human diet. Our eating habits have changed considerably since then. Today, at least in the Western world, food is too plentiful.

And, as a whole we are not terribly healthy.

Eating grains in moderation is acceptable, as it adds variety and texture to our diet. However, imbibing on excessive grains or starchy carbohydrates can lead to a host of *potential problems*:

- Grains contain *phytic acid*, which tends to bind essential minerals, such as iron, calcium, zinc, and magnesium. Therefore, their absorption in the intestines can be adversely impaired. What's the big deal here? *Deficiencies in these minerals* can result.
- Grains are *fairly low in nutrients* when compared to natural foods such as fish, chicken, meat, eggs, nuts, fruits and vegetables. Remember most grains are processed in some manner. After all, I don't see any bread trees out there! Do you?
- Wheat, the most common grain, contains *gluten*, which is actually a protein. Many people in the general population are extremely sensitive to gluten, and not simply those with the condition known as celiac disease.

Starchy carbs, regardless of whether they contain added sugar, eventually break down to simple carbohydrates. Basically, we are talking about *sugar*. I don't have to tell you how pro-inflammatory sugar is to our diet. It's like pouring gasoline over a fire!

This is my bottom line: If healthy aging is one of your goals, you might well consider limiting your intake of grains, starchy carbs and sugar. They promote _inflammation_, which we now know is *the bane of our existence when it comes to _aging._*

MYTH #4: TOO MUCH PROTEIN IS BAD FOR YOUR BONES AND KIDNEYS

It's true that protein promotes calcium excretion from the bones, but that is for the short-term. Long-term studies have demonstrated that the opposite occurs. Bone health is improved and there is a lower risk of fracture. [8]

I'd like to set the record straight about *high protein diets and kidney health*. There are still many physicians and dietitians who believe that high protein diets are injurious to the kidneys. This is simply not true when speaking about normal functioning kidneys. Those with impairment of renal (kidney) function, however, constitute a different population. One of the end products of protein is urea, which may further compromise a diseased kidney *if* there is excessive protein intake.

In essence, there is no association between a high protein diet and kidney disease in healthy individuals. If that were the case, I would be a goner for sure, since I have maintained a high protein diet for over 20 years. That's the usual case for bodybuilders interested in gaining muscle mass. I'm happy to say that my kidney function remains normal.

Eating a high protein diet is not deleterious to one's health and, in fact, may improve bone health and reduce the risk of fracture. Additionally, these diets can lower blood pressure and improve diabetes—lessening the possibility of kidney failure.

MYTH #5: LOW FAT FOODS ARE STILL THE WAY TO GO

Hopefully, no one reading this book still entertains this notion. For those of you who may still be holding on to your low-fat and non-fat salad dressings, cookies, and cereals, *the trash can awaits.*

We all remember the non-fat foods of the 90s, such as Entenmann's no-fat brownies and cakes. It amazes me that they were allowed to pass as being healthy. They certainly did nothing to help the battle of the bulge.

The country just got fatter and fatter.

By switching to low-fat and non-fat foods—while shunning healthy fats—we embraced processed foods like never before. Just reading the ingredients on the package must make you realize how unnatural these items are to our diet. As a substitute for fat, you

CHAPTER 28: You Are What You Eat

can count on there being plenty of *sugar*, most notably in the form of *high fructose corn syrup*. Then you will undoubtedly find a few unhealthy *artificial sweeteners* along the way. Let's not forget *fillers* to give it some texture.

And here we are in the 21st century. If maintaining your memory is near the top of your list when it comes to healthy aging, you need to feed your brain what it craves the most: **FAT**.

Yes, you heard me right! FAT!

Your brain is the fattest organ in your body and is at least 60% fat. Therefore, it should surprise no one that it thrives on a healthy high fat diet. (This obviously excludes fats from processed foods, fried foods, trans fats, fatty cuts of beef, lamb and pork, as well as fats from cured or processed meats such as hot dogs, sausage, and luncheon meats.)

Thankfully, there are plenty of *healthy fats*. I recommend a variety: avocados, olives, olive oil, fatty fish, nuts, nut butters and even peanuts—which are not nuts at all but legumes. Coconut and coconut oil are excellent choices as well as whole eggs.

*Here's a good rule of thumb: If it's **natural** or **unprocessed**…it's **healthy!***

Bottom line: avoid most non-fat or low-fat foods that are highly processed and laden with sugar or artificial sweeteners. Instead, opt for a higher fat diet comprised of mostly *natural foods*. Contrary to popular thought, such a diet won't make you fat and won't jeopardize the health of your heart.

Your brain will thank you.

MYTH #6: CARBS SHOULD BE YOUR BIGGEST SOURCE OF CALORIES

This statement refers to the food pyramid that was revised in the 1990s. The thinking was that a diet low in fat and high in carbohydrates (50-60 % of total calories) was optimal.

At the base of the pyramid was a recommendation of 6-11 servings/day of "breads, cereals, rice and pasta." At the very top of the pyramid, fats and oils were to be used "sparingly."

That's about as wrong as you could get. I would rather see an inverted pyramid with *healthy fat at the base. Carbs would become the macronutrient on top,* to be used sparingly.

Fortunately, for reasons previously mentioned, the high carb diet is not nearly as popular today. *Too many calories* are comprised of grains and starches, which eventually break down to sugar. Too much sugar clearly leads to *fat gain, metabolic syndrome, diabetes,* and *systemic inflammation.*

And as already mentioned, a diet like this is clearly *not the best for optimal brain function.*

It's clear; our thinking has changed over the last several years. And because I don't believe that one size fits all, I don't maintain an exact percentage of carbs that works for everyone. That said, unless we are talking about an extremely lean athlete who has a difficult time putting on muscle mass, I generally recommend that *starchy carbs* constitute *no more than 30-40 % of total calories* in the *average* American adult. In certain populations, such as those with diabetes and metabolic syndrome, I would recommend an even smaller percentage of carbohydrates.

In conclusion, the high carb, low fat diet has proven to be a **miserable failure.** It has repeatedly been shown to be inferior to *lower carb, higher fat* diets.

MYTH #7: DIETS HIGH IN VEGETABLE OILS ARE GOOD FOR YOU

Formerly it was felt that polyunsaturated vegetable oils, otherwise known as omega-6 fatty acids, were healthy because they lowered the risk of heart disease. Okay, but there is an even more important class of fats: fish oil or *omega-3 fatty acids.* These fats, by far, have a greater impact not only our heart health, but our health in general. Omega-3 fatty acids, both eicosapentaenoic acid (EPA) and docosahexaenoic acid (DHA) have potent *anti-inflammatory* properties.

We actually need both omega-6 fats and omega-3 fats in our diet, but in a certain ratio. Excessive amounts of omega-6 fats are found in the average Western diet, mostly in the highly processed foods commonly consumed by our society.

Too many omega-6 fatty acids are pro-inflammatory, and promote diseases of aging, including heart disease. Such an unfavorable ratio averages somewhere in the range of 10:1 - 25:1 (omega-6 to omega-3). A healthier ratio would be in the range of 6:1 or even less. [9] [10]

Besides their anti-inflammatory properties, omega-3 fatty acids increase bleeding time, decrease blood viscosity and therefore, decrease the tendency to form blood clots. This can prove to be useful in cardiac and stroke-prone patients.

There's more. They can significantly lower triglycerides—thus improving one's lipid or blood/fat profile.

The many benefits of omega-3 fatty acids go beyond the scope of this chapter, but a lower ratio of omega-6: omega-3 fatty acids is more desirable in reducing the risks of many of the chronic diseases prevalent in Western society.

MYTH #8: **LOW CARB DIETS ARE DANGEROUS**

This reflects what has been discussed above. The lower carb diets were demonized by the media and nutritionists in the 1990s. They continue to be shunned by many. The truth? Low-fat diets have worse outcomes. Every randomized controlled trial comparing low-carb to low-fat diets have demonstrated the following *benefits of a low-carb diet.* [11] [12] [13]

- *Lowers blood pressure*
- *Lowers blood sugar* (especially important in the diabetic population)
- *Raises HDL* or good cholesterol
- *Lowers triglycerides*
- *Lowers body weight* more effectively than "healthy eating" in both diabetic and non-diabetic patients

It is clear that high-carb diets are harmful for most of us. They have been shown repeatedly to have adverse consequences when it comes to health. Conversely, *controlling carb intake is a scientifically proven method* to not only lose weight and keep it off, but also to reduce the risk for cardiovascular disease and diabetes.

MYTH #9: HIGH FAT FOODS MAKE YOU FAT

This sounds rather intuitive, doesn't it? We've been hearing this for years. Thinking like this paved the way for all those unhealthy processed low and non-fat foods that proliferated in the marketplace back in the 1990s

We now know that *carbs play a greater role in weight gain than fat.* This is despite the fact that one gram of fat yields nine calories, and one gram of carbs yields four calories. It's difficult to know exactly why, but in relatively small amounts, *healthy fat tends to satisfy us.*

Most of the maligned fats in our society are actually bad fats combined with lots of sugar. It should be a no-brainer that such processed high fat and sugar-laden foods make us fat. Additionally, combining fat and sugar tends to be never-ending.

We simply want more.

Fat isn't some demonic three-letter word! Yes, there are plenty of unhealthy fats out there: trans fats, fried and processed fats, fast foods, fatty cuts of meat, pork, and lamb, as well as fats in typical desserts.

Fortunately, you have several *healthy* fats to choose from. They've been previously mentioned in this chapter.

A Few Fat Facts

- Fat is a potent source of *stored energy* and is essential to *brain health*, especially as we age. Fat has other vital functions, such as absorbing various vitamins and minerals.
- Fat plays an important role in *building cell membranes.* The cell membrane protects the interior of each cell in our body from the outside environment.

- Fat also builds the myelin sheaths surrounding nerves. These are vital in insulating the nerve cell. Moreover, they are essential for proper functioning of the nervous system.
- According to the 2010 Dietary Guidelines for Americans, adults should get 20-35% of their calories from fat. This is an oversimplification. I generally recommend a higher percentage of fat for my patients.

In conclusion, even though a gram of fat yields nine calories, you'd be hard pressed to become fat on a healthy high-fat, low-carb diet—when coupled with regular exercise.

MYTH #10: SUGAR ISN'T THE MAJOR PROBLEM

Really? Nothing can be farther from the truth. Sugar contains lots of calories of essentially no nutritional value. However, that is merely the tip of the iceberg. Table sugar, commonly known as sucrose is actually a combination of two simple sugars, fructose and glucose. This combination of these two simple sugars makes it a disaccharide which happens to be deleterious to your health.

The high fructose content affects metabolism in such a way that can lead to rapid weight gain and other metabolic problems. These include elevated triglycerides, non-alcoholic fatty liver disease and metabolic syndrome. Fructose is metabolized in the liver but only in small amounts. Due to the liver's inability to handle a high fructose load, excess fructose is converted into fat and subsequently dumped into the bloodstream as VLDL (Very Low Density Lipoprotein) particles.

What eventually occurs is a *significant rise in triglycerides*. A host of metabolic problems ensues, most notably insulin resistance. Such is the case when the skeletal muscles no longer recognize the body's insulin. Sugar then can't be stored in the muscles as glycogen. It *remains in the bloodstream* which isn't good. The pancreas then tries to compensate by dumping more insulin into the bloodstream. This only compounds the problem.

Metabolic syndrome, obesity, and type 2 diabetes result.

An interesting point about sugar is that it stimulates a biochemical urge that drives humans to desire and *eat even more sugar!* It is now believed that many in the general population are genuinely addicted to sugar, which makes it as much as a public health problem as smoking and alcohol.

Is cake the new crack? This kind of addiction truly exists. It's been said that as many of seventy-five percent of overweight individuals, as well as many of those of normal weight are addicted to carbs.

Oh, come on Dr. Elkin, how do you compare sugar to cocaine?

Good question. Here's the answer: they both *give folks that* **rush**. As with coke, this rush can lead to **cravings** *in your brain and* **intrusive thoughts** *when you go too long without a fix.*

Unlike cocaine, *carbs do more than rewire your nervous system.* They *reprogram your metabolism* in a way that is *contrary to optimal health.*

With a healthy diet, your metabolism stores fat as energy so that it can be used later as fuel. But a diet laden with carbohydrates increases your insulin level which commonly leads to insulin resistance and fat gain. The end result is your metabolism *locking your food away as unburnable fat.*

Insulin also *lowers blood sugar*, so imbibing on carbs can make you *hypoglycemic* and *ravenous*, not to mention *irritable*. You subsequently tend to crave the same food that started you down this path of chemical dependency.

The only difference? *This is not an illicit street drug, but a commonly ingested food product.*

Last thought: **sugar is the most <u>pro-inflammatory</u> substance known to man.** I've said it here, I've said it in my videos, and I'll say it once more: eating sugar is *like pouring gasoline over a fire*. It's like lighting a fire from within. Indeed, this is truly a disaster for healthy living. Inflammation is the basis behind the four most common chronic diseases that we see in the aging population:

- Heart disease
- Cancer
- Autoimmune disorders
- Alzheimer's disease

There is a reason why I chose the title of this chapter. You are indeed what you eat! We can cut back on the incidence of chronic disease by eating healthy and choosing wisely.

As an example, reducing the incidence of coronary heart disease with diet is possible. [14] But it's not merely about cutting back on fat and cholesterol, it's about maintaining a healthy diet and limiting inflammation by reducing your intake of sugar.

What's my bottom line? The harmful effects of sugar go way beyond empty calories. Sugar wreaks havoc on your *metabolism,* and sets the stage for *addiction, weight gain* and *serious diseases* rooted in inflammation.

∼

WHAT DIET TO FOLLOW?

With all the available diets out there, things can get a bit confusing. Is there any science behind all the marketing hype? Again, I'm not a proponent of any one particular diet, as I like to pick and choose from a variety of options. That said, let's investigate some of the current, popular eating trends.

The Mediterranean Diet

Probably no diet has been studied more extensively than the Mediterranean diet, and for good reason; such a diet is essentially *healthy* and *unprocessed.* It emphasizes fruits, vegetables, whole grains, breads, legumes, potatoes, nuts, and seeds. Also included are hefty amounts of both extra virgin olive oil and red wine, and moderate amounts of fish, poultry, dairy, and eggs. Red meat is eaten only rarely.

When it became apparent in the 20th century that heart disease was this country's number one killer, researchers asked why? They found that people living around the Mediterranean (such as Italy and Greece) had very little heart disease compared to Americans. The researchers surmised that the reason for their low rate of heart disease was their diet.

Although this diet has been consumed for quite some time around the Mediterranean, it only recently gained mainstream popularity to improve health and prevent heart disease. Numerous studies have been conducted on this diet, including several *randomized controlled trials,* which are considered the gold standard in medical science.

The PREDIMED study made headlines in 2013 for having caused a substantial reduction in cardiovascular disease. The subjects were randomized into three different diets:

- A Mediterranean diet with added extra virgin olive oil (Med + Olive oil)
- A Mediterranean diet with added nuts (Med + Nuts)
- A low-fat control diet

The results favoring the Mediterranean diet were published in several prestigious peer-reviewed journals. Here are some of the conclusions:

- The risk of combined heart attack, stroke and death from heart disease was reduced by 30% in the Med + olive oil group, and 28% in the Med + nut group (when compared to the low-fat control group).
- Patients with hypertension, elevated cholesterol and/or triglycerides, and obesity responded best to the Mediterranean diet.
- There was no statistically significant effect in women and there was no reduction in *overall* mortality. [15]
- There have been numerous other published papers on the beneficial effects of the Mediterranean diet.
- The prevalence of metabolic syndrome decreased by

6.7% in the Med+Olive Oil group and 13.7% in the Med + Nuts group. [16]
- The levels of oxidized LDL, known to be the culprit in initiating plaque formation in coronary heart disease, were decreased in both Mediterranean Diet groups, but not in the low-fat control group. [17]

10-11% of the subjects in the Mediterranean diet became diabetic, compared to 17.9% in the low-fat control group. Indeed, the Mediterranean diet reduced the risk of developing type 2 diabetes by over 50%. [18]

Compared to a low-fat control group, a Mediterranean diet can have beneficial effects on various risk factors for heart disease, such as blood sugar, blood pressure, and C-reactive protein (a key marker for inflammation) [19]

The landmark Lyon Diet Heart Study demonstrated that the group following the Mediterranean diet was 72% less likely to have developed a heart attack or to have died from heart disease. [20]

In summary, the Mediterranean diet is not prescribed as a weight loss diet, but rather is seen as a sensible diet that can help *prevent heart disease and premature death*. It seems clear from looking at the data that it is indeed healthy. Such a diet may help prevent some of the Western world's greatest killers.

It is obviously a *much better option* than the standard *low-fat diet* that somehow continues to garner support today.

The Paleolithic Diet

Commonly known as simply the paleo diet, it has become the *world's most popular diet* as of 2013. It is still quite *controversial* among health professionals and mainstream nutritionists. Some experts call it healthy and reasonable. Others call it downright harmful.

Fortunately, science can give us some answers, as there have been human studies performed on the paleo diet.

The diet of hunter-gatherers. My description of the diet is this: if it doesn't run in the wild or grow in nature, it probably doesn't belong on your plate. It is based on the premise that our ancestors did not suffer from the chronic deteriorating diseases of modern man.

This diet advocates consumption of animals and plants, including meat, fish, eggs, vegetables, fruits, nuts, and seeds. *Processed foods such as dairy, sugar, and grains are avoided.*

There are some studies done on humans and published in peer-reviewed scientific journals. It is based on the premise that our ancestors did not suffer from the chronic deteriorating diseases of modern man. A few are noted below:

- The paleo diet improved glucose tolerance (an indicator of insulin resistance and diabetes) more than the Mediterranean diet. Additionally, it led to a decrease in waist circumference. [21]
- The diet demonstrated weight loss and a decrease in blood pressure. [22]
- Compared to the traditional diabetic diet, the paleo diet resulted in more weight loss, and several improvements in cardiac risk factors such as an increase in HDL (the "healthy" cholesterol), a decrease in triglycerides, and improved blood sugar control. [23]

The diet resulted in the following health benefits: [24]
1. Decrease in total cholesterol.
2. Decrease in LDL cholesterol.
3. Decrease in triglycerides.
4. Improvement in glycemic control (management of blood sugar).
5. Decrease in blood pressure.

- A paleo diet demonstrated a decrease in fat deposition in obese postmenopausal women. We know that fatty liver is associated with metabolic disease, such as metabolic syndrome and diabetes. In this study, the women had an average reduction in liver fat of 49%. The subjects lost an average of ten pounds as well as experienced significant improvement in various cardiac risk factors previously mentioned [25]

There are several obvious *limitations* to the studies listed above:
- All the studies are *small*, ranging from 9-29 participants.
- The studies were of *short* duration, ranging from 10 days to 12 weeks.
- Only 2 out of 5 studies had a *control group*.

Naturally, it is difficult to make any firm conclusions based on the 5 studies above, since they are all too small and too short in duration. What we need are large scale studies with subjects being followed for a much longer time frame.

Especially useful would-be large-scale studies comparing the Mediterranean diet to the paleo diet.

There are aspects to this diet that appeal to me personally, especially the fact that *nothing processed* is eaten. How nice is that?

My take on the paleo diet is that it is more than likely *healthy*, and poses *little health risks*. But I also realize that such a strict diet can get a bit *boring*, since it *lacks variety*.

Therefore, the diet I follow myself is somewhere between the Mediterranean and Paleolithic diets.

OTHER DIET TRENDS

Gluten-free Diets

As the name implies, these diets exclude gluten, a protein found in wheat and related grains such as barley and rye. Oats do not actually contain gluten, but are processed in a similar manner, so, therefore, they are generally excluded as well.

Many of us are gluten intolerant. The most serious are afflicted with celiac disease, an inherited autoimmune disorder. This is diagnosed by a biopsy taken from a section of the small intestine. These patients have structural damage to the lining of the intestinal wall—a result of ongoing inflammation.

The culprit is gluten. An intense immune response takes place whenever an affected patient ingests the offending agent. This immune response eventually alters the lining of the bowel.

As a result, these patients fail to absorb vital nutrients. A host of medical problems can result, including other autoimmune disorders. *Currently there is no cure*, but complete abstinence from gluten keeps the disease at bay in most cases.

Celiac disease. It's on the rise. It's seen four times more frequently today than it was fifty years ago. No one knows why, but it could be because the gluten found today in wheat products is different than the gluten found years ago.

As far as mainstream medicine is concerned, celiac disease is currently the only indication for a gluten-free diet. If you don't have celiac disease, is there any benefit in going gluten-free?

Well, countless food manufacturers out there sure think so! The number of gluten-free products grows daily. Formerly showcased at specialty grocers such as Whole Foods and Trader Joe's, one can now find gluten-free items on the shelves of conventional grocers, like Ralphs and Vons.

This trend is here to stay. Along with many preventative-minded wellness and anti-aging physicians and nutritionists, I do believe there's a role for gluten-free diets in special cases. However, the current trend to go gluten-free is almost viral, with up to 30% of American adults embracing gluten-free living.

This is despite a lack of scientific clarity, regardless of health benefits. There is this sense that gluten is simply not good for us, but there's little evidence that going gluten-free equates to good health.

Personally, I see no harm in going gluten-free. Wheat products are essentially all processed and fortified. There certainly are no vital nutrients found in wheat products that cannot be found in nature. Therefore, I leave this choice to the individual.

In certain patients, I do believe in attempting a gluten-free diet for a limited time. An example could be individuals suffering from chronic disorders and health issues for which there is no attainable cure. This would include autoimmune disorders.

For one of the best sources available, I highly recommend reading *The Gluten Connection,* by Shari Lieberman, PhD, CNS, FACN. [26]

About 1% of the general population has celiac disease. However, a much larger group of people is estimated to have "non-celiac gluten sensitivity." According to the *National Foundation for Celiac Awareness*, as many as 18 million Americans may have some form of non-celiac sensitivity to gluten.

If you are losing weight, suffer from chronic fatigue, abdominal pain, gas, bloating, constipation and/or diarrhea, are deficient in iron, are anemic or have a family history of celiac disease, you might well consider a trial of gluten-free living.

Let's face it: The Western world is currently plagued by chronic disease, with approximately half of the adult population in the United States affected. Some sources report that up to 30% of our population has gluten sensitivity. In her book, Dr. Lieberman fervently believes that this is no coincidence. [26]

In her lifetime, in addition to classic celiac disease, she worked with scores of patients suffering from chronic diseases such as the following:

- *Skin disorders* such as psoriasis, eczema, acne and hives.
- *Neurological disorders* such as migraine headaches and behavioral problems.
- *Digestive disorders* such as irritable bowel syndrome (IBS), reflux, and ulcerative colitis.
- *Autoimmune disorders* such as lupus, scleroderma, rheumatoid arthritis, multiple sclerosis, thyroid disease, and osteoporosis.
- *Undiagnosed diseases* and conditions such as fibromyalgia, chronic fatigue syndrome, asthma, and unexplained weight loss or gain.

Dr. Lieberman, amongst others in the nutritional field, discovered that by altering patients' diets and eliminating gluten, amelioration of symptoms can result. There may even be halting of the underlying disease process.

Most of the research performed on gluten-free diets is based on observational studies involving small numbers of patients. We lack large, randomized placebo-controlled trials, the gold standard in medical research. However, there is plenty of evidence in the literature that supports gluten elimination in select cases.

My view on this? I believe in tenaciously *doing whatever it takes to obtain relief* of symptoms. Until we have a cure for some of these potentially debilitating illnesses, I recommend *healthy diet manipulation.* In many cases this may include going gluten-free.

Wheat, which contains gluten, is by far the most commonly ingested grain. It has no true nutritional value. There is certainly nothing harmful about following a gluten-free diet.

Here are a few of *my own case studies*:

1. CH is a relatively healthy female who continues to be employed as a vital marketing consultant well into her seventies. Besides a bout of early-stage breast cancer, she has suffered a host of autoimmune and other conditions including Graves' disease (a form of hyperthyroidism), osteoporosis, fibromyalgia, and severe chronic fatigue.

   She had an extensive work-up including a small bowel biopsy which was diagnostic for classic celiac disease. Eliminating all gluten from her diet, including most condiments, gluten-coated envelopes, as well as many gluten-containing lipsticks, her symptoms have greatly improved.

2. PG who is actually my niece suffered from chronic hives. This began in high school and persisted into her college years. She saw numerous top-notch dermatologists in New York City who offered her little relief. Upon going gluten-free her symptoms

CHAPTER 28: You Are What You Eat

resolved and she continues to lead a very active and full life.

3. LEL is my beloved mother who is over ninety years of age as of this writing. As early as her forties she was plagued with Irritable Bowel Syndrome (IBS) marked by severe abdominal pain, gas, bloating, and constipation alternating with diarrhea.

She saw numerous physicians over the years who offered her little relief. She was constantly told that it was a "nervous condition" and that she would "have to live with it." As you might suspect, she was prescribed an abundance of tranquilizers along the way. Her physicians actually appeared annoyed when she would continue to complain of these symptoms.

Upon my advice she read Dr. Lieberman's book at age 87 and it resonated with her. She made the conscious decision to go gluten-free, and her symptoms improved by nearly 75% within a short span of three weeks.

Now going gluten-free at any age takes work, but imagine assuming this degree of dietary change in your late eighties! And of course, she would cheat every so often and her symptoms returned with vengeance.

Here's how I see it; for those suffering from chronic illnesses where there is no cure in sight; a gluten-free diet is a therapeutic move worth considering.

Before starting a gluten-free diet, definitely *consult your physician.* There is *food sensitivity testing* that can nail the diagnosis. Such testing requires a simple blood sample sent to a specialty lab. It is regularly performed here at *HeartWise Fitness and Longevity Center.* Moreover, we employ a certified nutritional counselor. Her expertise is invaluable in guiding patients through such a dietary change.

At the very least, one can simply go gluten-free without the requisite testing and simply evaluate the response. Working with a qualified nutritional counselor is clearly important.

This *diet requires re-education and planning.* Furthermore, it is important to go *completely gluten-free* for a minimum of *2 months* before coming to any conclusion regarding the effectiveness of the diet.

Half-way measures do not work.

If you don't believe me, ask my mom!

GOING VEGAN?

What about the current *vegan craze?* I live in Los Angeles, one of the trend centers of the world. A new vegan restaurant or green juice bar pops up daily! For the past 20 years, 5% of the American population identifies as vegetarian, with 2% claiming to be vegan. A vegan diet disallows animal products of any kind, including eggs and diary.

What are the *benefits of a vegan diet?*

- May help *lower cholesterol*, more specifically the *LDL* or lousy cholesterol.
- May help *lower blood pressure.*
- May be useful in *losing weight.*
- *Increases antioxidant intake* while consuming a diet of fruits, vegetables, beans, and legumes.
- May *promote greater self-control* since one is following a regimented diet with inherently multiple restrictions.

Self-control is self-control. It can be extended to any behaviors requiring commitment and dedication, such as exercise and stress management. (Of course, the same could be said for folks following any heavily structured eating plan.)

What about the **disadvantages of a vegan diet?**

- **A radical change:** Going vegan takes a lot of *planning*. It can also be extremely *complicated*. This is especially true if one wishes to avoid certain ingredients such as soy, a good source of a plant-based protein. One would have to put together complimentary foods to form complete vegetarian proteins.
- **Potential interference with existing medical conditions:** Examples include chronic disease states such as diabetes and osteoporosis, where diet is a mainstay of treatment. Too many

CHAPTER 28: You Are What You Eat

carbs in the form of starches, commonly consumed in vegans, can make diabetes worse. Shunning all dairy products may make adequate calcium intake difficult. This could lead to osteoporosis.

- **Difficulty when dining out:** Living in Los Angeles, I admit that this is not a major obstacle. There are probably more vegan restaurants here than anywhere else in the world. However, this is not the case in Mobile or Bozeman—or for most of the United States.

- **Loss of essential nutrients, such as protein, vitamins and minerals:** This is my biggest concern for those who go vegan. *Protein is our most important macronutrient.* Protein is essential for growth and maintenance of all cells within our body. Eliminating all animal products from the diet can make this a challenge. Yes, there are good plant sources of protein such as tofu, beans, and nuts. The vegan, however, must become well-versed in nutrition to ensure adequate protein intake on a daily basis.

  Vegan diets do not contain *vitamin B12*, an essential nutrient. One study showed that 92% of vegans are deficient in this critical nutrient. [27] Vitamin B12 can be obtained, however, from fortified foods and from supplements.

  Vegan diets tend to be *low in calcium and vitamin D*. However, there are vegan sources of these nutrients as well. *Iron deficiency* is also a possibility since beef and shellfish are disallowed. This can be especially problematic for women of child-bearing age who are actively menstruating.

- **Unrealistic expectations:** You may believe that going vegan makes you automatically healthy. Maybe, but it's doubtful. Keep in mind, there is *no good data proving that being vegan equates to optimal health.*

A few additional concerns that I have with the vegan diet:
- **Protein.** It is likely that *protein intake from animal sources* provides *better preservation of muscle mass index*, a critical factor in healthy aging. [28] [29]
- **Aging.** Other markers of aging are also diminished in vegans, most notably *testosterone*. [30]

  Studies have shown that vegans are deficient in *creatine*, which is important in generating energy at the cellular level. A lack of creatine has potentially harmful effects on muscle and brain function. [31] [32]

  Additionally, *carnosine* which is only found in animal products, is protective against various degenerative diseases in the body. This nutrient is also lacking in vegans. [33]
- **No controlled trials.** Despite the claims of vegan proponents, there are no controlled trials demonstrating the benefits of going vegan.

Since vegan diets are often high carb and low protein, it certainly is not the diet for me. I actually attempted a vegetarian diet several years back when I was involved in aerobic sports. By going vegetarian, I excluded red meat only. I still imbibed on chicken and fish. I avoided cheese, butter, and egg yolks, eating only egg whites, all to limit my intake of saturated fat and cholesterol.

What I experienced was one respiratory infection after another. Furthermore, my energy stores, strength and recovery all suffered. Unfortunately, I failed to measure my testosterone level, but I assume it was down. My iron and zinc intake were obviously suboptimal since I avoided all red meat.

Basically, I was following the diet of the day for endurance athletes, which was the proverbial high-carb, low-fat trend. I believe that my relatively low protein intake contributed to a diminished immune system. (Obviously, these are all conjectures, but nonetheless here I am twenty some years later, feeling healthier, stronger, and overall much better.)

CHAPTER 28: You Are What You Eat

If you're going to dive in: Going vegan is a major decision, which requires quite a bit of planning. This diet speaks to many, as seen by the proliferation of cookbooks and restaurants popping up to support the followers.

I recommend *intracellular nutrient testing*, along with *appropriate supplementation* for those deficient in any of the nutrients listed above. Furthermore, I also suggest working with a *qualified dietitian or nutritional counselor* well versed in vegan diets.

Going vegan is a personal choice with many factors playing a role in the decision-making. My belief is while such a diet may benefit some, it is clearly not for everyone.

THE DR. DEAN ORNISH PLAN

I can't really leave the topic of a vegan/vegetarian diet without commenting on the Dr. Dean Ornish's plan, which rose to popularity in the 90s. He demonstrated that strict adherence to his plan can prevent, or in some cases actually reverse heart disease. [34]

Although I found his diet plan to be overly-restrictive, and his exercise program a bit lame, I supported his emphasis on stress reduction and the use of support groups. In fact, for a couple of years I maintained a weekly after-hours support group in my office, based on his model.

Twenty some years later we know quite a bit more about cholesterol, more specifically the difference between small and large LDL particle size. Moreover, since that time we have witnessed a major rise in obesity, metabolic syndrome, and diabetes.

The Ornish diet does not address these pressing issues. His diet recommends 10% fat, 20% protein and 70% carbohydrates. Even though simple carbohydrates were restricted, even complex carbs eventually break down to sugar.

To me this diet may make sense for *overweight cardiac patients* or patients with *multiple cardiac risk factors* who have elevated total cholesterol with an elevated large LDL particle size and normal triglycerides. A vegetarian diet can lower these values quite nicely.

However, for *diabetic patients*, and those with *metabolic syndrome* and *elevated triglycerides*, I believe *this diet is not ideal*. In fact, it may make matters worse.

Furthermore, we've already discussed the preferred diet for optimal brain function; a diet high in carbohydrates definitely fails to fit this bill. Again, *I would recommend a higher healthy fat, lower carb diet for general health and aging.*

THE ANTI-INFLAMMATORY DIET

We all know that inflammation is part of the body's immune system. Without it, we can't heal.

But when it's out of control, it can cause significant damage to the body. As I've previously mentioned, the major cause of diseases of aging, including heart disease and cancer, is inflammation spun out of control.

Sugar and starchy carbs are your main culprits. Eliminating these is your first step in maintaining an anti-inflammatory diet. In addition, making the foods listed below staples in your diet can further help maintain an inflammatory-free zone:

- *Fatty fish* and *fish oil* supplements. These are naturally anti-inflammatory in nature.
- *Dark leafy greens*
- *Nuts*
- *Peppers* (see below)
- *Beets*
- *Ginger* and *turmeric*
- *Garlic* and *onions*
- *Olive oil*
- *Berries*
- *Tart cherries*

One caveat to the above is the *nightshade* family. These include *tomatoes, peppers, potatoes,* and *eggplant*. These can potentially be pro-inflammatory, but in reality, the number of individuals sensitive to the effects of nightshades is relatively low. Being high in antioxidants, they do confer definite health benefits. If a patient is bothered by joint pain, for example, I have him or her hold all nightshades for three weeks. If their symptoms significantly improve, there's the answer.

THE ALKALINE DIET MYTH

When a diet seems too good to be true, you can pretty much bet that it is. Such describes the alkaline diet. Proponents say that replacing acid-forming foods with alkaline foods can improve health, but the data is simply not there.

That said, the alkaline diet is actually quite healthy, I am not opposed to it. It encourages a high consumption of fruits, vegetables and healthy plant foods while restricting processed junk foods.

The diet is based around the idea that the foods you eat can alter the acidity or alkalinity (the pH value) of your body. Putting it simply, proponents claim that eating acid foods makes your body acidic, while eating alkaline foods makes your body more alkaline.

Acidity is thought to make you more vulnerable to disease and illness, whereas alkalinity is considered protective. Acidic foods include meat, poultry, fish, diary, eggs, grains, and alcohol. Examples of alkaline foods include fruits, nuts, legumes, and vegetables.

So, what's the big deal? Remembering the basics from high school chemistry class, the pH value ranges from 0 to 14:

> 0-7 is acidic.
> 7 is neutral.
> 7-14 is alkaline.

Your blood. What you need to know is that the *pH value varies greatly within the body*. Some tissues are more acidic than others. There is no set value. For example, the stomach secretes hydrochloric acid which is necessary to break down food. This imparts a pH value between 2 to 3.5. On the other hand, *human blood is always* *slightly alkaline*, with a pH value 7.35 to 7.45.

With normal functioning lungs and kidneys, the human body maintains acid-base homeostasis. In other words, the pH value of the blood never deviates outside this range. Only in serious disease states will this range vary. Therefore, *what you eat from* one day to the next *has nothing to do with the pH of your blood.*

It is critical that the pH of your blood remains within that narrow range noted above. If it would fall out, as it does with life-threatening disease, your cells would cease to function normally. As a result, you would die if this condition is not reversed in a timely fashion.

What's with all those folks measuring their urine pH with test strips? Food can clearly change the pH value of the urine. After eating a large steak, your urine will become more acidic within a few hours. It's how our bodies maintain that homeostasis by excreting acids.

Food cannot change your blood pH. It may change the pH of your urine, but that is actually a very poor indicator of overall body pH. Therefore, even if one uses test strips to test the pH of the urine or saliva, this has little relevance to the alkalinity of your blood—and your overall health.

Many alkaline diet enthusiasts also believe that acid-forming diets found in animal products cause a loss in bone density, leading to osteoporosis. This is known as the "acid-ash hypothesis of osteoporosis." They attribute this to the leeching of alkaline minerals such as calcium from the bones to buffer the acid from acid-forming foods.

Not true. The respiratory system and the kidneys are responsible for buffering any excess acids. The *bones are actually not involved* in this process at all. [35] [36]

Acidity and cancer? Extensive review on this topic has failed to demonstrate a valid relationship between acid-forming foods and cancer. [37]

Proponents argue that cancer only grows in an acidic environment and can be treated and possible cured with an alkaline diet. It would be nice if it were true.

As mentioned above, food cannot influence blood pH. In fact, cancer grows in normal body tissue which, as I have pointed out has a slightly alkaline pH of 7.4. Various studies have confirmed this by successfully growing cancer cells in an alkaline environment.

While tumors may grow faster in acidic environments, the tumor cells themselves are responsible for creating this acidity. *It is not the acidic environment that creates the cancer, but the cancer that creates the acidic environment.*

An alkaline diet is actually quite healthy. It *emphasizes healthy foods* and *restricts junk foods*. But acids are not some bad offshoot of our metabolism. They are some of the most important building blocks of life, including amino acids, fatty acids, and our DNA (deoxyribonucleic acid).

The alkaline diet is healthy because it is based on *real, unprocessed foods*. But this has nothing to do with the creation of an alkaline environment within our body.

CONSIDERING GOING KETO?

The ketogenic diet is an extremely *low-carb, high-fat* diet that confers many health benefits in combating several disease states. These include diabetes, cancer, epilepsy, and neurodegenerative disorders such as Parkinson's disease and Alzheimer's disease. [38] [39] [40]

Although formerly relegated to the backburner of diet enthusiasts, its popularity is clearly on the rise.

The keto diet is not new. Its use spans over 90 years for the symptomatic treatment of intractable epilepsy in children. The salutary effects of a ketogenic diet are being increasingly appreciated in the Western world.

Keto is a very low-carb, high fat diet that shares many similarities with the Atkins diet, but is generally stricter and more structured. It involves drastically *reducing carbohydrate intake* and *replacing it with fat*.

It is extreme. The marked reduction in carbs puts your body into a metabolic state called *ketosis*. As a result, your body becomes *incredibly efficient at burning fat for energy.* The process turns fat into ketones in the liver, which can supply energy for the brain.

There are several versions of the ketogenic diet. The most studied has been the *standard ketogenic diet*. This is a very low-carb, moderate-protein and high-fat diet. It typically contains 75% fat, 20% protein and only 5% carbs. However, many ketogenic diets go as far as 20% carbs or perhaps a bit more.

Potential benefits of a ketogenic diet:

- **Weight Loss:** Research shows that going keto is far superior to a low-fat diet. [41] [42]

  A ketogenic diet tends to *reduce hunger* due to the satiety effect of a high-fat intake. Furthermore, there are hormonal and metabolic changes that take place that aid in *preserving muscle mass.* [43]

  The end result is an improvement in body composition with an increased muscle-to-fat ratio. This may be the ideal diet for anti-aging.

- **Metabolic Disorders:** [44] [45]

  High blood pressure

  Abdominal obesity

  High levels of "lousy" LDL cholesterol

  Low levels of "healthy" HDL cholesterol

  High blood sugar

  Elevated triglycerides

  The bottom line: potential improvement in many aspects of the metabolic syndrome such as enhanced insulin sensitivity and subsequent weight loss, and possible disease reversal in diabetics and prediabetes.

- **Heart disease:** The ketogenic diet can improve cardiac risk factors such as obesity, HDL levels, blood pressure and blood sugar. [12] [46]

- **Cancer:** Cancer seems to thrive in a glucose-rich environment. Following a very low-carb diet may be efficacious in cancer patients. [47] [48]
- **Neurodegenerative disorders such as Parkinson's disease and Alzheimer's disease.** [49] [50]
- **Brain injuries.**
- **Epilepsy.**
- **Polycystic ovary disease:** These patients have significant insulin resistance and tend to be overweight. A ketogenic diet might prove extremely therapeutic in such cases. [51]
- **Exercise performance:** It has long been thought that glucose is essential for peak performance. Maybe not. There are emerging trends in the literature that counter that old school thinking. Going ketogenic does not seem to adversely affect exercise capability. [52]

This is the one diet to keep watching. As you can see, the ketogenic diet has a myriad of potential health benefits. Perhaps the easiest way to appreciate this diet is by the following case study.

THS is an *extremely active woman* in her early fifties. She is a former fitness pro, currently owning a thriving personal training business. So, she knows a thing or two about healthy living!

THS became a bride at the age of 40. Because of her excellent health and fitness background, she figured getting pregnant would be a "slam dunk." Unfortunately, her first pregnancy ended in miscarriage. "This was the start of a very long and painful journey," she remarked.

For the next two years the couple tried everything recommended to them by fertility experts. This included lots of meds and three rounds of in vitro fertilization, all of which ended in failure. This proved to be both financially and emotionally exhaustive. Furthermore, the fertility treatments led to weight gain, fatigue, digestive issues, and hormonal imbalance.

But miracles do happen! After two long years of fertility treatments, they were able to conceive their first daughter naturally. They clearly proved the experts wrong who told the couple that there was less than a 1% chance of THS conceiving with her own egg.

Two years later the couple attempted one more pregnancy. This time, however, they decided to use an egg donor, to minimize THS's exposure to "a bunch of fertility meds." However, in prepping for the embryo transfer, she was obliged to take a multitude of synthetic hormones, some of which were by daily injections.

Her first embryo resulted in pregnancy, but failed to progress. Over the next year she went through this process six additional times.

The doses of the medications were increased, and prednisone was eventually added to suppress her immune system. This was necessary to minimize the chance of her body attacking the embryo.

After one solid year, four miscarriages and one failed embryo transfer, she was finally successful. The second pregnancy was quite a bit more taxing. She developed gestational diabetes and "a lot more aches and pains that I did not have with my first pregnancy."

She went on to require steroid injections, bed rest and labor induction with "a lot of antibiotics and drugs."

Post-delivery of her second healthy daughter, THS dealt with elevated blood pressure and blood sugar, worsening gut issues, insomnia, and extreme fatigue.

Taking the bull by the horns like a true Medical Advocate, THS did tons of research. The ketogenic diet resonated with her. She started her keto journey two months post-partum. A significant decrease in her blood sugar and blood pressure resulted. Weight loss subsequently followed.

Furthermore, cholesterol and triglyceride levels normalized, and her insulin resistance vanished.

She never feels hungry on this diet. Her gut issues have resolved, and her energy has returned. "At the age of 51 I feel as if I've reclaimed my health. Now my goal is to be healthier and more fit than I was in my 30s. I am convinced that I will attain my goals with the ketogenic way of life."

Admittedly THS's story is incredibly unique as it represents what can possibly go wrong metabolically when synthetic hormones, steroids and other potent medications are used in an otherwise healthy, fit individual. But let's not forget that the end result was well worth it, as two beautiful healthy girls were born.

As a true Medical Advocate, THS did her own research and found the ketogenic diet doable. She continues to follow it daily, and currently counsels her clients on the diet's benefits. Furthermore, she continues to thrive in every way.

A couple of years ago I would have turned my back on anything remotely akin to the ketogenic diet. Having done my own research and having met and worked with THS, I now feel markedly different.

WHAT ABOUT FASTING?

This is a hot topic! Proponents claim fasting can disrupt chronic illnesses such as diabetes and cancer, reduce the effects of aging, and support weight loss. [53]

A long time ago, we hunters-gatherers managed our eating patterns according to food availability. By necessity we alternated between eating and fasting. While fasting we lived off our fat stores.

Now we just eat! We no longer eat and fast. And we eat a lot more than we need!

Intermittent fasting isn't a diet in the usual sense. It doesn't specify what foods to eat, but rather *when* you should eat them.

Common fasting practices involve fasting for 16 hours with an eating time of eight hours. But there are no golden rules. Variations are many and based on the individual. The objective is to have a long interval where there is no food intake. Other practices involve fasting for 24 hours once or twice a week. For example, not eating from dinner one night until dinner the next.

Why consider it?

There are a number of changes that occur at the cellular and molecular level with fasting. Your body adjusts various hormones to make stored body fat more accessible.

Some of the changes that commonly occur:
- **Human Growth Hormone (HGH):** Levels of HGH tend to skyrocket with fasting, increasing as much as five-fold. This benefits both *fat loss* and *muscle gain*. [54]
- **Insulin:** Insulin sensitivity increases as insulin levels drop dramatically. Lower insulin levels make *fat stores more accessible*. [55]
- **Cellular repair:** Fasting initiates cellular repair processes. Most notably is *autophagy*, where cells digest and *remove dysfunctional proteins* that build up in our cells. [56]
- **Gene expression:** Gene function can change as the result of fasting. These changes can promote longevity and guard against chronic disease. [57] [58]

There are other potential benefits of fasting:
- **Combating inflammation**
- **Heart health**
- **Cancer prevention**
- **Brain health**
- **Longevity**

I have been been practicing intermittent fasting for over three years now. I've lost a few pounds, rarely, if ever feel hungry, have easily maintained my muscle mass, and continue to have boundless energy. Moreover, people comment, telling me I look younger. What could be better than that!

Fasting Mimicking Diet. I can't possibly leave this discussion without mentioning a popular form of fasting that is currently taking the diet industry by storm. *FMD* is pioneered by its founder Dr. Valter Longo of the Longevity Institute at University of Southern California (USC).

This diet is called fasting mimicking because *you don't actually fast*. Instead, you drastically *reduce your caloric intake* for *five* consecutive days of the month for *three* consecutive months. Thereafter it's repeated quarterly, or according to your individual goals.

Here's the deal (and it doesn't matter what gender you are, how much you weigh or your fitness level): You have a total of 1200 calories on day 1, which drops to 700 calories on days 2-5.

That's it! Cut and dry! I've done the requisite three consecutive months followed by multiple quarterly cycles. I love the necessary discipline, akin to all those years of competitive bodybuilding. FMD is clearly up my alley. By the fourth and fifth day I'm in ketosis from caloric deprivation. My hunger disappears and my energy is incredible. My staff even comments that I'm nicer!

There is a company called Prolon that pre-packages your five-day meals in attractive little boxes. All you do is follow the directions day by day. There is no requisite calorie counting, as it's all been done for you. Alternatively, you can create your own five-day meal program.

Basically, this is a plant-based, low starch carb diet with all-natural ingredients.

When I first heard Dr. Longo speak at the 2017 American Academy of Anti-Aging Medicine meeting in Las Vegas, I became keenly interested, mainly because of the positive effects on longevity. The research is bourgeoning, and this eating plan is worth watching. [59]

MY BOTTOM LINE

As I repeatedly say, "one size never fits all." *Fasting is not for everyone*. It should generally be avoided in *underweight individuals, those with an eating disordeer, insulin-requiring diabetics, pregnant or lactating women, hypoglycemic individuals*, individuals that run a *low blood pressure*, and those suffering from *adrenal or chronic fatigue*.

As always, I recommend getting cleared from your physician.

GOING ORGANIC

No discussion on nutrition can be complete without detailing the benefits of eating organic, and for good reason; the organic-food industry is booming. About 70% of Americans purchase organic food occasionally and nearly a quarter buy it weekly, according to the Hartman Group, a prestigious market research firm.

Why all the hoopla? The reason is simple; we want natural food that's genuinely good for us and for the environment. But buying organic has one major drawback, the cost. You can expect to pay as much as 50% more in some cases.

Also, because preservatives are not used in organic crops, *food tends to spoil more easily* which means more *frequent food shopping*.

Though organic food can be produced with certain synthetic ingredients, it must adhere to specific standards regulated by the United States Department of Agriculture (USDA). Crops are grown without synthetic pesticides, artificial fertilizers, irradiation (a form of radiation used to kill bacteria), or biotechnology. Animals on organic farms eat organically grown feed, aren't confined 100% of the time, and are raised without antibiotics or synthetic hormones.

Research states that organic foods may have greater nutritional value than conventional food. The reason is that in the absence of pesticides and fertilizers, plants are able to boost their production of phytochemicals (vitamins and antioxidants) that strengthen their resistance to bugs and weeds.

Pesticides. It may be arguable how important a role they play in undermining our health, but most of us believe that pesticides are *simply not good for us.* Especially at risk are pregnant women, fetuses and children with their less-developed immune systems. This is because of the negative effect on our microbiome. Life in utero and in infancy is a setting for autoimmune illnesses, asthma, and allergies.

Meat and dairy products. Many scientists are concerned about the antibiotics administered to most farm animals. Too often, these same antibiotics are used in humans and their overuse complicates our ever-growing problem of *bacterial resistance*. This resistance can make these antibiotics *less effective in fighting life-threatening infections*.

The use of *synthetic hormones* is also a potential problem. It is conjectured that the use of synthetic estrogens plays a role in the growing incidence of low testosterone levels in men, along with premature menstruation in girls as young as ten.

Environmental boost. *Organic farming reduces pollutants* in groundwater and creates *richer soil* that aids *plant growth* while *reducing erosion*. So says the Organic Trade Association. Furthermore, it *decreases pesticides* that can end up in your drinking water.

Organic farming used *50% less energy* than conventional farming methods according to one 15-year study.

$$$. With all the plusses noted above, why would you elect to purchase anything but organic food? It boils down to money. If you can afford it, I always recommend buying organic.

Even if you can't afford to go completely organic, try to go the extra mile when it comes to buying the fragile fruits and vegetables listed below, which often *require more pesticides* to fight off bugs compared to heartier produce.

The dirty dozen:

Peaches	Nectarines	Strawberries
Apples	Spinach	Celery
Pears	Sweet bell peppers	Cherries
Potatoes	Lettuce	Imported grapes

When shopping for organic foods, *always look for the USDA seal* on any packaged food. For meat and dairy, this seal ensures you are getting antibiotic and hormone-free products.

Research. What about the nutritional value of organic over non-organic fare? Many experts have said that there is no conclusive evidence that eating organic has a distinct advantage.

Unfortunately, there really *hasn't been much data* in evaluating the nutritional benefits of organic products. Why? There simply is no money to conduct such research. Only pharmaceutical companies have enough capital to conduct large, randomized placebo-controlled trials, the gold standard in medicine. As a result, there is actually very limited information in humans on health outcomes with consumption of these products.

A few studies have demonstrated that organic produce contain higher amounts of vitamin C, minerals, and antioxidants. These are thought to protect the body against diseases of aging such as heart disease and cancer. But the differences are small and the impact on overall nutrition may not be that great.

Again, it boils down to personal choice. If you can manage the *higher price*, and if the idea of *fewer pesticides* and more *environmentally friendly* production speaks to you, going organic may well be the way to proceed.

Organic food appears to be *safer*, possibly *more nutritious*, and *better tasting* according to most advocates. True, we lack the research that links organic foods to improved outcomes, but hopefully that will be forthcoming.

As part of a healthy diet, I believe in the power of going organic whenever possible. Promoting holistic health and overall wellness, it just seems right to me. It's clearly safer and better for the environment.

GO GO GMO?

Genetically modified foods (GMO's) are *highly controversial* these days. They are also ubiquitous in nature, found in all sorts of food products, often without labels. The term generally refers to *food that has had its genes changed through biotechnology*. With genetic modification, science can produce *new* varieties of plants that are able to resist viruses or pesticides.

Genetic modification is a scientific technique employed to alter the genetic material of an organism. It is usually done by transferring one organism to another, giving it new traits. Besides making plants *more resistant to disease and pesticides*, it can also *increase the nutritional value* of a plant. Such modification can allow it to *grow faster* or *taste better*. Listed below are a few examples:

- Herbicide-resistant **corn** and **soybeans**: This allows farmers to kill off weeds by spraying their fields with powerful herbicides such as Roundup.
- Virus-resistant **papaya**: In Hawaii, this practice allows the fruit to be able to withstand a virus.
- **Golden rice**: Developed in Switzerland, a yellow rice has been developed that produces the antioxidant beta-carotene.

What disturbs health-conscious consumers and activists is that the amount of GMO food found on the market is *increasing worldwide*.

In the United States, GMO foods do not need to be labeled in contradistinction to Europe, where all such food is required to be labeled. GMO food is much more available in US markets. More than 95% of all food-producing animals in the US consume GMO feed. If you eat soybeans or processed soy products, it is likely that they came from a GMO crop. [60] More than 90% of all soybeans are genetically modified. To make matters worse, most processed foods in the US contain soy, corn, or canola. So, if you're eating processed food, then you're most definitely eating some genetically modified ingredients.

What's the controversy? There is no question as to the magnitude of GMO foods in the US. Opinions on GMO foods are often based on *ethical, religious,* or *philosophical* views. For many of us, GMO connotes an *unnatural* phenomenon. It just doesn't sound right.

But is the science on our side?

There are plenty of unanswered questions. Some scientists are concerned about the potential *impact on the environment*, both positive and negative. Supporters of GMO foods argue that genetic modification is necessary to *prevent worldwide food shortages*. Those who avoid GMOs believe these *foods are unhealthy*.

Until recently, there was no definitive evidence of GMO foods causing harm to humans. [61] However, *Roundup* (glyphosate)—an herbicide sprayed on vegetables, has been shown to increase the risk of certain cancers. It has been demonstrated that there is a definite link between glyphosate and Non-Hodgkin Lymphoma. [61]

But is the culprit the herbicide or the genetic modification itself?

Unanswered questions remain. Again, it is a matter of personal choice. The research is scanty at best, and may be biased by the widespread practice of genetic modification.

My opinion? This whole GMO thing is awfully scary.

I am extremely concerned about environmental health, so I do my best to avoid any possible environmental contaminant or pollutant.

I believe in keeping food in its natural state to the best of our ability. There are enough factors in the environment which are beyond our control. We do, however, have control over what we put in our mouths.

∼

In summary, I could have written a complete book on nutrition alone. (My editor says I did!)

Even though I never had a single class in nutrition in medical school, eating healthy has remained a major interest of mine since my internship and residency. That's when I learned how nutrients in tube feedings and parenteral or intravenous feedings were essential in keeping critically ill patients alive.

My interest grew from there and it continues to flourish.

My objective here was to give you a thorough review on nutritional principles and controversies. As stated a number of times, I earnestly believe in keeping it simple and as natural as possible. Fad diets don't move me, and I believe patience is indeed a virtue when implementing dietary changes.

Think of this as a life-long plan to optimal health and wellness. We are all in this for the long term. Consistency is the key to success.

As far as I am concerned, choosing a physician conversant in all aspects of nutrition and wellness is essential. I also highly recommend a wellness-based dietitian or nutritionist as a member of *your* Dream-Team.

CHAPTER 29

SUPPLEMENT YOUR HEALTH

THROUGHOUT MY TRAINING and years of practicing medicine, I have constantly heard this banter from both physicians and dietitians alike: "If one truly follows a healthy diet with plenty of fruits, vegetables and whole grains, there really is no need for supplements."

In fact, as late as August 2013, Carol Haggins, a registered dietitian and consultant to the NIH, actually said, "It's possible to get all the nutrients you need by eating a variety of healthy foods, so you don't have to take supplements." [1]

I don't think that well-informed Medical Advocates today still believe that statement.

Insufficient Research. As I see it, the problem is the lack of truly well-designed studies demonstrating the efficacy of supplementation. Funding is one of the biggest challenges. Because of their economic resources, it's relatively easy for Big Pharma and profitable medical device companies. However, large, double-blinded placebo-controlled studies that evaluate vitamins, minerals, and various supplements are generally lacking. There simply aren't enough funds.

It's not that there is a dearth of useful information touting the effects of appropriate supplementation. On the contrary, information abounds. However, the studies tend to be small and observational in nature. Therefore, they are unable to meet the criteria favored in gold-standard medical studies.

To make matters worse, the studies that have made it to the attention of peer-reviewed medical journals are often flawed by design. As a result, the conclusions may state that there is no true benefit in taking a particular supplement. Worse yet, they may report negative sequelae or adverse effects as a result.

But it doesn't end there. These studies tend to be gobbled up by the media. Before long, you find negative press everywhere. It disturbs me greatly how this negative information is interpreted by the public.

This is what I often hear from patients, confused by what they've heard: "Dr. Elkin, now that vitamin E (or vitamin D or calcium or beta carotene, etc.) is supposedly bad for me, should I just hold off on taking supplements?"

My response: "I...THINK...NOT!"

Does it make any sense to *avoid prevention* and *wait until disease strikes*? Then we will all be compelled to take pharmaceuticals.

You get my drift here? Medical Advocates want and deserve more.

To me, this is truly a travesty and akin to disempowering patients' intelligence and right to choose. As a lay person, you might find it extremely difficult to fully evaluate the validity of what you've read. Don't feel bad. Many physicians are far removed from their days of training when they actually learned how to interpret medical studies. Without scrutiny. they tend to take a peer-reviewed study at face failure.

They simply yield to the study's conclusions.

This is truly a dangerous situation, because folks come to physicians to make sense of what they've heard from the media. But physicians tend to shun what they don't fully understand. Often, they are so overwhelmed with the caring of patients and the practice of medicine, they simply don't have the time to scrutinize the results. Sadly, your average physicians will often reiterate what they've heard from the media.

Worse, they might actually dissuade you from what your commonsense dictates.

I have a question for you fledgling Medical Advocates: *where is it written that you can't **question** or **disagree** with your **doctor**?*

CHAPTER 29: Supplement Your Health

Skeptic at heart. I'm certainly not better or smarter than the average physician, but I personally have to fully understand and research all that I read in order to believe it and subsequently put it into practice. That's just me, and I've been that way since I was a student. In medical school some of my fellow students would chide me, "Howard why do you have to be so difficult and ask so many questions? Can't you just memorize this stuff like the rest of us?"

I wasn't trying to be difficult. It just came naturally! I still maintain this quality—if you want to call it that—to the present day. When a pharmaceutical rep enters my office to detail a new heart drug, they are often surprised to learn that I'm a step ahead of them.

Usually, I am already familiar with the medication. I then pose enough questions that they leave in bewilderment: "Great questions Doctor. I'll contact my research division, and someone will get back with you."

I believe that most physicians are genuinely caring. I mean, there must be a common link that attracted us to this profession. But as I stated above, doctors often shun what they don't understand. I made it through medical school without a single class in nutrition. Now you don't think they taught us about supplements, do you?

Throughout my training in medical school, my residency in internal medicine, and my fellowship in cardiology, there was never a word uttered about supplementation. Granted, this was over thirty years ago, but I don't believe much has changed.

I learned this firsthand when I was hospitalized with back surgery at Cedars-Sinai Medical Center. This is a well-known and respected teaching institution. However, the students, residents and attending faculty physicians knew nothing about supplementation. This was evident when they viewed the shoebox of supplements at my bedside. They appeared both stupefied and clueless.

This seemed incredulous when you consider that I was 20-30 years their senior!

I am still amazed when I see a patient for the first time. I carefully view the shopping bag of supplements at their side. I ask them if they have discussed these supplements with either their cardiologist or primary care physician. The response is too often: "Oh no, they don't believe in supplements," or worse yet, "If they knew I was taking all these, they would drop me as a patient."

Can you imagine? I mean, who is paying who here?

The truth of the matter is we physicians have no formal education when it comes to supplements. My zeal came about from my interest in sports nutrition, athletic performance, and preventative health. A few years later I entered the practice of anti-aging medicine and acquired a formal education in supplementation through my fellowship program. This ultimately led to board certification.

Today, there are many physicians, chiropractors and nutritionists who believe in sound, appropriate supplementation. You need to seek these medical providers.

Remember, fledgling Medical Advocates, this is how you exercise your patient bill of rights discussed previously.

If you honestly believe in supplementation, should you not seek the attention of a physician who appreciates your interest? I'm talking about optimizing patient care and making you, the patient, accountable for your health.

And you need your Dream-Team to be on your side to make this happen.

Why supplement in the first place? It's obvious. Look around. The appeal is there. Common supplements include vitamins, minerals, and herbal products, known as botanicals. More than half of all Americans take one or more dietary supplements either daily or on occasion. We spend more than 28 million dollars on supplements annually.

Supplement your health. Even though supplements can't claim to cure an illness, evidence does suggest that they can enhance health in different ways. A few simple examples:

CHAPTER 29: Supplement Your Health

- Calcium and magnesium support bone health.
- Vitamin D helps the body absorb calcium and hosts several other useful properties.
- Vitamins C and E are antioxidants and help squelch free radicals and prevent cell damage while maintaining optimal health.
- Fish oil may boost both heart and brain health. There is probably more research on fish oil to support its use than all other supplements

DIMINISHED NUTRITION

Do we really get adequate nutrients by eating healthy? Despite good intentions, I doubt that the average American attains this goal.

Here's why:

Nutrient Depletion in the Soil. Unfortunately, because of modern farming techniques, fertilizers are used that actually deplete the soil of essential nutrients. If the plant lacks vital minerals from the soil, it cannot produce essential vitamins. Naturally if the plant lacks it, we won't be getting it!

I'm talking about the nutrients we need by eating the plant. It's that simple. Remember a few years ago when we were admonished to eat a minimum of five fruits and vegetables per day? Given the current trend in farming, we probably need more like ten per day.

How many folks out there are eating ten fruits and vegetables per day?

The Ill Effects of Commercial Harvesting, Shipping, Food Storage, Processing, and Additives. These all degrade the nutrient content of food. The bottom line here is that unless you are growing your own or have the luxury of eating a very fresh plant, the end product is a far different product than what was initially harvested.

Pesticides, Herbicides, and Chemicals Found in the Modern Food Supply. These are combined with chemicals in water. Then there is environmental contamination from elements such as degraded plastics, and air pollution from carbon monoxide. Add some lead and mercury to the mix. You can see how these elements vastly increase your need for extra vitamins, minerals, and nutrients to combat free radical formation which adversely affects your immune system. This *ultimately undermines your health.*

The Ability to Absorb Nutrients from Food Decreases as We Age. There are two ways to solve this issue. One is to *eat more food to obtain more nutrients.* Does that sound like a good idea to you? Caloric restriction may play a vital role in increasing longevity. That said, the last thing I would recommend is to eat more food—which boils down to more calories. Keep in mind that many medications interfere with proper nutrient absorption. The best solution in my opinion is to *supplement when appropriate.*

Exercise Increases Nutrient Needs. For those of us who are athletes or who exercise frequently, we simply need more antioxidants from nutrient consumption. This is to squelch the free radicals that accompany heavy exercise.

Any way you look at it, appropriate supplementation in the 21st century is as vital as sound nutrition for optimizing your health. But make no mistake about it, supplements are merely supplements. They should be adjunctive to a healthy diet. They are not meant to function as food substitutes. *Whole food should remain the backbone for optimal health and wellness.*

Choosing supplements. A few tips. I recommend purchasing products from *reputable companies* that are of *pharmaceutical grade.* Unlike pharmaceutical companies, *supplement manufacturers are not regulated* by the Food and Drug Administration (FDA). What's in the actual product is not necessarily what's listed on the bottle. Pharmaceutical grade products, such as my own line of products available at HeartWise Fitness and Longevity Center, meet the highest regulatory requirements for purity, dissolution, and absorption. Such products can, at any time, undergo post-production analysis

CHAPTER 29: Supplement Your Health

by independent laboratory evaluation.

Like my own line of supplements, I recommend that the contents be *gluten-free, dairy-free,* and *soy-free.* This is to avoid any food allergies or food intolerances. Other common allergens such as *nuts* should also be excluded.

Going the extra yard, my supplements do not use any excipients (inactive substances) other than USP Microcrystalline Cellulose and veggie capsules.

My objective in this chapter is to provide you with the tools necessary to make wise decisions regarding supplementation. There isn't room for me to have a lengthy discussion on all the supplements I favor. However, I do have a few that deserve special mention.

The ones listed below are for *general health and wellness,* and are *most valuable for those over the age of 40*:

- OMEGA-3 FATTY ACIDS
- COENZYME Q10
- VITAMIN D
- MAGNESIUM
- PROBIOTICS

OMEGA- 3 FATTY ACIDS aka FISH OIL

These incredibly healthy fats have important benefits for your heart, your brain, and your body in general. However, people eating the typical Western diet are not consuming enough, not by a long shot. [2][3]

Omega-3 fatty acids are named *essential* fatty acids because they are needed for health, and yet, *the body cannot produce them.* We must obtain them from our diet. There are three main types of omega-3 fats:

- **EPA** (Eicosapentaenoic acid). This fatty acid has many vital functions, most notably its ability to *decrease inflammation.* Additionally, EPA can lower the triglyceride levels in your blood.

- **DHA** (Docosahexaenoic Acid). This fatty acid also possesses anti-inflammatory properties. It is a structural component of cell membranes, particularly the nerve cells in the brain and eyes. 40% of the fat found in our brain is DHA. [4]
- **ALA** (Alpha-Linolenic Acid). ALA is the most common omega-3 fat in our diet. It is found in high-fat plant foods such as flax seeds, walnuts and chia seeds. However, it is not very active in the body. It needs to be converted into EPA and DHA for it to become active. The conversion process is not terribly efficient in humans. Therefore, ALA should never be relied on as the sole source of omega-3 fatty acids.

In essence, both EPA and DHA are the most vital omega-3 fats that we consume. One of their most important functions is their *anti-inflammatory* action. [5]

Throughout this book you have read about the *ill effects of inflammation on the aging process*. Consuming adequate amounts of both EPA and DHA is vital to help curb this deteriorating process.

Being a cardiologist, I have a keen interest in the effects of fish oil on heart disease prevention. Even though omega-3s have not been shown to prevent heart attacks and strokes, there are other cardiac benefits. We know that omega-3 fatty acids have a *blood thinning* effect. They also have an *antiarrhythmic* effect in so much as they decrease the incidence of abnormal heart rhythms that can potentially lead to sudden death.

Other possible benefits of Omega-3 fatty acids:
- Decreasing blood triglycerides
- Reducing risk of cancer (colon, prostate, and breast cancer) [6]
- Improving symptoms of depression and anxiety [7] [8]
- Reducing risk of cognitive decline [9]

CHAPTER 29: Supplement Your Health

Still other reported benefits are reducing the fat content in non-alcoholic fatty liver disease, asthma prevention, and improving baby's intelligence and eye health in pregnant and lactating mothers.

Something fishy here. There remains controversy regarding the benefits of fish oil supplementation, but most agree that it is safe. Furthermore, omega-3 fatty acids have been studied more thoroughly than most other supplements.

The question I am often asked is how much fish oil one should take for optimal health. The American Heart Association recommends eating fatty fish at least twice a week to ensure optimal omega-3 fat intake and to prevent heart disease. That sounds appropriate to me.

Note of caution. Many of us refuse to eat *farm-raised fish*. Sometimes referred to as "sustainable", farm-raised fish is anything but healthy. I don't know about you, but I find it increasingly difficult to find wild fish either in restaurants or in supermarkets. This topic is beyond the scope of this book.

Suffice it to say, I don't think the average American is eating two *healthy* fatty fish meals weekly. Therefore, there is most likely a need for supplementation.

Both the World Health Organization and the European Food Safety Authority recommend a total of 250-500 mg combined EPA and DHA daily. [10]

Personally, I recommend 1,000 mg daily for the average healthy American adult. For pregnant or lactating women, I would add an additional of 200-500 mg DHA for optimal fetal and infant brain development.

Special needs patients, such as those with heart disease, elevated triglycerides, arthritis, depression, and dementia will more than likely require higher doses. However, such recommendations should come from a health care professional conversant with supplementation.

Is there such thing as too much? Most experts in the field believe that taking *up to 5,000 mg daily of combined EPA and DHA is safe.*

[11] However, this is *not universally accepted*. Check with your physician. High intake, however, is certainly not required by most people. Moreover, taking more than 5,000 mg daily has not been shown to provide any additional benefit.

One word of caution. In high doses, omega-3s can cause blood thinning and excessive bleeding. It is imperative that you speak to your physician if you are on a blood thinner, or if you have a bleeding disorder before taking these supplements. Moreover, I recommend you stop fish oil supplements ten days prior to any surgical procedure to minimize any operative or post-op bleeding.

COENZYME Q10 (CoQ10)

Anyone who knows me is aware of how much I tout this particular supplement. But I have to give credit to my teacher and mentor Dr. Stephen Sinatra. It was he who truly introduced me to the benefits of CoQ10. [12]

Cellular energy is what sustains us. Whether it's a heart cell, a brain cell or a muscle cell, *each cell in your body must generate energy*. Without that cellular energy, the cell will die, and eventually the organism will perish. Co-enzyme Q 10 is a vital co-factor in the electron transport chain. This chain is located within the mitochondria, known as the powerhouse of the cell. This is where ATP (adenotriphosphate) is generated. ATP is the primary source of energy in all living cells.

CoQ10 doesn't act alone. In my video entitled *"Nutrition for the Heart,"* I discuss the use of L-carnitine and D-ribose. Suffice it to say these three compounds are vital to normal heart function.

Nutritionally deprived hearts. A diseased heart is seen in those who have sustained heart damage from a heart attack. Similarly, the same is true for those with valvular heart disease, or with cardiomyopathies. Diseased hearts often lead to a potentially lethal condition known as congestive heart failure (CHF).

CHAPTER 29: Supplement Your Health

Fortunately, through the use of medications and the implementation of new cardiac-assist devices, *this disease state can often be managed.* As a result, patients have better control of their symptoms, are hospitalized less frequently, and have a survival advantage.

But make no mistake about it; these measures do nothing to support the nutritionally starved heart. That's where CoQ10 and the other two supplements mentioned above come into play. I have seen numerous patients with sick hearts benefit from the use of these supplements. The response can be dramatic with such patients being able to do more with less effort.

I always start with *CoQ10*. It's the *cornerstone of bioenergetics* for the heart as far as I am concerned. It is also a potent antioxidant by decreasing oxidative stress while squelching free radicals. It helps support *healthy blood pressure* as well.

A good brand is always suggested. This is not a supplement where I recommend price comparing. Known as ubiquinone, CoQ10 is ubiquitous in nature. However, it is a large molecule and some of the *cheaper brands are not well absorbed.* Bioavailability is a major factor when supplementing with CoQ10. Being fat-soluble, *it should be consumed with food.*

Besides heart health there are other potential benefits of CoQ10. It might aid in *reducing migraines, improving* symptoms of *Parkinson's* disease and *depression, warding off dementia,* and even *halting* the *aging* process.

In summary, CoQ10 helps to:
- Promote *heart health* and function.
- Enhance overall *energy* levels.
- Provide *antioxidant protection.*
- Replenish *depleted levels* seen in those taking statin drugs and beta blockers, and in those who exercise vigorously.

The exact dose depends on your age, how often you exercise and whether you take cholesterol-lowering statin drugs or beta blockers. These medications actually deplete your native CoQ10 levels. This is why these drugs often have the reputation of causing muscle weakness and pain. CoQ10 helps to mitigate those commonly seen side effects. I generally recommend 100-200 mg daily. In those with diseased hearts, a condition known as a cardiomyopathy, the dosage may be as high as 400 mg daily.

CoQ10 benefits just about anyone. It is generally considered safe and well-tolerated. There have been some reports that CoQ10 may lower blood sugar levels. This may be considered a good thing when dealing with diabetics or those with metabolic syndrome. Blood sugar levels should be monitored in such patients.

Caution is also advised in those with bleeding disorders or in those taking blood thinners and aspirin. Again, there have been very few reports of bleeding associated with the use of CoQ10.

As mentioned repeatedly throughout this book, it is important to ensure that your health care provider knows that you are taking CoQ10. For that matter, this goes for any supplement. Ideally, he or she supports appropriate supplementation.

VITAMIN D

Vitamin D is like no other vitamin. It acts more like a hormone. Structurally it is produced from cholesterol when your skin is exposed to the sun. Practically speaking, there is no other source of vitamin D other than the sun. Adequate amounts are rarely found in multivitamins. Furthermore, food sources of this vitamin are poor at best.

Enter the world of vitamin supplementation.

Like all vitamins, vitamin D is absolutely essential for optimal health. Yet deficiency is extremely prevalent. Data from 2005-2006 demonstrated that 41.6% of the US population lacks adequate amounts of this vitamin. This percentage goes up to 82% in blacks and 69% in Hispanics. [13]

Vitamin D is one of the four fat-soluble vitamins (A, D, E and K). This means that it dissolves in fat and can be stored in the body. There are actually two main forms:

- Vitamin D3
- Vitamin D2

Of the two, D3 is what interests us. It is the more effective of the two forms at increasing levels of vitamin D in the blood.

Vitamin D goes through quite a conversion process for it to become active within the body. The first conversion takes place in the liver. That is the storage form of the vitamin. Vitamin D is subsequently converted to calcitriol in the kidney. Calcitriol travels throughout the body and becomes truly active by sun exposure.

Sunshine is still the best way to get vitamin D. The ultraviolet B (UVB) rays provide the energy for this reaction to occur at the skin level. The challenge is that you need to expose a large portion of your body for 20 minutes or so multiple times a week. Furthermore, wearing sunscreen will limit this chemical reaction.

So sunshine is not practical for most of us who work and play indoors.

Vitamin D deficiency is a major deal. As you might imagine it is one of the most common nutrient deficiencies. *Dark-skinned individuals* are greatly at risk because the melanin pigment in their skin blocks the chemical conversion to the active form of the vitamin. *Elderly* people are also at great risk. [14]

People with certain illnesses are likely to be deficient. *Heart attack patients* tend to have low vitamin D levels. I have personally witnessed this phenomenon in my own practice. One study showed that 96% of heart attack patients had low vitamin D levels. [15]

Researchers continue to uncover cardiac benefits of vitamin D. Recently an important study was presented at the American College of Cardiology 65th Annual Scientific Sessions. It concluded that supplementation with vitamin D3 may *improve heart function* in patients with chronic heart failure. The study assessed a simple and promising treatment for the five million Americans with heart failure. [16]

Deficiency of vitamin D has been linked to *osteoporosis*, reduced mineral *density of bone*, and increased risk of *fractures* in the elderly. [17]

Studies have also shown that people with low vitamin D levels are at greater risk of *heart disease, diabetes, cancer, dementia,* and various *autoimmune disorders* such as multiple sclerosis. [18]

Vitamin D deficiency has also been linked to *all-cause mortality* in critically ill patients, and in nursing home residents. [19] [20]

Vitamin D deficiency is a well-known cause of *bone disease* but has also been linked to a myriad of other illnesses, as well as *reduced life expectancy*. What is unclear is whether vitamin D deficiency actually contributes to these diseases, or whether people with low levels are just more likely to contract these illnesses.

What is becoming more apparent is the association between vitamin D deficiency and inflammation. [21] [22]

As stated repeatedly in this book and in my videos, _inflammation_ is the bane of our existence when it comes to healthy aging. It should be of no surprise that inflammation is often increased in those with vitamin D deficiency.

In conclusion, vitamin D supplementation has been shown to have numerous benefits related to bone health, cancer, heart disease, mental health, and autoimmune disorders...to name a few. There certainly is *no reason why anyone should be deficient in this critically needed vitamin*.

The only way to know if you are deficient is to have your blood level measured. The proper lab test is 25- hydroxy vitamin D. The range is ridiculously broad; anywhere from 30-100 is considered within normal limits. Those of us in the anti-aging / functional medicine field are so bullish about vitamin D that we tend to shoot for levels in the 50-70 range. Toxic levels are extremely rare.

In general, the only people who might possibly limit their intake of vitamin D are those with diseases of the parathyroid gland, lymphoma, sarcoidosis, and those with recurrent kidney stones. Too much vitamin D in these conditions may cause elevated calcium levels.

Vitamin D supplementation is potentially life-enhancing if not lifesaving. Fortunately, it is also relatively inexpensive. It is imperative that you have your baseline measurement obtained before supplementing. Make sure to check your levels two-three months later.

Once settling on a dose, I recommend that levels be *checked at least annually.*

MAGNESIUM

Magnesium is the fourth most abundant mineral in the body. It plays an important role in over 300 enzymatic reactions. These functions include transmission of nerve impulses and muscle relaxation.

About 60% of magnesium is found in bone. The rest is in muscles, soft tissues, and body fluids, including blood. *Every cell in our body contains magnesium.* It's essential for life.

Unfortunately, studies reveal that at least 50% of people in the United States and Europe are deficient in this vital mineral. Surveys conducted over a thirty-year period suggest that this is related to rising calcium–to-magnesium food intake ratios among adults. [23]

Below are some of the vital roles involving magnesium as a co-factor or "helper molecule" in various enzymatic reactions within the body: [24]

- **Energy creation:** Helps convert food into energy.
- **Protein formation**: Helps to form protein from amino acids.
- **Gene maintenance:** Helps create and repair DNA and RNA.
- **Muscle performance:** Helps muscles to both contract and relax.
- **Nervous system regulation:** Helps regulate neurotransmitters so that nerve impulses can be conducted properly.

But that's not all. Magnesium has other important roles in optimizing our health.

Magnesium may boost exercise performance. Exercise itself increases one's requirements for magnesium. This is a result of mineral loss from sweat and urine. This additional need for magnesium may be as high as 10-20%. [25]

Magnesium helps mobilize blood sugar into your muscles while disposing of lactic acid, a by-product of exercise. Such a process may boost exercise performance in athletes [26]

Although not all studies have shown a positive response, magnesium may enhance exercise performance.

Magnesium can help fight depression. Magnesium plays a big role in *brain function* and *mood*. Low levels of the mineral are found in depressed subjects. [27] [28] Several studies have shown that supplementing with magnesium may reduce symptoms of depression. The results can be dramatic. [29]

There is no downside in supplementing magnesium in depressed individuals. They tend to be deficient in the mineral and stand to gain improvement in their symptoms.

As you can see this one mineral can play a huge role in our quest for wellness. Some other potential uses include:

- **Decreasing the risk for developing type 2 diabetes.** Supplementing may lower blood sugar in certain individuals. [30] [31]
- **Lowering blood pressure in hypertensive patients.** [32][33]
- **Combating inflammation.** Low magnesium intake is often seen in chronic inflammation. Magnesium supplementation can reduce CRP and other inflammatory markers. [34] [35] [36]
- **Relieving PMS symptoms.** [37] [38]
- **Preventing migraines.** [39]

There are two other roles of magnesium that I have personally found to be particularly useful: treating cardiac arrhythmias or *rhythm disturbances,* as well as *promoting sleep.*

Heart palpitations, flutters or racing heart rhythm are common complaints that I see almost daily in my cardiology practice. After ruling out any potentially life-threatening arrhythmias and/or true heart disease, I am left with how to best treat my patients' symptoms. I have found that these bothersome palpitations can either clear up or improve dramatically by taking magnesium once or twice daily.

Magnesium depletion can lead to a host of cardiovascular problems ranging from *high blood pressure* to *arrhythmias*. There are many kinds of arrhythmias, but they all have one thing is common; they involve abnormal conduction of the heart's electrical impulses. It is these impulses that govern heart rate and heart rhythm. Such electrical disturbances in turn result in a heart rate that is irregular, too fast, or too slow. [40] [41]

Magnesium is ultimately involved with these electrical impulses and repletion of this vital mineral with appropriate diet and supplementation can play a role in ameliorating these commonly seen symptoms.

Sleep deprivation is one of the most common health problems that Western society faces today. It seems as if more and more is expected of us in the workplace, and this may adversely affect our sleep. Disturbed sleep is clearly a serious issue.

Magnesium is well known for its ability to *relieve insomnia*. It's been shown to help decrease the stress hormone cortisol which can keep us up at night. It also helps muscles relax. Studies have documented its usefulness as a natural sleep aid. [42] [43]

Magnesium is vital for the function of GABA receptors which are found throughout the brain and nervous system. Magnesium binds to and activates GABA receptors. GABA is a calming neurotransmitter that the brain requires to switch off the excitatory neurotransmitters. Without GABA we remain tense, our thoughts race, and we lie in bed staring at the ceiling.

I think you can see that I could go on and on espousing the benefits of magnesium supplementation. Unfortunately, the amount we can glean from our diet is limited. This is due to the lack of vital nutrients found in our soil. Over-farming and the use of pesticides are causative processes that lead to this mineral deficiency. For *most of us*, supplementation is the only practical way of repletion.

Magnesium is tops when it comes to heart health. It is useful for normal muscle function, and the heart is indeed a muscle. Our bodies require a steady supply of magnesium to maintain proper muscle function both in relation to the heart muscle itself, as well as to the smooth muscle comprising our blood vessels.

Magnesium plays a pivotal role in cardiovascular disease prevention. However, as you can see its effects are far-reaching, and go way beyond heart health. Low levels predict cardiovascular and all-cause mortality.

Correcting low magnesium levels may actually prolong life. [44] [45]

Are you magnesium deficient? It's an assumption as far as I am concerned. Most individuals are deficient. This is especially true in the *elderly*, and in those with *heart disease*. *Athletes* are especially vulnerable.

Measuring magnesium blood levels is pretty useless, since the majority of this mineral is in bone and soft tissue, and not circulating in the blood. Additionally, a blood level tells us nothing about a deficiency in the heart or brain. A truly low level in the blood is an ominous sign and must be treated immediately. This is often found in heart failure patients and in those taking diuretics.

For most of us, there is truly little danger in taking magnesium supplements. However, folks with kidney disease are at potential risk. Such individuals must weigh the benefits versus risks. It is essential that this be discussed with their physician.

Generally speaking, taking 300-500 mg of magnesium before bed should be sufficient for most. I recommend a chelated form such as citrate or glycinate. Avoid oxide salts as they are poorly absorbed and often cause diarrhea.

CHAPTER 29: Supplement Your Health

*In essence, **magnesium is absolutely essential for life**. Both food and supplementation should be used to reap its many health benefits.*

PROBIOTICS

Probiotics support the live, friendly microorganisms that reside within our gastrointestinal tracts, commonly referred to as the gut. In adequate numbers they confer huge health benefits. Normally we are referring to bacteria, but there is also a type of yeast that can function as a probiotic.

What's fascinating is that the number of *bacteria in our body outnumbers our body's cells* **10 to 1.** It's having the right bacteria present that impacts our state of wellness.

Such benefits include *weight loss, improved digestion, enhanced immune function, better skin,* and the correct balance of *neurotransmitters.*

Throughout my training in medical school and residency in internal medicine, I learned that the GI tract was essential for digestion, absorption, and elimination. But its role encompasses so much more.

Having learned in my anti-aging medical fellowship that you are only as healthy as your *gut,* I can now say without reservation: *IF YOUR GUT ISN'T HEALTHY, YOU AREN'T HEALTHY.*

This is where probiotics come into play. Probiotics are foods or supplements that contain these friendly bacteria. What they do is colonize our guts with health-boosting microorganisms. This complex community of microorganisms in the gut is referred to as the *gut flora* or *microbiome.* Most of the gut flora is found in the colon, or large intestine. The colon is the last part of the digestive tract.

The many activities of the gut flora act like an actual organ such as the heart, liver, or brain. In fact, some scientists are now referring to the gut flora as the "forgotten organ." [46]

Probiotic foods include yogurt, kefir, sauerkraut, kimchi as well as any fermented fruits or vegetables.

Make no mistake about it; *taking care of your gut is one of the most important steps you can take to enhance your health!*

There are literally dozens of probiotic bacteria that are beneficial. The most common groups include Lactobacillus and Bifidobacterium. There are many different species within each group and each species has many strains. *Different probiotics work best for different health conditions.*

Many probiotic supplements combine different species together. These are known as broad-spectrum probiotics.

The gut flora performs many activities essential to your health. For example, they *stimulate the immune system* and help *maintain the integrity of the gut.* This helps prevent unwanted substances from leaking into the body and provoking an immune response that could cause harm. [47]

What's important to understand is that not all organisms are gut friendly. Some are good, and others are bad. The gut flora is extremely sensitive to insults and an unbalanced gut flora has been linked to numerous diseases. [48]

This is clearly a bourgeoning field in medical science. A healthy gut flora increasingly appears to play a significant role in disease prevention. Some of the disease states seen with an imbalance of gut flora include: [49] [50] [51] [52] [53]

- Obesity
- Metabolic syndrome
- Colorectal cancer
- Alzheimer's disease
- Depression

Probiotics to the rescue! Whether it's from food or supplements, probiotics can help correct this imbalance. It's about maximizing the function of forgotten organs. Probiotics help our gut flora perform optimally.

Although much of what we have learned about gut flora and probiotics is relatively recent, probiotics have been extensively studied when it comes to digestive health. [54]

CHAPTER 29: Supplement Your Health

Everyone knows that antibiotics often cause diarrhea. It's a common side effect. The reason is that *antibiotics kill the healthy gut flora*. This shifts the balance and allows the unhealthy bacteria to thrive. Countless studies have demonstrated that probiotic supplements can help obviate antibiotic-associated diarrhea. [55]

Probiotics have also been shown to be beneficial against *irritable bowel syndrome*. Additionally, they may play a protective role in the treatment of *inflammatory bowel disease* such as ulcerative colitis and Crohn's disease. They may even be useful against Helicobacter pylori, the main force behind *ulcers* and *stomach cancer*. [56] [57]

Probiotics have been shown to have numerous health benefits. They may reduce *depression* and *anxiety*, improve *heart, and gut health* and enhance *immune function*.

The role of probiotics in enhancing the immune system has garnered quite a bit of interest lately. This should be of no surprise because 70-80% of your immune system resides in your gut. The lining of the small intestine is full of lymph nodes. When necessary, inflammation in the intestines creates a pathway for the immune system to carry out an attack against invading viruses and bacteria. However, when inflammation is present but not warranted or desired, illnesses such as allergies, flu and chronic infections can occur. Probiotics offer a beneficial defense against the effects of unwarranted inflammation.

In essence, *probiotics keep the gut healthy*. They ensure that the immune system functions well. Probiotics can also modulate the immune system, enhancing the body's innate immunity. It's becoming more evident that *inflammation begins in the gut*. This modulation helps to alleviate inflammation within the gut, thereby boosting immune function.

Most of us can benefit from regular usage of probiotics, but there needs to be caution in the immuno-compromised population such as those with full blown AIDS, transplant patients and in critically ill patients in intensive care units.

Maintaining a healthy gut has been shown in recent years to impact one's state of wellness positively. Lifestyle factors such as a *nutritionally sound diet* are essential as is *adequate rest*. In addition, probiotic foods and supplements may play a particularly important role.

～

Last word about supplements. You have been given a plethora of information regarding supplementation; why supplement in the first place, who may benefit, etc. I also discussed my personal favorites.

But there is much more to the story. There are numerous other supplements that may play a role in your individual quest for optimal health.

When choosing supplements. Always consider your individual goals. What exactly do you seek that you currently lack? *Be objective* as possible. Are you in need of *more energy*, an *enhanced immune system*, or *improved brain function*? What about supplements to help *balance hormones*, to improve the *quality of sleep*, to *enhance athletic performance*, or to help *ward off the aging process*?

This is exactly the thought process I utilize in assisting my patients in selecting their supplements. I do not believe that more is better. I cringe whenever I see patients with a shopping bag or two of expensive supplements. Don't be overly influenced by all the marketing hype on the Internet and infomercials. Like medications, supplements are not the end-all-be-all.

Use discretion.

Testing? Is there testing to see if we are nutritionally sound? Are our supplements actually working? Are we absorbing our supplements adequately? Or do we literally have expensive urine? Are we merely peeing out what we ingest?

TEST...DON'T GUESS

These are important questions. Fortunately, such testing exists. Commonly known as micronutrient testing, there are specialized laboratories that perform this function.

Standard lab tests measure the concentration of a particular substance, such as cholesterol, sodium, potassium, liver enzymes or thyroid hormone in the plasma portion of the blood. This tells us nothing about the nutritional status of the patient. For that we need to examine what's happening at the cellular level.

One such lab that performs this well is Spectracell Laboratories whose headquarters are in Houston, Texas. They measure the function of selected vitamins, minerals, antioxidants, and other essential nutrients within your white blood cells. Intracellular nutrient testing is the only way to truly examine the functional nutrient status of a given patient. [58]

Another laboratory that we frequently employ is Genova Diagnostics, headquartered in Asheville, North Carolina.

Why is this testing useful? *50% of those taking vitamin/mineral supplements are still nutritionally deficient.* There are several factors that enter the picture and explain why one size does not fit all.

- Biochemical individuality
- Absorption
- Chronic illness
- Aging
- Lifestyle

Some need more. Obviously, it stands to reason that *hard-core athletes* might well need additional antioxidant support than someone leading a more sedentary lifestyle. Certain individuals absorb their nutrients more efficiently than others. Folks with *chronic disease* may well require more micronutrients.

Intracellular nutrient testing takes all this into consideration. The end result is providing a given patient with a blueprint of what he or she needs *today*. Naturally, this may change over time. Repeat testing from time to time might prove useful.

This process takes the guesswork out of supplementing. You end up with the nutrients you need in the dose that you need them. You also avoid wasting money on supplements you don't need. This does away with what I call expensive urine!

∽

I'll say it again: **supplements are not meant to be a stand-alone.** They are adjunctive to whole foods. Most importantly, any usage of a particular supplement must be cleared by your physician. He or she knows the details of your state of health and should be able to guide you.

And if your physician frowns upon the use of supplements, it may be time to make a change.

After all, whose body is it? It's *your body.*

Your health care providers **must** be able to accept your position as a Medical Advocate. When it comes to your health, *this is how you stay in the driver's seat.*

CHAPTER 30

YOU GOTTA MOVE

What can I possibly say about the need to exercise that hasn't already been said? Along with following a healthy diet, exercise is probably the most preventable way to avoid premature death and disability as we age.

Even when afflicted with chronic illness, exercise can help mitigate the effects of the disease process. In fact, people who work out on a regular basis are thought to have up to a *50% lower risk of dying from chronic disease.* [1] [2]

The rewards of exercise. As previously mentioned, the more active individuals are at any age, the less the incidence of *heart disease.* The benefits of exercise, however, have far-reaching effects, greater than seen in heart disease alone. *Regular exercise* plays a role in preventing or staving off *hypertension, type 2 diabetes, osteoporosis,* and *various cancers.* [3] [4] [5]

Honestly, given all the facts and figures we have in the 21st century, there really should be *no reason to NOT exercise.* To not exercise is to have a death wish as far as I am concerned.

My mother is in her mid-90s, but age doesn't stop her, nor does infirmity. Peripheral artery disease, arthritic knees and balance issues don't impede her will to keep mobile. While still in bed, she begins her morning routine with stretching and core-work. Although walking is difficult, even with the assistance of a walker, she never ceases to desire to do more.

I once had a patient with pancreatic cancer who did his best to remain active, gardening on a regular basis. I witness folks at Golds Gym in Venice, California in wheelchairs who are either paraplegic or who lack lower limbs.

Nothing tends to stop committed individuals.

But the reality is that most of the people living in the United States are not convinced. According to the Center for Disease Control (CDC), only 20% of American adults meet the government's recommended guidelines for physical activity. The statistics are even grimmer when you consider out nation's youth. [6]

The U.S. government recommends adults get at least two-and-a-half hours of moderate-to-intense aerobic exercise each week OR one hour fifteen minutes of vigorous-to-intense activity, or a combination of both. Adults are also encouraged to engage in muscle-strengthening such as lifting weights at least twice a week.

I think I've heard just about every excuse there is to not exercise, and I am absolutely unyielding about one point: *don't tell me you don't have the time.*

Make the time!

You can't use that one on me. There are 24 hours in a day, 168 hours in a week. You may scoff at my drive from Whittier to Venice, California four days a week to exercise. Even I admit that is over the top. But I do it because it works for me. So please, don't tell me you don't have the time.

In a week, I believe every adult can find a minimum of 2 1/2 hours out of 168.

You say you want to *lose weight, lower* your *blood pressure, prevent depression,* or just *look better.* Regular exercise can play a huge role here.

Need more reasons to exercise? Check these out:

Exercise boosts brain power. This alone should be an impetus to get moving. As mentioned previously, mental well-being is one of the 5 dimensions of health. No one wants to age with a faulty memory. Studies have shown that for older adults, physical activity correlates with better overall cognitive performance. This appears to hold true for those with seemingly normal cognition, as well as for those with mild cognitive impairment. [7] [8] [9] [10]

CHAPTER 30: You Gotta Move

The exact explanation is unclear but could well be due to *increased blood flow to the brain* which results from exercise.

Exercise reduces stress. Seriously, I don't know where I would be if exercise didn't play such a vital role in my life. Exercise delivers a relaxation phase that serves as a positive distraction. By the way, *you aren't the only one who will benefit* from stress reduction. So will *family, friends,* and *co-workers.* Whenever my office manager asks if I can start early on a particular day by skipping my training, I almost always refuse.

When I say, "You don't want me around if I miss my training, do you?" She immediately backs down!

Exercise energizes. Endorphins accompany exercise. These feel-good chemicals are released into your bloodstream—energizing you all day. With the improved strength and stamina from exercise, it's easier to accomplish everyday tasks such as carrying groceries and climbing stairs.

Fitness-in-common can help build relationships. This one is rarely on anyone's list. Whether it's with a spouse, a sibling, or a friend, there is something to be said about partnership. It's all about working for a shared goal. It can be a lot more fun to exercise with a partner. Accountability is an important benefit. We are less likely to miss an exercise session when a partner is involved.

Exercise allows you to eat more. How's that for a benefit? This one is common sense: The more calories burned with exercise; the more calories one can eat. Just don't go overboard with this one. Discretion is advised.

Exercise can play an important role in weight loss. Exercise is often advised for weight loss, but *the focus should be on fat loss.* Dieting without exercise will likely produce muscle loss along with fat. In fact, it's been estimated that when people lose weight, about a quarter of that weight is muscle. [11] How's that for a disappointment? Ever wonder why diets without exercise fail? It's because you lose muscle with the fat. Less muscle lowers your metabolism. Your weight loss then comes to a screeching halt.

A lesson in futility.

Adding an exercise program alongside your diet helps reduce the amount of muscle you lose. [12] [13]

Exercise enhances performance. *In any sports activity.* Regular exercise can positively impact your golf game, your racquetball game, your tennis match, or your long-distance swim. With age comes an expectant drop in performance. This can be mitigated by regular exercise.

Maximizing. Okay, we've established the *need for all of us to exercise—without a shadow of a doubt.* The next step is implementing and/or revamping an existing exercise program to achieve maximal health benefits. My recommendation is to incorporate all three of the following:

- Aerobic exercise
- Resistance training
- Stretching

AEROBIC EXERCISE (CARDIO)

The most recent guidelines from the American Heart Association and the American College of Sports Medicine recommend 30 minutes of moderately intense aerobic exercise five days a week. An alternative schedule is 20 minutes of high intensity aerobic exercise three days a week. [14] The overall aim is to *maintain good health* and *reduce your risk of heart disease.* [15]

Clearly *aerobic exercise is the most beneficial exercise for maintaining a healthy cardiovascular system.* Moderate means exercising at a level that allows you to maintain a conversation with the person next to you. Although 30 minutes at a stretch is the recommended interval, research shows that aerobic exercise is beneficial even when done in shorter interrupted segments.

CHAPTER 30: You Gotta Move

Other benefits of aerobic exercise:
- *Increases* your *stamina* and *endurance* (because of the positive effects on your heart, lungs, and circulation, you more than likely will be able to do more with less effort).
- *Increases your stamina and endurance.*
- *Reduces stress* through activation of the endorphin system.
- *Reduces anxiety* and *depression.*
- *Strengthens* your *immune system.*
- *Strengthens* your *joints* and *bones.*
- *Decreases* your *appetite.*
- *Increases* the number of *calories burned.*
- *Decreases* a woman's risk for *breast cancer.*
- *Decreases* your *blood pressure* while lowering the lousy or LDL- cholesterol and raising your good or HDL-cholesterol.
- *Manages diabetes, pregnancy,* and *aging.*

One caveat about aerobic training and calorie burning: aerobic exercise doesn't have a major effect on muscle mass when compared to weightlifting. However, it is highly effective at burning calories. Aerobic training can play a role in burning fat, especially the dangerous belly fat that increases your risk of developing type 2 diabetes and heart disease. [16]

I always recommend performing aerobic exercises that are both safe and effective *for you*. Most importantly it should be something you enjoy; walking, jogging, swimming, hiking, stairclimbing, gardening, and cycling indoors or out are all excellent choices.

And to avoid boredom *don't forget to mix things up a bit!*

A question I often hear: What's the *best time* to exercise? My recommendation: do what best suits you and your lifestyle.

I personally enjoy training in the morning because of the energy boost, and because I feel grounded, positive, and truly ready to go about my day. But I'm a morning person. Some prefer training at night. Choose whatever time *you* believe is best for *you.*

RESISTANCE (WEIGHT) TRAINING

All types of physical activity have benefits and can help you burn calories. Resistance training, such as weightlifting, has benefits that go beyond that.

Even though I am a cardiologist, I would list weight training as the form of exercise most beneficial for our aging population.

Weight training helps increase your strength while improving the tone and amount of muscle you have. This is vital for long-term health since inactive adults lose anywhere between 3-8% of their muscle mass per decade. [17]

Resistance training for the older adult, age 65-and above has been extensively studied. The health benefits are well known and include the following: [18] [19]

- Increases *muscle strength* and *endurance*.
- Increases *muscle mass* which translates into improvements in functional capacity (combating sarcopenia or muscle wasting).
- Increases *bone density* (combating osteoporosis).
- Increases *insulin sensitivity* (combating diabetes and metabolic syndrome).
- Mitigates pain from *arthritis*.
- Improves *sleep*.
- Reduces *depression*.

Most of us would like to spend our final days living independently, not stuck in a nursing home. How is this decided? Besides having the necessary cognition to live alone, *physical strength* is what generally separates the strong from the infirm.

Seriously, it often boils down to who can perform the necessary activities of daily living with ease. Being able to shut a window, open a jar, or close a garage door is what I am talking about here.

My bottom line: *we need to maintain muscle mass and strength as we age.*

With increased muscle mass and strength, as well as functional capacity, improved balance and coordination generally follow. With better balance, one is less likely to fall. With stronger bones, the risk of fracture is less.

You get my drift here? Weight training is essential when it comes to longevity and enhanced quality of life. One of the most common complaints I hear from my older patients is loss of balance. Loss of balance leads to falls and serious injuries. It doesn't have to be this way.

As mentioned above, weight training promotes bone development by increasing bone density. Studies have shown a 1-3% increase in bone mineral density in those who regularly train. This can lessen low back pain while easing discomfort associated with arthritis and fibromyalgia.

Another great benefit of weight training is fat loss. You've already heard that cardio burns calories during the actual activity. Weight training does more. It burns fat around the clock. [20] [21]

The physiology is fairly simple. A pound of muscle is considerably more metabolically active than a pound of fat.

In my opinion, this is the bottom line: *muscle is your greatest ally.* More muscle means greater fat-burning, even at rest. So, if fat loss is one of your goals, you truly need to add resistance training to your exercise program.

Get a trainer. If you're a novice I highly recommend seeking the assistance of a certified personal trainer, experienced in training both young and older adults. Another requirement: he or she should have experience in working with special populations such as those with injuries.

Once you have the basics down pat you should be able to train independently. *Proper form* is essential and *injury prevention* is of utmost importance.

Personally, I love working with the trainer of champions, Charles R. Glass. We've been together for over 20 years. He both motivates me and pushes me to my potential. I train more efficiently in his presence. Most important, I feel terrific after every session.

Folks are amazed when they learn that I commute from Whittier to Venice, California four days a week to train with Charles. But again, it works for me. It adds fun and purpose to my life.

What about strength training frequency? I concur with the recommendations of The American College of Sports Medicine: two to four training sessions per week depending on an individual's needs and goals.

Most everyone who discovers the benefits of weight training enjoys it. If you haven't already, it's your time to embrace this activity. It can play a vital role in your anti-aging strategy.

STRETCHING

I know what many of you are thinking about at this moment. "He wants us to do cardio, then weight training, and now stretching. How do I possibly fit all that in?"

Stretching often takes a back seat to your exercise routine. You may think that stretching your hamstrings or calves is merely something to be done if you have a few extra minutes after your cardio. After all, the main concern is exercising, not stretching, right?

Well, not so fast. Although studies about the benefits of stretching are mixed, stretching may help to improve your range of motion. In turn, this may help boost your athletic performance, and decrease your risk of injury. [22] [23]

Admittedly, studies show conflicting results. Some show that stretching helps. Others show that stretching either before or after exercise has little benefit and that it doesn't reduce muscle soreness. For certain, *stretching a cold muscle is rarely recommended* and I refrain from such activity.

Stretching also improves blood flow to the muscle. This may have far-reaching effects, as improved blood flow may help flush out waste products. The end result is less muscle soreness, but again the studies on this benefit are mixed.

Personally, I enjoy stretching immediately after my cardio, as well as between sets during my weight training. Being muscle-bound, I have lost quite a bit of flexibility due to age and the very nature of my physique. Stretching clearly helps keep me limber. Moreover, I believe it explains my relatively low injury rate despite all the years of heavy lifting.

Done right, I believe the benefits of stretching outweigh any potential risks. There are many good books and articles on proper stretching techniques. Don't hesitate to employ a certified trainer to get you started.

Here are my tips for ***safe stretching:***

- *Don't stretch a cold muscle.* This is not a warm-up activity.
- Focus on *major muscle groups* and remember to *stretch both right and left sides.*
- *Don't bounce.* Stretches should be smooth movements.
- Hold your stretch for up to *30 seconds* while breathing normally.
- Aim for *tension*, not pain.
- *Be consistent* with your stretching. If you don't use it, you'll lose it. This is especially true about stretching.
- *Keep it safe.* Stretching is great, but it won't prevent an overuse injury. If you have any health concerns, consult your doctor or qualified physical therapist.

∼

Exercise has played a very important role in my life. It's no longer about bodybuilding and competition. I believe, and research backs me up here, that exercise on a regular basis keeps us young and healthy. Moreover, it's vital for memory preservation.

Practicing cardiology for over 34 years and longevity medicine for twenty years, I always endeavor to lead by example.

Now it's your turn to either get moving or modify your current exercise program to reap some of the benefits discussed in this chapter. Always remember to consult your physician or health care professional before embarking on an exercise program.

Isn't it time to get this component of your life in order? I promise that you will have no regrets.

My final question to all of you:
Whose body is it? IT'S YOUR BODY!
SO GET MOVING.

CHAPTER 31

YOU GOTTA BREATHE

Admittedly, the last few chapters might seem a bit overwhelming. It takes a lot of energy and resources to achieve optimal health and wellness. I've tried to make things digestible. I honestly believe that becoming a Medical Advocate is doable.

It requires effort, but *the rewards are immeasurable.*

So now we get to the "easy" part. You just have to breathe!

Breathing is so simple that most of us don't even think about it. Like robots, we're constantly running from the moment we wake until the moment we finally crash. Some of us are so keyed-up that sleep is all-but-impossible.

This is not good. It's not the way our bodies were designed to function.

Working 24/7. More is expected of us in the workplace than ever before. Emails, faxes, texts, Skype and Zoom calls, conference calls, endless meetings—we're simply not equipped to handle these constant and often unreasonable demands.

Evolution moves quite a bit slower than this. Believe it or not, our bodies are built to function as they did in prehistoric times. That means that we work… hunt, gather and eat during daylight hours… and we sleep at night.

Do you actually get 8 hours of sleep a night? I've been doing an informal survey in my office. I have found that the average working woman gets 7-8 hours of sleep. Males only get 5-6, if not less.

Hmmm, ever wonder why women live on the average 7 years longer than men?

We live in stressful times. Most of us can agree on that. How we deal with that stress can make a huge impact on our state of wellness.

If health and wellness are your goals—and they should be—isn't it time to make some changes?

Living in the present moment. Here's what I'm talking about: Taking time out to not only *breathe* but to also *partake in a pastime that brings you joy*. With all the stress that we encounter on a daily basis, it's easy to get bogged down with either *obsessing about the past* or *fearing the future*.

We've become pre-occupied with "stuff" we can't control. This is disempowering, a total waste of precious energy. This sets the stage for generalized *anxiety* and *depression*.

These negative emotional states lead to unhealthy consequences.

There is a plethora of evidence that links *anxiety* and *depression* to *disease*. I've alluded to it throughout this book. So, what can we do about it?

We may not be able to change the world at large, but we can make changes within ourselves that can help diffuse stress.

One of my favorite HeartWise videos that I produced is entitled "Live Your Passion: Staying in the Present Moment." What I do in this video is lead by example.

Walking my Talk. I start with my *weight training* with Charles Glass, my long-term trainer. For me, it's no longer about competition, but maintaining my strength and muscularity.

I have other interests as well. *Dancing* with Lisa Nunziella brings me great joy. It also works on my balance and coordination. This is no small feat, considering the nerve damage I incurred from my back surgery. *Singing* never fails to bring me a natural high that lasts for hours. I've been working with William Hanrahan, my singing coach, for several years.

What do these activities have in common? They keep me in the *present moment*. There is no way I can obsess about anything else while bodybuilding, dancing or singing.

These are my pastimes. Hopefully, you have your own. It could

CHAPTER 31: You Gotta Breathe

be crafts, gardening, or playing bridge. The options are limitless. Engaging in activities that bring us joy keeps us *here-and-now*. And they help *deflect stress*.

It all starts with the breath. The first thing a healthy newborn baby does as he or she enters the world is take a breath. It becomes their new lifeline and remains so for the duration of their life.

Trudging through our hectic lifestyles, most of us don't take time out to appreciate the power of the breath. As a result, we suffer the consequences.

I'm a cardiologist. Chest pain, shortness of breath, racing heart rate, and dizziness often bring patients to my office, and for good reason. Symptoms like this can be terribly scary.

I easily see five such patients monthly in my office with these complaints. Keep in mind these are usually young folks without heart disease. I can usually detect the problem the moment I lay eyes on them: *STRESS!*

Most people aren't ready to hear that. Generally, I must first develop a relationship with the patient, and order appropriate cardiac testing to rule out any heart problem. Fortunately, the test results are almost always negative.

I tend to take a different approach than my peers. The response they often hear from the cardiologist previously seen is this: "Well, I have good news and bad news. The good news is that your heart is healthy, and all your tests are negative. The bad news is that you have to live with this."

LIVE WITH IT! *Who in hell wants to live with pain or discomfort?* I don't care if its physical or emotional, I, for one, do not want to live in pain. Personally, I will do everything in my power to either minimize or rid myself of pain.

So, I tend to act differently. I sit down on my giant medicine ball and give my patients a mini lesson on deep breathing. Trust me, the time is well worth it. It is often the beginning of a new chapter in their lives—using the power of the breath.

My work as a physician goes way beyond putting balloons and stents in diseased arteries and saving lives. Certainly, saving lives is incredibly rewarding. But empowering patients to become their own Medical Advocates is equally rewarding and important.

Breeeeaaatheee. There are scores of excellent sources both online and in bookstores on deep breathing and meditation practices. I will share with you my simplistic approach which has served me well for years, as well as many of my patients.

The first step is to realize that change is needed and that simply living on the time clock is no longer serving you. Novices can't see themselves meditating for 20-30 minutes at a stretch. It just doesn't seem within their reach.

So, we start slow, using simple steps. We start right in the comfort of my office. I demonstrate the technique. We then do it together with the patient repeating what I do. Sounds easy, right?

Most folks can take ten deep breaths while sitting in a chair. That generally takes about one minute.

Practice makes perfect. The adage "use it or lose it" holds equally true with breathing. So, here's the deal: *take ten deep breaths a minimum of three times a day.* You can certainly do this activity more frequently, but three times a day is a must. It's a start and it's doable.

I like performing this before each meal. Once the food is in front of you, begin with your ten breaths. Think of it as an adjunct to a grace or prayer.

Here's what happens: After ten deep breaths your heart rate and respiratory rate will drop, and your blood pressure will more than likely fall.

What's also nice is that you will probably eat less as a result. In this country we are so fast paced, we gobble down our food. It takes twenty minutes for your stomach to inform your brain that you've eaten enough. Deep breathing is a great way to engage in mindful eating.

Who knows? Weight loss may follow.

Mind without distraction. Once you've become adept with the above, hopefully you'll be ready to go a bit further and engage in a regular meditation practice.

What exactly is meditation? It's when the mind is in the *present moment* and there is *no hesitation or anticipation* as to what happens next.

It's a *delicate* and *effortless* way of doing *nothing*. Beyond all the mental chatter in our brains, there exists a silent, peaceful, blissful place that is *always intact* and *unbroken*.

The key for all of us is to find that state within and embrace it. The mind comes back home to peace and joy. I believe inwardly that we are born into this world and that we leave it with a clear, free mind.

It's about going beyond the intrusiveness of outer affairs and simply *relishing silence*. That's the joy of living in the present moment. We all have this ability and *the time to enjoy it is now.*

Over the years I have practiced various forms of meditation, both on a solo basis and in groups. To name a few, I've meditated while listening to Native American flute music, while chanting, voicing affirmations, performing visual imagery as well as body scanning. Everything seems to work. I recommend that you experiment and discover what works best for you.

It matters not when you commit to your daily meditation practice. What works best for me is to perform my practice alone before starting my day. I prefer the morning before I shower, shave, and get ready to either train at the gym or work in my office.

Why? Two reasons come to mind: 1) I am more likely to get it done and 2) My mind is fresh after a good night's sleep. I haven't built up much verbal clutter by 4:30 a.m.!

Personally, I don't need music or meditation tapes to get me going. But if you're a novice, feel free to use whatever aid is helpful in obtaining a relaxed mindset.

I generally have my back propped up along my bedframe or sofa. The last thing I want to do is fall back asleep! But keep in mind that it's not a perfect world. Most of the time I embrace my meditation practice from the onset. Other times it doesn't happen so easily. If I haven't slept well, I might find myself drifting off to sleep.

Practice makes perfect. Allow whatever happens to simply happen. There is no penalty here. After a while you will see that your practice becomes easier and that your experience will grow in a positive way.

1-2-3-4. I generally begin with breathing. I take in a deep breath through my nose while counting silently to four. I then hold my breath for about two seconds. Finally, I exhale deeply and audibly on a six count. Often, I make a hissing sound with my upper and lower teeth held together, simulating the sound of a tire deflating.

If you're wondering why I use this pattern, there actually is a reason. First, *inhaling oxygen is essential to life!* We never ever forget to inhale. Where we lose focus is on the exhalation. When we are excited or anxious, we often hold our breath and/or forget to fully exhale. This can lead to trapped air in the lungs and even hyperventilation.

The consequences are anything but relaxation.

By emphasizing the exhalation and by using both sound and a longer count, you eliminate this from happening. The end result is a breath which is relaxed, and which can be repeated for minutes or even hours.

(And if you're wondering, I've been able to maintain this breathing pattern for as long as two hours. A transformation takes over and I get this feeling of a non-chemical high.)

It's important to maintain your focus on the breath. Believe me, *your conscious mind will come into play.* Before you know it, you'll be thinking about what you need to wear today, or about an upcoming meeting. Or about what mom said in your last phone call!

Don't fret! This happens to all of us. When it does, I simply say to myself, "Stop, delete, cancel. I don't need to be thinking about this at this moment." Then I go back to my breathing. With practice you, too, will learn to overcome this natural human tendency.

CHAPTER 31: You Gotta Breathe

Need for structure. If my breathing program seems a bit regimented, you are correct. You may be someone who can easily get into your breathing without a particular format.

I'm a doer. My light switch is consistently in the *on* position. (Again, my coach says I'm a Type **A+** personality.) As a result, I can get terribly distracted by all that I am doing or need to do. Therefore, having some structure to my practice is useful.

It keeps me on track.

Once a breathing format is established, I might include a mantra or two for a more meaningful experience. It might be as simple as, *"God in"* on the inhalation and *"Fear out"* on the exhalation. Other times I might add a few forgiveness statements, such as "I forgive me for judging myself for not being good enough as a parent, a role model or a writer."

There is no right or wrong way regarding your meditation practice. Your aim is to simply establish a pattern that works for you.

Visualization. After several minutes of deep breathing, I begin the second phase of my practice. I actually visualize what I wish to see happen.

But it's *not just a wish or a whim*. I try to *make it real* in my mind as if I'm already there. For example, with the nerve damage from my back surgery, there are challenges that affect my everyday life. I *visualize walking upstairs*, *hiking, climbing,* and *getting on and off the floor* effortlessly.

Getting beyond those obstacles.

Sometimes I see myself doing *book tours*, *speaking* in front of 500 people, *being interviewed* by Oprah or Dr. Oz. It's a positive way of viewing my dreams and savoring the fruits of my labor.

Prayer. The third and final phase. Born and raised in the Jewish faith, I have a deep respect and fondness for my religion. That said, I don't consider myself terribly religious, but I am spiritually based.

I pray for my family, my friends, my patients, and those encountering tough times. *I give gratitude to my higher power.* My prayer isn't so much about me. It's my time to give back to God and to all who have been present in my life.

Prayer is the perfect way to end my meditative practice.

I feel grounded and ready to approach the day.

There are hundreds of meditation techniques to explore. The benefits are best described by Sri Ravi Shankar, founder of the *Art of Living*: *"Every day you brush, that is dental hygiene. Similarly, every day you meditate, that is mental hygiene."*

Whether you practice in groups or solo, with or without music, with a mentor or on your own, it won't take long for you to experience the power of the breath. With time your meditation practice will flourish.

Living from the inside out. This is what I mean when I mention the fourth dimension of wellness...your *spiritual well-being*. There is a gift deep within that we all possess. Seek it now and you will be forever grateful and healthy in mind and spirit.

CHAPTER 32

AVOIDING AGING UNGRACEFULLY EVER AFTER

ANTI-AGING IS ONE OF THOSE BUZZ WORDS you hear daily. Personally, I don't like the term. Let's face it; we can't avoid aging. I prefer the term *age management*, for the simple reason that we can and should be able to manage our aging given the proper tools. That's what this chapter is all about.

I can deal with aging. I mean it's inevitable. I just don't want to grow old!

There are *several theories* on the aging process. [1] This is a burgeoning field, and the interest is huge. Despite recent advances, the mysteries that control the human lifespan have yet to be unraveled.

Some of the questions that scientists continue to ask are these: *Why do we age? When do we start aging? What aging markers are available? Is there a limit as to how old we can be?*

Below is an outline of the generally accepted theories of aging. These can be broken down into two main categories: *Programmed Theories* and *Damage or Error Theories*.

PROGRAMMED THEORIES

1. **PROGRAMMED LONGEVITY**
   Proponents state that aging is the sequential **switching on and off of genes**. Our genes are inherently unstable. This instability leads to aging. [2]

2. **ENDOCRINE THEORY**
   Our **biological clocks act through hormones** to control the pace of aging.

3. **IMMUNOLOGIC THEORY**
   Our *immune systems are programmed to decline over time.* This, in turn, leads to incr*eased vulnerability* to infectious disease, autoimmune disease, cancer, and Alzheimer's disease. As we age, our immune response becomes dysregulated. It is an established fact that the effectiveness of our immune system peaks at puberty and gradually declines thereafter with age. [3]

DAMAGE OR ERROR THEORIES

1. **WEAR-AND-TEAR THEORY**
   Our cells and tissues have *vital parts that wear out over time,* resulting in aging. Like components of an aging car, parts of the body eventually deteriorate from repeated use. This leads to death of tissue and eventually death of the organism.

2. **CROSS-LINKING THEORY**
   According to this theory, an accumulation of *cross-linked proteins damages cells and tissues.* Bodily processes slow down as a result. Aging ensues. Recent studies show that cross-linking reactions are involved in age-related changes in the studied proteins. [4] [5]

3. **FREE RADICAL THEORY**
   This well-supported theory proposes that *free radicals cause damage to our cells over time.* [6] [7] Accumulated cell and organ damage leads to dysfunction and aging.

The body does possess natural antioxidants to squelch and curb the dangerous build-up of these free radicals. Unfortunately, the supply of these protective antioxidants declines as we age. For this reason, many of us make the conscious decision to supplement our diets with antioxidants to slow down the aging process.

There are still other theories on aging. Those mentioned here are the ones generally accepted.

CHAPTER 32: Avoiding Aging Ungracefully Ever After

Since the 1930s it has been found that *restricting calories* can expand lifespans in laboratory animals. Studies on human subjects remain limited. Scientists are earnestly attempting to elucidate the underlying mechanisms. Despite the lack of unequivocal evidence, there is a small-but-growing population reducing calories in attempts to retard the aging process.

When it comes to aging, no doubt you will hear about the *mitochondria*. These constitute the powerhouse of the cell. Mitochondrial preservation is a huge topic these days. It is clearly a goal of successful aging.

As you can see, there is no single theory on the aging process. These are exciting times scientifically. We're at the tip of the iceberg.

No one wants to get old. The question I pose is what can all of us do *today* to *age well*?

Hopefully, you have gleaned from my journey and from the contents of this book that I'm all about living *a vibrant life at any age*. Your history doesn't matter. Perhaps you've sustained a heart attack or by-pass surgery. You might be a cancer survivor or have an autoimmune disorder for which there is no cure.

Life free from disease might be our aim, but this may not be attainable in all of us. Not everything is within our control. However, *we can control our lifestyle choices.*

Truthfully, I didn't need an anti-aging fellowship to practice longevity medicine. As a matter of fact, when I embarked on that arm of my practice in 2000, I had yet to receive any formal training. However, I possessed the necessary zeal and passion. What the fellowship program did was provide me with the academic background, framework, and tools to further my practice of wellness medicine.

No fountain of youth. Sorry to disappoint you! That said, there are many avenues we can all pursue to achieve vibrant health. It's about *avoiding* what I call *aging ungracefully ever after.*

We've been talking about these measures throughout this book.

This is especially so in this "how do" section. It's first and foremost about maintaining *optimal nutrition*; a lifelong program versus a fad. It's all about keeping your *heart*, your *bones*, and your *brain healthy*. *Adequate rest* is essential. Sleep deprivation and its ill effects on one's health continue to emerge as big topics in longevity medicine. Then we detailed *supplementation*, the need to *exercise* and the need to *slow down*, *relax* and *breathe*.

HORMONES

I want to make it clear from the onset that the decision to take hormones is a *personal choice*. Getting as knowledgeable as possible is essential. I encourage all of you to be the ultimate Medical Advocates before making any definitive decisions.

Being an anti-aging physician, I admit my bias. I fervently believe that when it comes to the aging process, *most of us look better, feel better and think more clearly on* <u>hormone</u> <u>replacement</u> <u>therapy</u> (HRT).

Does that mean I recommend such therapy to all my patients? The answer is a resounding NO! Again, there is not one therapy for everyone. We must take into account one's *goals*, *past medical history* as well as one's present *medical*, *emotional* and *social challenges*.

WOMEN AND HRT

This has been a highly contested topic for as long as I can remember. Back in 1997, I was preparing for a Medical Ground Rounds held at my hospital. I was the keynote speaker, and my topic was *"Women and Heart Disease."* Concentrating on heart disease prevention, I discussed the prevalent thinking at that time: HRT was more than likely cardio- protective. The problem was that most of these studies were observational in nature.

What subsequently followed was a blockbuster, the release of the Women's Health Initiative (WHI) in the summer of 2002. This was an exceptionally large randomized, double-blind placebo-controlled trial, optimally conducted by medical standards. [8]

CHAPTER 32: Avoiding Aging Ungracefully Ever After

WHI was a primary prevention trial, and the objective was to examine if HRT had an actual role in *preventing* heart disease. The subjects in the treatment arm were postmenopausal women, ages 50 to 79. Each of these women had an intact uterus and was prescribed a combined estrogen and progestin.

The trial was stopped early based on health risks that exceeded health benefits over an average follow-up of 5.2 years. The subjects were shown to have an increased incidence of heart attacks, strokes, blood clots, and breast cancer.

What a huge shock...to both the medical community and the lay public. Suddenly women all over this country were taken off their hormones. Disabling menopausal symptoms resurfaced with vengeance.

But even well-designed, large, conducted trials can be flawed. Here are a few of the *flaws* inherent in this study: [9]

- *The age of the participants:* The age range of 50-79 years is huge. The older the patient, the more likely the risk of pre-existing heart disease. Many of these women could have had heart disease without even knowing it. The average age of women reaching menopause in this country is 51. Would the results of the study been different if HRT had been started at younger ages and/or at the onset of menopausal symptoms?
- *The drug regimen* used: Subjects were administered an untested regimen. Selected for the trial was continuous conjugated equine estrogen, derived from the urine of pregnant horses, along with a synthetic formulation of progesterone, medroxyprogesterone acetate (MPA).
- *No options* offered: Clearly a viable treatment option exists in the form of bioidentical hormones. This obviously was not considered or tested in the WHI.

Still, I want to be clear, the decision to use HRT is a personal choice.

That said, I will go on record by saying that *there is no reason for a woman to endure a painful menopause.* If you're suffering from menopausal symptoms, take heart in knowing you're in the majority. *Only 40% of women breeze through menopause.* 60% experience a plethora of disabling symptoms which include, but are not limited to the following:

- Night sweats
- Hot flashes
- Insomnia
- Anxiety
- Panic attacks
- Phobias
- Irritability
- Emotional swings
- Fatigue
- Brain fog
- Unfavorable changes in blood levels of cholesterol and triglycerides
- Loss of libido
- Recurrent urinary tract infections
- Painful joints
- Bone loss (osteoporosis)
- Palpitations
- Migraine headaches
- Vaginal dryness
- Painful intercourse
- Dry skin, thinning of hair

Your options? Considering all we know from the WHI, *synthetic hormones are clearly passé.* In my opinion there really is no role for these hormones in the 21st century.

Premarin is risky. Premarin is an equine estrogen derived from the *urine of pregnant horses.* Although it certainly can reduce hot flashes

CHAPTER 32: Avoiding Aging Ungracefully Ever After

and night sweats quite effectively, there are definite concerns down the road. The potency of synthetic estrogen is about 200 times that of natural estrogen. [10] That's downright scary!

Equine estrogens have little in common with what a woman normally produces during her reproductive years. It's akin to comparing apples to oranges as far as I am concerned.

Provera or **medroxyprogesterone acetate** bears little resemblance to natural progesterone. Does the name sound even remotely natural to you?

My recommendation? Stay away from these synthetic hormone preparations. Enter the world of **bioidentical HRT**. These compounds are structurally *similar to the hormones a woman naturally produces.* These are derived from wild yams and unprocessed soy. Experience has shown that they constitute a *safe, viable* alternative.

Treating menopausal symptoms with bioidentical HRT is relatively easy. The challenge is to achieve *hormonal balance.* There are *two major hormones* that a woman produces during her reproductive years, *estrogen* and *progesterone*.

ESTROGEN

Estrogen has nearly 400 functions in the body, just a few of which follow: [10]
- Enhances energy.
- Improves mood.
- Maintains muscle.
- Maintains bone density.
- Maintains memory and concentration.
- Decreases wrinkles.
- Decreases LDL or the "lousy" cholesterol.
- Increases HDL or the good cholesterol.
- Reduces overall risk of heart disease.
- Improves libido.

PROGESTERONE

Known as the *calming hormone*, progesterone plays a critical role in achieving true hormonal balance. While estrogen enhances energy and vitality, progesterone *allays anxiety* and *aids in restful sleep*. This is the first hormone that diminishes with age. Dwindling levels of progesterone are commonly noted in women in their late 30s and early 40s.

Early on in my practice I would evaluate middle-aged women complaining of bothersome palpitations. Palpitations or a sensation of rapid and/or an *irregular heart rhythm* is a common complaint that cardiologists evaluate.

After performing the requisite cardiac work-up, I usually found no detectable abnormalities. Even researching the cardiac textbooks offered no clues.

My discovery! During my anti-aging fellowship, I learned that such symptoms are associated with *low progesterone*. And I have found this to be the case in numerous female patients approaching menopause.

Amazing that it took a fellowship in longevity medicine to appreciate what I never learned during my fellowship in cardiology.

I've seen premenopausal and menopausal women experience *extreme anxiety*, *panic attacks* and occasionally *phobias*. I once had a schoolteacher as a patient who developed the fear to drive on the freeway or take a cruise with her family. This kind of intense anxiety can clearly interfere with a woman's sense of well-being.

Sadly, I often find that *these same women are often prescribed antidepressant and antianxiety medications!*

Instead of searching for the root of the problem, which is hormonal lack or imbalance, patients are treated with *psych meds*—which have their own inherent *side effects*.

This is a "Band-Aid" approach to medicine. It's the antithesis of how functional medicine is practiced.

Few U. S. physicians actually prescribe bioidentical hormones. Wonder why?

First, it is *not a part of the standard medical education curriculum.*

Second, both the public and physicians alike get *fixated on pharmacology* (the study of drugs). This is at the expense of physiology (the study of how the body functions). [11] Medical students and especially practicing physicians have *minimal exposure to physiology* and massive exposure to pharmacology.

We can't live without hormones. From a physiology standpoint, hormones are the chemical messengers necessary for life. Why then do we speak as though hormones are dangerous drugs?

Thanks a lot, **Big Pharma**. Amazing what a few billion dollars can purchase: *advertising* to sway the public and physicians alike, the hiring of a mob of *lobbyists*, coercing the *FDA*.

Get the picture here?

I am in no way disrespectful of the pharmaceutical industry or the FDA. As a practicing cardiologist, I have treated countless patients with medications. These folks have lived longer lives as a result.

The FDA is our governmental medical watchdog which helps to shield us from dangerous medical devises and medications. They certainly serve an important and protective role. But too many resources—time, effort, and money—are spent to manipulate physicians into thinking that "evidence-based medicine" means *the exclusive use of patentable pharmaceuticals.*

Pharmaceuticals are only a piece of the pie. It's not about a magic pill, a magic bullet, or a magic vaccine.

We need our medications. But we need more. With such outmoded thinking, we would never see vitamins, minerals, bioidentical hormones, or various supplements in the marketplace.

Being your own Medical Advocate. When it comes to your health, knowing all your options keeps you in the driver's seat. I envision a world that practices *functional medicine*—where we find *medications, supplements* and *hormones* used concurrently to enhance the quality of our lives.

Another reason why you hear so little about the use of bioidentical

HRT is because it is not a product of Big Pharma. In other words, *there's no money in it.*

They must recoup their money. Large pharmaceutical companies can spend millions on drug research and marketing of new products. That partly explains the exorbitant price tag we see on new patented medications.

Bioidentical hormones, on the other hand, are produced under strict conditions in small compounding pharmacies. These small outlets lack the necessary funds to market their fare. They certainly are not in a position to conduct large medical research studies.

But that doesn't mean that their products are ineffective and unsafe. Bioidentical HRT from compounding pharmacies is a viable option that should be considered in appropriate situations.

Functional Medicine. Physicians practicing functional medicine do things differently. We don't merely prescribe hormones and check for symptom relief. We follow our patients scrupulously. We routinely measure hormone levels in saliva and their by-products (metabolites) in urine.

The aim again is to obtain *hormonal balance* as it pertains to estrogen and progesterone. *Regular testing* provides for optimal safety while successfully treating disabling menopausal symptoms.

But it's *not just the symptoms* we wish to treat. We also want women to achieve the long-term benefits of bioidentical HRT. These include *bone health, memory preservation, optimal lipid levels* and the *prevention of heart disease.*

Are bioidentical hormones completely safe? Are there any risks involved?

We may never have the complete answer. Who is going to fund a large, randomized placebo-controlled study? With no pharmaceutical giant manufacturing these compounds, the interest and financial backing is simply not present.

As I've been saying, the choice to undertake HRT with bioidentical hormones is a personal decision. I urge you—Medical Advocate that you are—to examine your options and do your own research.

CHAPTER 32: Avoiding Aging Ungracefully Ever After

There is a plethora of useful information available. One of my personal favorites that made bioidentical HRT headlines is *The Sexy Years: Discover the Hormone Connection* by celebrity actress Suzanne Somers. This was followed by *Ageless: The Naked Truth About Bioidentical Hormones.* [12] [13]

It often takes someone of celebrity status to initiate a movement and Ms. Sommers has done it beautifully. Honored to know her personally, she exudes passion in her work. She has helped propel and propagate anti-aging medicine.

Seriously, once her book was published, I no longer had to search for articles to give my patients. She made my work easy. I simply said and continue to say, "Just read Suzanne's book. You will then have a clear idea of what bioidentical HRT is all about."

Last Word. Synthetic hormones are <u>unsafe</u>. They should no longer be prescribed. Hormone supplementation should be done with compounds identical to the natural molecule. Although more research is needed to make definitive conclusions, there is evidence for the benefits of *bioidentical HRT in the proper doses* and in *proper balance.*

Bioidentical HRT is the only clear choice.

MEN AND HRT with TRT (Testosterone Replacement Therapy).

Right off the bat, let me say that *treating men with HRT is totally different than treating women.* It's a whole lot easier. *Give a hormone-deficient male some testosterone and you instantly become his hero!*

Men are allergic to doctoring. The biggest challenge I have with my male patients is reminding them to obtain the necessary lab work once therapy has been initiated. Women almost never misplace their lab slips, and they tend to be much more compliant with follow-up visits.

It's less complicated with men because there is no need to exquisitely balance two separate hormones (e.g., estrogen and progesterone). We do have a balance issue in men, but the process is much simpler.

Steroids. The word *steroid* has unnecessarily earned a bad rap. Did you know that *estrogen and progesterone are steroids*? Indeed, both male and female sex hormones are considered steroids. This merely refers to the *ring-like biochemical structure* of these compounds.

Stacking. In anti-aging medicine we are not talking about supra-physiologic doses of testosterone. That refers to a practice whereby one *stacks* combinations of various orals and injectables. Stacking various derivatives of testosterone is *commonplace in competitive bodybuilding*, especially at the professional level. Combining mega doses of anabolic steroids can have adverse effects on one's health.

In anti-aging medicine we aren't trying to look like a massive, ripped competitive bodybuilder. Instead, our aim is to obtain *physiologic replacement* doses of hormones. Both male and female hormones peak at around age 25. From that point on we age from an endocrinologic standpoint.

Obtaining the hormonal milieu of a healthy 25-30-year-old male or female is our quest. Monitoring hormone levels carefully, this can generally be done successfully and safely.

The Low Testosterone Quiz. What are the symptoms associated with low T?

- Lack of energy
- Decrease strength and/or endurance
- Decrease in "enjoyment of life" or lack of what was once pleasurable
- Grumpy old man syndrome
- Decrease in sex drive
- Decrease in erectile function and/or loss of early morning erections
- Loss in height
- Falling asleep after dinner
- Decrease in sports performance
- Brain fog or trouble keeping one's mind on a given task

- Deterioration in work performance
- Change in body composition (increase fat-to-muscle ratio)

Many of these symptoms are seen with disorders other than hypogonadism or low T. However, collectively this list should give you a clue.

HYPOGONADISM: *Reduction or absence of hormone secretion or other physiological activity of the gonads.*

Before you ask, here's my take on treating men with hypogonadism. Remember, I'm an anti-aging physician *and* a cardiologist, so I believe that men (as well as women) look better, feel better and think more clearly with HRT.

That doesn't mean I recommend this therapy to all men. Each case should be taken individually. What I am adamant about is treating the cause. Too often we prescribe antidepressants for grumpy, depressed moods, or drugs to "get it up."

Again, I call that the Band-Aid approach to medicine. If hormone deficiency is the cause, should we not at least consider HRT?

Testosterone Talk. It's long been thought that testosterone causes *prostate cancer, heart disease, roid rage* and *man boobs*. **False**! I'm here to tell you that the science behind such studies is clearly lacking.

The association between testosterone and prostate cancer should be put to rest once and for all. This fallacy stems from the work of a urologist named Dr. Charles Huggins, who in 1941 linked high testosterone levels to prostate cancer. [14]

Without going into details, the *methodology* and *laboratory testing* used were *archaic* by modern standards. Furthermore, his conclusions were based on three castrated men with advanced prostate cancer which had already spread to their bones.

The proof that castration worked was merely based on a specific lab test that is no longer useful today. We simply lacked the appropriate testing to follow the true history of prostate cancer. Besides, he worked with an ill population in whom HRT with testosterone would not have been considered.

Mainstream medicine took his work as gospel. They awarded Dr. Huggins the Nobel Prize and his theory has been accepted ever since.

Or have they? Fortunately, medical science questioned the validity of his theory and numerous studies have shown that this association simply does not exist. A key player in unraveling this medical mystery is Dr. Abraham Morgentaler who tenaciously did his own research while studying at Harvard University. He found that *men with prostate cancer tend to have low testosterone levels.* Moreover, he challenged that testosterone-prostate cancer risk. [15] [16]

His battle was an arduous one. After all it's not easy to debunk a seventy-year-old theory. Fortunately, we can safely say today that testosterone therapy does not cause prostate cancer.

There remains a question regarding the safety of administering TRT in men *with prostate cancer.* Since prostate cancer is hormonally driven, its growth may be enhanced with testosterone administration. For this reason, such therapy is generally withheld. However, even this continues to be questioned and challenged.

Testosterone therapy and heart disease. Being a cardiologist *and* an anti-aging medical practitioner, this topic is quite dear to me.

I find it so important that I have written a blog on the topic as well as produced a short video (www.heartwise.com). Let's be real here. As a cardiologist practicing for over thirty years, what would prompt me to prescribe TRT if it was harmful to the heart? That would truly be an oxymoron—and an insult!

In early 2014, the media went viral as they cited a study that proclaimed that aging men on testosterone therapy suffered a greater risk of a heart attack. That was the second such study in a relatively short period of time reporting the negative effects of testosterone therapy on the heart. Together these two studies brought this topic to the limelight. [17] [18]

CHAPTER 32: Avoiding Aging Ungracefully Ever After

As predicted, within two months, ads appeared in our nation's major newspapers, on the Internet, and on national television encouraging men on testosterone therapy who had suffered a heart attack or stroke to notify the law offices of so-and-so.

This was nothing new. We've all witnessed the legal profession's zeal to encourage the public sector to sue whenever there is a remote chance of an association between a given drug and an unfavorable outcome.

The last study was so flawed that I found this entire media outrage beyond ludicrous.

Let me set the record straight: There have been *countless studies* over the years demonstrating the *cardiac benefits of TRT*. This doesn't even take into consideration the myriad of other positive effects that testosterone has on men's health and well-being.

Below is your reality check. The evidence points to the fact that **low testosterone** is associated with **heart disease**.

- Men with coronary disease had a significantly *lower total testosterone and free testosterone*. [19]
- Men with low testosterone levels have an *increased mortality* due to heart disease. [20] [21]
- Men with coronary disease under the age of 45 had *total and free testosterone levels lower* than age-matched controls. [22]
- Men with low testosterone levels were shown to have *atherosclerosis* (hardening of the arteries) involving the carotid arteries. [23]
- Men with low testosterone levels had an *increased incidence of all-cause mortality* independent of numerous risk factors. Serum testosterone levels were inversely related to mortality due to cardiovascular disease and cancer. [24]

What does the literature have to say about **TRT and heart disease?**
- Testosterone replacement has been shown to *increase coronary blood flow* in patients with coronary heart disease. [25]
- Testosterone has been shown to *improve chronic angina* by increasing exercise tolerance versus controls receiving placebo. [26]
- Testosterone has been shown to *decrease inflammation and lower total cholesterol.* [27
- Testosterone replacement has been shown to be *helpful* in patients with *severe heart failure.* [28]
- Testosterone replacement for three years *did not boost atherosclerosis* in older men. [29]

The studies cited above are just a few examples of the numerous studies in the medical literature that have shown that:
- *Low testosterone* is associated with an *increased risk of heart disease.*
- *Testosterone replacement therapy* (TRT) decreases *that risk* and may even be beneficial in patients with preexisting coronary heart disease.

So how in the world did two studies conclude that male patients treated with TRT had a high probability of developing heart disease? There were 4 *major flaws* in these studies:
- *Estrogen levels were not measured* in the subjects of these studies. It is a known fact that high estrogen levels in men increases the risk of heart attack and stroke. [30] [31] [32] [33]
- *Hemoglobin/hematocrit levels were not measured.* Erythrocytosis (polycythemia) or elevated red blood cell counts can result with TRT. If left unchecked, clumping and sludging can occur which could conceivably lead to blood clots. [34]

CHAPTER 32: Avoiding Aging Ungracefully Ever After

- *Follow-up testing of testosterone levels was not consistently done* in the study patients. We don't actually know if the doses used in these studies were higher than therapeutic or lower. Too high a level may cause oxidative stress and damage to arterial walls, potentially leading to negative consequences. [35]
- *Dihydrotestosterone (DHT) levels were not obtained.* In some patients, elevated DHT levels can enhance atherosclerosis.

In Summary. We have a plethora of medical studies supporting the *beneficial cardiac effects of properly prescribed testosterone*. It becomes obvious that the studies cited above were poorly designed, and their conclusions flawed.

Some of the patients did not have testosterone levels measured and may have had levels greater than warranted. In addition, DHT, estrogen levels and circulating red blood cells were not addressed.

Even though I hinted that HRT in men is a bit simpler than that in women, the term *balance* again is the key. It is essential to monitor estrogen levels, red blood cell levels and DHT levels in all male patients undergoing HRT. The aim is to avoid any complications of therapy. Naturally, measuring prostate activity with a PSA level is also essential.

One Size Doesn't Fit All. *HRT in both men and women can be greatly beneficial in selected patients.* Again, I can't stress enough the need to individualize such therapy. Anyone that knows me can attest to the fact that I am completely, 100% against the cookie-cutter approach to medicine. This is especially important when considering HRT.

My advice is to find a physician well-versed in anti-aging medicine; a practitioner who can guide you safely through your hormonal regimen. Ongoing monitoring of hormone levels and ensuring hormonal balance is critical in both male and female patients.

I am rather bullish about a couple of other anti-aging hormones; **DHEA** and **melatonin**.

DHEA

DHEA (short for dehydroepiandrosterone) is a hormone produced mostly in the adrenal glands. DHEA is the *most abundant* of all the circulating *steroid* hormones.

Like all steroid hormones, your levels of DHEA drop exponentially with age. By the time you reach 70, your levels are likely to be 75-80% lower than at age 25. Even though mainstream medicine often fails to measure DHEA levels, don't fall into the trap thinking this should be taken lightly.

A study of more than 2,600 men aged 69 to 81 demonstrated that men in the lowest 25% of DHEA levels were: [36] [37]

54% more likely to die from any cause
61% more likely to die from cardiovascular disease

Studies have demonstrated that *women are also vulnerable* to the effects of low DHEA levels. Low levels have correlated with an increased risk of dying from heart disease. Stroke risk in women has also been shown to increase with low DHEA levels. [38] [39]

Evidence indicates that maintaining DHEA levels is a good way to fend off some of the most immediate threats to our longevity, namely cardiovascular disease. One study has shown that increasing DHEA levels can *decrease the risk of a heart attack*. [37]

There are additional reasons to supplement with DHEA. This vital hormone has been shown to *boost the immune system* as well as *protect against bone loss*. [40] [41] [42]

Moreover, DHEA supplementation can play a role in *weight loss*, improved *lipid values*, and improved *insulin sensitivity*. This not only benefits the cardiovascular system, but it also aids in averting metabolic syndrome and diabetes. [43] [44]

A few words of caution: Although DHEA does not have an effect on prostate cancer risk, men on aggressive hormone ablation therapy may need to discontinue DHEA during this time.

Because DHEA supplementation can influence estrogen and testosterone levels in women, women should consider getting tested for these hormones before initiating therapy. If you have been diagnosed with an estrogen-dependent cancer, you should consult your physician before embarking on DHEA supplementation.

DHEA supplementation is remarkably *inexpensive,* making it affordable to include in one's healthy longevity program. A daily dose of 10-50 mg generally brings us to therapeutic levels. I never recommend starting any hormone blindly. Always obtain a baseline value and undergo regular blood testing thereafter.

MELATONIN

Known as the "sleep hormone," melatonin has been used for years in helping us achieve a *better night's sleep.* While melatonin is involved in regulating our internal body clock, there are several other health benefits.

Based on extensive research, scientists have discovered that melatonin plays important roles in everything from *heart disease* and *diabetes* to *bone health* and *obesity.* Even more exciting is that it may *protect our genetic material* and guard against *age-related disease* and decline. [44]

Emerging evidence now suggests that melatonin plays a crucial role in a variety of metabolic functions, including *antioxidant* and *neuroprotection, anti-inflammatory defense,* and *immune system support.* [45] [46] [47] [48]

Because melatonin production drops with age, experts believe that its decline contributes to both the aging process and a generalized deterioration in health. We are beginning to see how melatonin can play a major role in *combating the aging process.* [49] [50]

Melatonin is amongst the strongest of all antioxidants. As a result, it plays a powerful role in *fighting free-radical-related diseases of aging,* from *heart disease to cancer,* and practically *everything in between.*

These are just a few of melatonin's potential roles in promoting our health and well-being:

- Antioxidant defense [51]
- Protection against heart disease [52]
- Protection against cancer [53] [54]
- Immune system modulation
- Protection against diabetic complications
- Brain Protection [55]
- Obesity modulation
- Prevention of osteoporosis [56]

Melatonin was formerly known as the "sleep hormone." While many of us indeed find that it helps to restore restful sleep, scientists are finding far more consistent applications for its use in brain protection. Indeed, it may soon become known as the "brain hormone."

Most promising is that supplementing with melatonin in middle age and beyond may *protect against Alzheimer's disease*, the most common cause of dementia in the elderly population. Other roles in neuroprotection include *reducing the risk of Parkinson's disease, shrinking the size of brain injury* at the time of stroke, and *minimizing brain swelling* and dysfunction post-head injury. [57] [58] [59]

Last words on aging. Aging is a *multi-factorial process*, involving a heavy load of *free radicals*, as well as *alterations in metabolic, hormonal, and immune function*. Mitochondrial function and regeneration are paramount. [60]

I've stated throughout this book and in my videos that inflammation is the bane of our existence as it relates to aging. A new term known as *inflammaging* describes the chronic, sterile, low grade inflammation which contributes to the pathogenesis of age-related diseases (e.g., heart disease, cancer, autoimmunity, and Alzheimer's disease). [61]

Epigenetics. Herein lies another term which is clearly in vogue these days. Epigenetics is the study of changes in gene activity which are

CHAPTER 32: Avoiding Aging Ungracefully Ever After

not caused by changes in DNA sequence. So, it's not so much the study of the individual genome (which is fixed), but the study of gene expression, or the way in which genes bring about their effects.

Why is epigenetics important? Changes in epigenetic factors can play a critical role in disease. Our DNA sequence may be fixed, but epigenetic patterns can be modified; examples include diet, obesity, physical activity, alcohol, environmental pollutants, stress and working night shifts.

The bottom line is that we can't merely blame our outcomes on our genes. They may contribute up to 20 % when it comes to one's lifespan/healthspan. Lifestyle and epigenetic changes, however, play a larger role. Personally, I prefer focusing on what we can all do to combat and stave off the deteriorating effects of aging.

When patients my age *and younger* present in my office, too often I hear these words. "Well Doc, we are all getting older!" I refute that statement because it's not entirely true. While we are all aging chronologically, our biologic age is variable based our diet and lifestyle.

As an example, a recent clinical trial found that a combination of growth hormone, DHEA and metformin helped to reverse the size of the thymus gland (which normally shrinks as we reach adulthood). As a result, biological/epigenetic age was reversed. Even though I am not advocating the universal use of these agents, this happens to be one of the first reports of an increase in predicted human lifespan. [62]

Biohacking. The field of anti-aging is a burgeoning one. Many are taking the leap and checking out biohacking. Biohacking involves the study of one's own body for the purpose of learning to optimize it while living life to the fullest. The biohacker aims to discover patterns which serve his body best and which keep him happier and healthier.

Sound's good, right? Who wouldn't want this? Well, keep in mind that such experimentation is not done in an academic setting, but in a private lab, or in one's own personal life. Many purists consider biohacking dangerous. After all, biohackers are using their own bodies as a form of experimentation. There is generally little to no scientific data to back their claims. On the other hand, it is possible that we can learn more about ourselves and the way our bodies function at their best from biohacking. Who knows? It may well be a way to learn to live an optimal life.

This entire field fascinates me. I mention it for the sake of completeness. There is little doubt that you will soon be hearing more and more about these unconventional practices.

I have adopted some of these practices myself, in aims of augmenting my overall performance, mitochondrial function and longevity. For example, I routinely take cold showers, and imbibe in both cryotherapy and ice baths. In addition, I adhere to intermittent fasting and practice Intermittent Hypoxic Training (IHT).

Although we may lack conclusive data at this time, this doesn't much matter to me. I believe in what I am doing. The setting is carefully controlled, and I genuinely enjoy the challenge. Speaking for myself, you won't hear me say, "I'm not going to try that until it's clearly been shown to work."

But that's me. It is not necessary for my readers to follow my lead. In fact, such practices should not be attempted without the expressed approval from your medical professional. My purpose here is to merely introduce you to the gamut of anti-aging practices.

This portion of my book is *all about choice*. As I've said earlier, I can deal with aging. I just don't want to get old!

Choice means a *healthy nutrition plan* with *appropriate supplementation*. *Exercise* is an absolute must. Even if you are one that finds exercise abhorrent, do it for your memory. It's so important to keep that blood flowing to your brain. It is especially important to add resistance training to your exercise regimen. Frailty doesn't bode well with aging. Weight training and maintaining muscle is absolutely essential.

CHAPTER 32: Avoiding Aging Ungracefully Ever After

Restful sleep is an essential component of optimal health. Gone are the days in which we jokingly bragged that we could get by with 4-5 hours of sleep per night. Who were we kidding?!

Taking time out to *meditate and relax* is also a vital part of your optimal wellness plan. Most important, remember that all we really have is the *present moment*. Dwelling on the past and fearing the future is simply an energy drainer. *Live your passion* and *do it NOW*.

It all starts with pulling in the reins and becoming your own best Medical Advocate. By getting in touch with your body you will become more self-reliant. This will place you in a more favorable position to communicate with your physicians and allied health providers.

This book is a primer. Use it. Ask *questions*. Do your *research*. Seek *second opinions* when appropriate.

It doesn't matter if you're in great shape, a cancer survivor, a cardiac patient or one with orthopedic and/or neurologic impairments. Our work as Medical Advocates never ends. There is always more we can do to add vitality and happiness to our lives.

I am a mere example. I'm my own Medical Advocate. It wasn't my medical degree that got me here. It's a never-ending tenacity to march forward and never look back.

Now it's your turn. Follow my lead and become your best Medical Advocate.

*After all, whose body is it? It's **your body**, so make the most of your special time on this planet.*

It's your **birthright.**

PART FIVE
Journal
(Life Without an Outline)

PREAMBLE TO THE JOURNAL

I tend to thrive with organization. From the very start I knew how my book was going to begin and how it was going to end. I had prepared a detailed outline early on, which commenced with chapter titles. Sure, I made a few changes along the way, but adherence to that outline was my basic rule. After all, I'm a Leo, a fixed sign, and we don't do well with surprises.

Nothing could have prepared me for what happened on May 2, 2015. A sudden relapse affecting my back was the last thing I expected. I mean I had endured enough pain and misery already. There was no room for an unhappy ending.

I chose to journal my journey which proved invaluable to my healing. I literally had to live life on life's terms. This didn't mean I was going to give up in any way. It meant I had to take it day by day. I didn't have the answers, didn't have a crystal ball, and I definitely didn't have an outline this time around.

～

The following section is excerpted from my journal, written over a period of four years. Writing to yourself in the first person is quite different than "talking to the reader." Selected sections were combined, deleted and tweaked to make it more reader friendly.

Because this portion of my book was literally written as it happened, extemporaneously, it has had a profound effect on my development.

I'm most proud and humbled by this section, and I am happy to share this with you.

[Note from the editor. *After Dr. Elkin felt his book was ready to publish, I requested to touch up the journal and make it a bit more compatible for your readership. I do consider the journal a very important part of Dr. Elkin's exceptional journey.*
— Jack Barnard]

THE JOURNAL

May 2015

Just when I thought things were going well, the inexplicable happens. Suddenly I'm dealing with a major relapse of some kind that affects my back and particularly my right lower extremity. I'm having difficulty walking. But fortunately, I have no pain.

This clearly is not part of my wellness plan!

It's Saturday May 2, 2015. My Heartwise staff and I are hosting a booth complete with our own team, entitled TONY'S TIGERS. This is no ordinary event. Furthermore, Tony is not some fictitious character. This is the American Cancer Society's Relay for Life fundraiser. We are walking, honoring cancer survivors. Tony is a dear friend currently being treated for advanced kidney cancer.

Walking casually and intermittently for 12 hours with patients and friends shouldn't be too taxing. After all, I'm in pretty good shape.

The truth of the matter is that I simply am not used to walking on uneven grass for a prolonged period. I can generally handle a treadmill or a track, but something about walking on grass just doesn't bode well with me.

By the late afternoon I'm walking with my friend Moira. I'm noticing how much effort I'm expending just to keep up with her. Something is clearly wrong here.

The next morning I'm determined to forget all this. I attend an event at the Farmer's Market at Third and Fairfax in Los Angeles. I'm feeling ok at this point, so I proceed to the bluffs atop Santa Monica Beach where I typically perform my weekly earthing exercises. Normally walking barefoot on grass is really soothing. I do this on a regular basis. It feels good and I know

From Both Sides of the Table: When Dr. Becomes Patient

I'm doing something beneficial for my health.

But today is anything but pleasurable. In fact, it's downright miserable.

From there I go to my dance instructor's studio for my weekly lesson. Nothing satisfies me more than dancing with Lisa Nunziella. But suddenly I'm having problems with my balance.

It's difficult to describe in words but it feels like I'm losing contact with the ground. I'm scared shitless. I'm doing all I can do to avoid falling.

By this time, I feel totally diminished. I return home, nap and simply take it easy.

Over the next couple of weeks, I make little to no progress. I don't get it. Despite seeing Dr. Cloud for spinal decompression, Michele for physical therapy and Russ for bodywork, I am experiencing extreme fatigue while walking. I'm used to having difficulty with dorsiflexion (not being able to fully plant my right heel on the ground in front of me to initiate a step). It's been that way since my surgery. *But now I can't complete the step with plantar flexion.* Suddenly pushing off from the ground is difficult.

So, if I can't plant my right foot on the ground and subsequently push off, I ain't going anywhere! This truly sucks. I even self-medicate with a corticosteroid pack which only gives me temporary relief. WTF! Every step is with effort.

I next talk to my dream-team leader, retired chiropractor Dr. Ralph Abitbol. He thinks it's time to get an updated neurological consultation. I couldn't agree more.

The most upsetting thing about this setback is my lack of proprioception. There is some inability that I have about sensing my own body. I don't know if it's because my brain isn't receiving the proper input or what, but my balance and spatial orientation are way off. I really notice this when I dance. Then my confidence goes out the window. This sucks because I generally feel so comfortable on the dance floor.

Oddly enough I'm currently rehearsing for this year's WHITTIER DANCE WITH THE STARS. I am part of an alumnae group opening act. This should be simple for me. Last year as a solo performer, I was truly dancing. Now I'm doing a fairly easy group dance number. But I'm just so damn tentative with my moves. And rightfully so... If I'm not overly mindful, I could lose my footing and fall. This is not like me at all.

Then I look around and see guys who lack my dance skills but who are able to turn and lift. So now I'm getting super envious. Gosh, it sucks feeling less than. I'd love nothing more than to get out of this commitment. Yet I still have a week before the actual performances.

Walking on either land or treadmill remains extremely difficult. And we are going on 3 weeks!

Thank God it's finally the week of WHITTIER DANCE WITH THE STARS. I can't wait to get this over with. Ambulating from the parking lot to the stage door of the Whittier Community Theatre for 3 performances literally sucks the wind out of me. We are talking about the equivalent of a half city block.

It's the end of yet another week. By this time, my negatively charged brain is in full swing. I'm obsessed with negative thoughts that are starting to consume me:

- Could I become permanently disabled? Is this as good as it gets?

- Will I actually need another back surgery? Just the mere thought of going under the knife again scares the hell out of me.

- Am I going to have to re-write my book? I already have a great ending. I'm not supposed to end on a negative note.

I'm anything but the ultimate Medical Advocate at this point. How can I possibly take charge of my health? I'm making decisions as necessary, but I am totally out of my comfort zone. I'm feeling a major loss of control here.

Suddenly I'm living in fear and am becoming a prisoner to my own thoughts. Fortunately, I just hung up the phone with dream-team leader Ralph. We both realize that I can't allow this pattern to continue. It will only undermine my efforts to heal.

Living in constant fear and making premature conclusions about the unknown simply isn't working. I've got to drop this obsession.

May 30, 2015

I'm doing my best to earnestly believe that this is just temporary. I'm not going down the river of amnesia with all that self-loathing. Been there, done that. But honestly, I don't know what's going to transpire.

My friend Ralph busts my bubble this evening. "Dude," he says, "I'm going to tell you like it is, and I'm coming from a position of love. You are too freakin' big. You need to downsize."

Happy I'm not. I bark back in defiance. "Ralph, I've spent 15 plus years of training and competition to attain my present size."

When he mentions something like I should be 25 pounds lighter, I feel my blood boiling. At this point I just have to get off the phone. I'm feeling truly diminished.

My modus operandi is to be super defensive. I'm not fat. I carry a lot of muscle. But let's face it; having not competed for a couple of years, I am nothing like competition lean.

I may be stubborn, but stupid I'm not! Ralph has a point. I listen begrudgingly.

What Ralph did was give me a rude awakening. At 228 pounds and only 5 feet 9 inches, I am too large for my frame. Damn it he's right. I really don't need to be THIS BIG anymore. Besides, I really have been thinking about downsizing a bit. But 25 pounds is preposterous! Ok, let's shoot for a 10-15-pound weight loss at which time I can reevaluate.

It all comes down to this. I have an injured spine and both acute and chronic nerve damage dating from my back surgery. I'm having difficulty walking. I need to be proactive. With one spine per lifetime, I heed to his advice and agree to work on decompressing my spine by downsizing.

Next, I go see Michele, my physical therapist. She confirms what I was expecting. My measured dorsiflexion is at an all-time low. My calf strength is also down. THIS SUCKS!

One good thing about objective measurements; it confirms what I already know. It's not all in my head. Here's the deal; I'm walking with great effort. What's scary is that I've deteriorated over the last week. It's gotten so bad that now I'm literally hiking my right hip up and then relying on my left leg to propel me further.

I can't fight it anymore. Michele has been after me in the past to consider an ankle foot orthosis (AFO) which forces my right foot into dorsiflexion. This allows me to clear the ground and avoid the possibility of falling.

In the past, the very notion of wearing a device of sorts seemed way too orthopedic and convalescent-like to me. I mean this is a tool to consider when you have no option, right? Guess what? That time is NOW!

So, I get fitted and employ the AFO which does help me get from point A to point B.

I meet with my speaking coach and editor of this book. He's really excited about this relapse. "You bastard," is all I can say. He may be smiling, but I'm certainly not!

Jack earnestly believes that this relapse puts a new twist on my writing project. The original outline of my book was about my journey as this doctor cum patient who sustains a heart attack and emergency back surgery AND who evolves to become his own Medical Advocate. I, in turn, am in a position both as a physician and a patient to motivate my readers to do likewise.

Then WHAM! Just when things are looking hunky-dory in the concluding chapter of the book, I get hit with the biggest challenge since my actual back surgery seven years prior.

"Wow, this really IS huge," are my actual words after hearing him out. What appeals to me most is that there is no outline for this portion of my book. It must be written extemporaneously.

So, this portion of my book will be titled PART 5: THE JOURNAL. I see Jack's point. For me, this is essentially my ongoing journey. It's paramount to not only the marketability of this project, but to my life in general.

In PART 5, I am truly living the life of a Medical Advocate. The scary and "human" part of all this is that I'm in the midst of a struggle and I'm not quite sure of the outcome. Now my strength and perseverance are on the line. No doubt this is my truest test in life. Reality is slapping me in the face.

June 6, 2015

I go to my long-awaited neurology consultation at Cedars Sinai Medical Center. This doctor is incredibly old school and anything but the touchy-feely type. But I must say I've never had a more thorough neurologic exam.

The bottom line, as he sees, is that I am not a surgical candidate as I have no pain. He believes I have a burnt out L5 nerve root. Duh, no surprises here!

He doesn't seem terribly excited to see me and he doesn't offer me any real answers. But he does want me to have both an MRI and an EMG, otherwise known as a nerve conduction study.

Ok, I'm still training at the gym, doing what I do best; weight training. Fortunately, my strength is still there. But I don't stop there. Forty minutes of boring cardio gives me ample opportunity to look around and observe others. I don't like what I see.

I'm watching others skipping rope, running on the treadmill, and jumping up and down on platforms of various heights. Many of these folks aren't nearly as physically fit as I am.

Yet, they can do things that I can't.

The obsessive thoughts return. "What if I am unable to perform any of these exercises again? I'm a piece of shit. I'm only good for hoisting around heavy weights. I'm a total failure when it comes to functional fitness. What if I can't dance again? What if I can't walk more than a city block without that damn AFO?"

My brain just won't quit today.

But it gets even worse. "I must have done this to myself." That's what I'm starting to think. I mean seriously, here I am blaming myself as if I willed this relapse. It's total nonsense. But this is how my brain works when that mood overcomes me. Today was especially dark.

I know where this comes from. I've harbored a feeling for the past few months that my right foot and ankle were getting slowly and progressively worse. I mentioned this repeatedly to both Russ and Michele, but it wasn't so obvious to them.

It was an inner feeling. I knew deep down inside that I was getting worse, but a part of me wasn't ready to accept yet another blow.

So now I'm in this self-questioning, self-guilt ridden, self-loathing mode and it sucks.

Even though it wasn't obvious to others, why didn't I take action? If I noticed my right foot and ankle getting weaker, maybe I should have stopped or tapered my resistance training to better suit my ill spine. Maybe God is punishing me for being excessive with bodybuilding and competition.

It's like I go down this downward spiral called a rabbit hole whenever I get triggered by observing others do what I can't. So here I am getting envious and angry.

I just need to accept this character defect of mine. Or is it truly a defect? I have this unyielding drive to always push forward. Generally, it serves me well, as I am never satisfied with the status quo.

What I'm learning now is that this drive is both a blessing and a curse. I can't let it run me or it will clearly affect my progress in a negative way.

What is my reality anyway? The reality is that no one knows where this is going. That's the disconcerting part. My reality is that I am doing a hell of a lot. I'm doing everything in my power to push past this.

I have to let go of those negative thoughts or at least put a lid on them. There can be no more "What ifs." It's simply counterproductive to both my physical and emotional healing.

Now I want to do everything possible to maintain the integrity of my spine. Although I was initially unyielding about downsizing and losing muscle, I realize now how necessary that is to decompress my spine. Ralph is right. I'm just too damn big given my age and my broken spine. Besides, since competing in no longer a goal of mine, who needs all this mass anyway?

So, I need to do more cardio and make some changes in my diet. I've already implemented some changes but it's obvious I need to do more. So far, the pounds don't seem to be coming off so fast.

Come to think of it, I haven't dieted in two years, which was for contest preparation. I'm not looking to diet this time around, but to make lifestyle changes. I expect the weight loss will be slower and more permanent.

It feels weird having a different goal. Never having a true weight problem, my goal in the past was to diet for a contest. That was anything but healthy. Losing 25+ pounds in 14 weeks seems absolutely crazy to me today.

Now it's a different story and a new goal. This time I'm purposely downsizing for the health of my spine and to achieve a more balanced look.

I'm a lot more content this week. I feel gratitude for the first time in a while. I continue my daily practice of meditation and prayer. But I'm also adding a new visualization component. I visualize myself walking effortlessly in the gym, on the street and up mountains.

I'm like a pit bull who won't quit! That said, my vulnerability is at an all-time high right now. I try my best to stay upbeat, but I get triggered easily. Staying positive in the face of adversity is difficult.

I work on this daily with affirmations, visualization, meditation, and prayer. Even with my daily practice, however, I often slip when my negative voice resurfaces. Such feelings of inadequacy don't simply vanish.

I'm challenged each day I walk into the gym. Being somewhat of an elitist, given my former athletic training and background in gymnastics, I often come back with, "Why can't you do that?" Then I hear, "Well, loser, it's because you are handicapped." I actually hear my critical voice coming back at me in the second person. These puppets in my head are driving me nuts.

This is really tough to take. No matter how much I work on the positive, I am constantly reminded of my limitations daily. Well, maybe not every day, just every day when I'm in the gym!

So, I have to come up with new affirmations. My latest one is, "OK, what these guys are doing is cool, but I can't measure my progress based on what they do. I am doing the best that I can at this moment. This is me NOW."

June 27, 2015

Improvements are happening weekly at this point. I am increasing my walking time on the treadmill. Currently I'm up to 27 minutes. From there I jump onto either the elliptical or the recumbent bike to complete my 40 minute of cardio which I now do 5 days a week.

I'm getting into this downsizing thing. It may include some muscle, but there's a fair amount of fat that I can clearly afford to lose. But hell, whether it's fat or muscle, I need to downsize to save my back. That's the bottom line. No more hiding behind my muscles.

I've lost a total of six pounds in three weeks which doesn't sound like much. But the only dieting I've ever done in the past is drastic dieting for a bodybuilding contest. A two-pound weight loss per week is actually a doable, healthy way to go.

I am enjoying the discipline of sticking to a healthy eating plan. I'm trying to eat clean 90% of the time. Drinking tons of water and decaffeinated, unsweetened tea, while leaving out any sodas and drinks/juices laden with sugar is the rule here. I have truly cut down on starchy carbs, all of which must be consumed for breakfast and lunch. After 2:00 pm my meals consist of lean protein and lots of veggies.

It's funny but I'm working as hard now as I previously worked preparing for a contest. I'm truly grateful for my background in competition, because it has given me the tenacity and the will to keep pushing.

July 4, 2015

No doubt this will be another challenging week. It's Monday and I make my trip to Cedars-Sinai Medical Center for my scheduled EMG. Being punctured with an inch-long needle in both legs, calves, ankles, buttocks as well as in my spine 20 plus times over the course of an hour is pretty traumatic. I feel like a human pin cushion. But that's not all. Next the neurologist delivers a series of electric shocks to measure nerve conduction to various muscles.

All I hear from him is, "Well, this is pretty abnormal. You've got a motor neuropathy." By this time I am pretty fed up with this character who insists on inflicting me with pain and showing no mercy whatsoever. So, I come back with, "No shit Sherlock! Tell me something I don't know." Seriously, I can easily understand how someone might develop PTSD (Post Traumatic Stress Disorder) from this procedure alone.

My MRI results aren't good. Ok I have this new herniated disc that is huge at the level of L1-L2. If that isn't bad enough, my spinal stenosis has deteriorated from "moderate" in February 2009 to severe in the present study. I mean, "Really?" That's why I had the damn surgery in the first place. There are a few other abnormalities, but this is what I recall.

Despite being a nonsurgical candidate, the neurologist reached over his desk and handed me a business card of a respectable neurosurgeon, "just in case". This was after offering me absolutely no therapeutic plan, while admonishing me to give up bodybuilding and any physical activity for that matter, at least for the present time. Imagine, all this without knowing my physical capabilities and potential. I stormed out of there, tossed the business card in the wastebasket, and vowed never to see this grim reaper ever again.

Well, a surgical candidate I'm not, so my rehab plan continues.

November 2015

It's been 6 months. My walking is pretty good at this point. I think it's a combination of the weight loss of 15 pounds, the elapsed time with months of ongoing rehab, some custom-made orthotics and my unstoppable drive. Whatever, I no longer need the AFO. I can push off from the ground and even appreciate a right heel strike while walking. Ok, maybe not always, but often.

I am beyond fortunate is having a dream-team that helps me every step of the way. (pun intended). But the last thing on my mind is searching for yet another team member. I've tried it all: physical therapy, chiropractic care, Rolfing, and sports medicine practitioners, injection with stem cells. What else can I possibly try?

Enter Tony Molina of Rewire Project. A friend tells me I absolutely must meet this guy. He supposedly performs magic.

So, I meet Tony at his facility in Santa Monica. He immediately turns me off when he states that heavy weightlifting isn't working to my advantage; that I need to consider changing my priorities.

CHANGE! That's the last thing I want to hear at this point.

From Both Sides of the Table: When Dr. Becomes Patient

Seriously Tony? I'm not about to give up an activity that has brought me praise (from years of competition), strength and confidence. Even if I can't walk worth a damn, I'm quite strong. Besides, I'm really good at bodybuilding. No one is going to take that away from me. No one is going to take me off track.

My years in bodybuilding have given my joints stability and have played an important role in maintaining the integrity of my "broken spine." Overall, it's kept me unbroken for the most part.

But I'm listening. Tony starts talking about type 1 and type 2 muscle fibers. I'm a doctor with a lot of knowledge about all this. Hell, I'm a strength athlete. That makes me a type 2 fiber or fast twitch kind of guy. He says I'm off balance; that I need to recruit more type 1 or slow-twitch fibers.

I stormed out of there vowing to never see this character again. But then I start thinking. Some of what he says makes sense. Perhaps I'm jumping the gun?

I calm down, come to my senses, and speak with Tony a couple of days later. What he was attempting to do was render an opinion. Nothing needs to be changed at this time. It's me going to that place where it's *all or none*.

Something about Tony Molina compels me to do a double take. He carries a sense of adventure and positivism which clearly resonates with me. Performing the most extensive muscle testing ever experienced, he believes that my overall machinery is working. Nothing is 100% dead. Yes, there is major weakness in my right foot, ankle, calf, and hamstring. But he believes that there is major potential for improvement.

Reflecting on my rehab over the past 5 months, I think I'm doing fairly well. I believe I'm pretty much back to my baseline state prior to the relapse. *But I want more!* I'm just not ready to cash in and say, "Well, guess this is as good as it gets."

Because Tony gives what I believe is honest hope, I decide to add him to my dream-team. We've been working together for a few weeks now and I can truthfully say that my walking has improved.

Why, just this evening I'm walking two city blocks to a meeting. I notice that something is distinctly different. Suddenly walking doesn't seem to be a major effort.

Tony's business is aptly named Rewire Project. I'm not quite sure what that is supposed to mean, but I get it. To me "rewiring" means stimulating the nerve to muscle connection. The goal is improving strength and function. Is it possible? Tony seems to think so, so I'm game.

So, the journey with Rewire begins. I'm doing new activities that are foreign to me. Even though the word *change* scares me, I get terribly excited when exploring new things.

I'm taking Tony's lead. I'm going full force ahead. Here's my take on this: If my muscles can contract on some level then that means there is something there. I'm going to do all that is humanly possible to better my lot.

So, we use a combination of therapies at Rewire. I'm doing electro-stimulation both at Tony's facility and at home with a device of my own. Then we're combining electro-stim with whole body vibration on a machine called the Power Plate. It's all to help rehabilitate my truly weak areas. He's outlining a protocol specifically for me and I swear it's like having a second training session in the course of a day... very brief but intense.

I'm exhilarated. It's working on both my balance and coordination. This is really important since these areas have really suffered as a result of the surgery itself and this recent relapse. The result is renewed self-confidence.

Tony is an interesting fellow. He seems to take in everything and come out with very intuitive conclusions. He remains an integral member of my team.

That relapse in May 2015 has truly been a major wake-up call. I've learned that my previous lifestyle was no longer serving me. My back disease had been progressing for some time. I just continued to ignore it. Maintaining all that mass and training as heavy as I did brought me to my knees in May 2015.

It's different now. I am constantly in a state of flux and am opening myself up to new ideas and challenges. To be able to say that at year's end is pretty cool.

MAY 2017...Two Years Later

Life goes on. There continues to be ups and downs, including a couple more athletic injuries. Through lots of rehab, a 20-pound weight loss, and training a bit lighter and a whole lot smarter, I continue to do well.

The back surgery was in 2008. My first post-op relapse was a mere seven months later. My next major relapse was 2015. In 2016, I sustained two accidents in a span of two months. I'm reminded that I am not immune to ongoing mishaps.

But it's not over. I don't use the words battle or fight, because I don't wish to see my life as a constant struggle.

However, in April 2017 I'm hit with yet another bump in the road. This one's a big one. I'm noticing something new. When I stand in one position for a few minutes, I notice the sensation of pins and needles in my right foot. It feels as if my foot is falling asleep. I soon learn that this phenomenon is known as paresthesias. It comes from pressure on a nerve or from a damaged nerve itself.

I fall into both categories. I know from the MRI in 2015 that my back disease had progressed. Furthermore, I suffer permanent nerve damage from the actual back surgery. It hardly seems possible that this could happen, although this can't be a complete surprise when you consider my anatomy and functional status.

The emotional trauma hits hard. I've been extremely diligent in hopes of avoiding worsening of my back disease. Again, I ask, WHY DID THIS HAPPEN AND WHAT ELSE COULD I HAVE DONE TO PREVENT THIS?

Well, I've learned to forgive the whys in life. All I can do is keep doing my best.

March 2019

I'm coming up on 4 years from that infamous relapse. I hate it when I hear folks say, "I have good days and bad days." But I get it. Somedays I feel terrific and have no paresthesias. Other days I may experience 2 or 3 brief episodes while standing in one position and sometimes while walking on a treadmill or even during my dance lesson. It's scary but I can't allow those puppets inside my head to take over.

Fortunately, these episodes are brief. Interestingly enough, when I hiked Mount Baldy a few months back I had no such episodes.

They tend to be sporadic and unpredictable. It bothers me, but it doesn't run me.

I don't have a lot of options. I'm not a good surgical candidate. I could say I'm learning to live with it. But I'd rather say I'm *working* with it.

But I take nothing for granted. I maintain my regimented lifestyle on a weekly basis. Everything from my training in the gym, my work with Tony Molina, and my regular visits to my physical therapist, chiropractor and Rolfer is what sustains me.

Then there's maintaining a healthy lifestyle. It's about diet and stress management. My regular meditation practice is essential.

My dream-team director and good friend Ralph Abitbol told me 5 years ago that I'm "too freaking big." Although I didn't want to believe him, he was right. I've maintained a weight loss of 20 pounds for the last few years. At 205 pounds, I am big enough. As a result of my weight loss, I possess a much healthier body image. I've never looked or felt better. Furthermore, weighing less helps to decompress my damaged spine.

Naturally keeping a positive attitude and embracing the fact that the glass is always half full is vitally important. I can accept these obstacles that get in my way, yet I never give up. I'm always open to new discoveries and new therapies that nourish my body and soul.

THE JOURNAL

Promise has become my buzz word. I'm clearly a work in progress.

It's all about being my own best Medical Advocate. I wasn't about to take the words of that grim reaper of a neurologist who did not know me nor my potential, but who suggested I see a neurosurgeon for a possible redo surgery. He also recommended that I refrain from my usual exercise, while giving me no options. There's no room for this kind of negativity in my life.

Instead, I made and continue to make necessary changes that benefit my health and wellness. What's great is that I don't have to do it alone. I have my own dream-team that are present and who rally me to success.

It all boils down to this: It's not just about my broken back, my nerve damage, nursing 2 injuries in 2 months, convalescing from therapeutic injections of stem cells into my shoulder, or bothersome paresthesias. It's about staying in the game and refusing to give up *no matter what*.

I'm always putting myself on the line here, and it's not because I'm this paragon of perfection. I'm simply a living example of what's humanly possible. A lot of folks scoff at what I do and think it's too far-fetched and unreachable; that I'm out in left field.

I don't believe that's true. Life is, to a certain extent, a choice. I chose to be unstoppable. I won't stop until I've tried everything possible to reach my wellness goals.

REFERENCES

PART 2

Chapter 19

1. Benjamin EJ, Muntner P, et al. AHA 2019 Heart Disease and Stroke Statistics-2019 Update: A Report from the American Heart Association. *Circulation* 2019; Jan 31.

2. Elkin H, Winter A. Grounding patients with hypertension improves blood pressure: A case history series study. *Alternative Therapies* 2018 Nov/Dec; 24(6):46.

3. The SPRINT Research Group. A randomized trial of intensive versus standard blood pressure control. *NEJM* 2015 Nov; 373:2103-2116.

4. Bangalore S, Toklu B, et al. Optimal systolic blood pressure target after SPRINT: Insights from a network meta-analysis of randomized trials. *The American Journal of Medicine* 2017 ;130(6):707-719.

5. Butt DA, Mamdani M, et al. The risk of hip fracture after initiating antihypertensive drugs in the elderly. *Arch Intern Med* 2012 Dec 10; 172 (22):1739-44.

6. Gonzales D, et al. For the Varenicline Study Group. Varenicline, an alpha4beta2 nicotinic acetylcholine receptor partial agonist, vs. sustained-release bupropion and placebo for smoking cessation: a randomized controlled trial. *JAMA* 2006 July 5; 296:47-55.

7. Moore TJ, Furberg CD, et al. Suicidal behavior and depression in smoking cessation. *PLoS One* 2011; 6(11):e27016.

8. *FDA Drug Safety Communication:* Chantix (varenicline) drug label now contains updated efficacy and safety information. Issued on 12-12-12.

9. Ross SM. Neurofeedback: An integrative treatment of substance use disorders. *Holist Nurs Pract* 2013 Jul-Aug; 27(4):246-50.

10. Karch S, Paolini M, et al. Real time fMRI neurofeedback in patients with tobacco use disorder during smoking cessation: Functional differences and implications of the first training session in regard to future abstinence or relapse. *Front Hum Neurosci* 2019; 13:65.

11. Rizzo M, Berneis K. Who needs to care about small dense low-density lipoproteins? *Int J Clin Pract* 2007; 61(11):1949-1956.

12. Backers J. Effect of lipid-lowering drug therapy on small-dense low-density lipoprotein. *Ann Pharmacother* 2005; 39:523-526.

13. Myers J. Exercise and cardiovascular health. *Circulation* 2003; 107:e2-e5.
14. Eckel RH. Obesity and heart disease: A statement for healthcare professionals from the nutrition committee, American Heart Association. *Circulation* 1997; 96:3248-3250.
15. Vest A, Heneghan H et al. Bariatric surgery and cardiovascular outcomes: A systemic review. *Heart* 2012; 98:1763-1777.
16. Diabetes and Coronary heart disease. *Diabetes Spectrum* 1999 Nov; 12(2):80-83.
17. Wingard DL, Barrett-Connor E. Heart disease and diabetes. *Diabetes in America* 2nd *edition*. Harris ML, ed. Bethesda, Md., National Institutes of Health (NIH publication no.95-1468) 1995:429-48.
18. Grundy SM, Benjamin IJ et al. Diabetes and cardiovascular disease. *Circulation* 1999; 100:1134-1146.
20. Centers for Disease Control. National Diabetic Fact Sheet 2011.

Chapter 20

1. Miller M, Stone NJ, et al. Triglycerides and cardiovascular disease: a scientific statement from the American Heart Association. *Circulation* 2011 May 24; 123(20):2292-333.
2. Nordestgaard BG, Chapman MJ, et al. Lipoprotein (a) as a cardiovascular risk factor: current status. *Eur Heart J* 2010; 31(23):2844.
3. Danesh J, Collins R, et al. Lipoprotein (a) and coronary heart disease. Meta-analysis of prospective studies. *Circulation* 2000; 102(10):1082-5.
4. Smolders B, Lemmens R, et al. Lipoprotein (a) and stroke: a meta-analysis of observational studies. *Stroke* 2007; 38(6):1959-66.
5. Sotiriou SN, Orlova VV, et al. Lipoprotein (a) in atherosclerotic plaques recruits inflammatory cells through interaction with Mac-1 integrin. *FASEB J* 2006; 20(3):559-61.
6. Marcovina SM, Kennedy H, et al. Fish intake, independent of Apo(a) size, accounts for low plasma lipoprotein levels in Bantu fishermen of Tanzania: The Lugalawa Study. *Arteriosclerosis, Thrombosis, and Vascular Biology* 1999 May 19(5):1250-6.
7. Sharpe PC, Young IS, et al. Effect of moderate alcohol consumption on Lp(a) lipoprotein concentrations: Reduction is supported by other studies. *BMJ (Clinical research Ed.)* 1998 May; 316(7145):1675.
8. Suk DJ, Rifai N, et al. Lipoprotein (a), hormone replacement therapy, and risk of future cardiovascular events. *J. Am. Coll Cardiol* 2008 July; 52(2):124-31.
9. Stampfer MJ, Malinow MR, et al. A prospective study of plasma homocysteine and risk of myocardial infarction in US physicians. *JAMA* 1992 Aug 19; 268(7):877-81.

REFERENCES

10. Loscalzo J. The oxidant stress of hyperhomocysteinemia. *J Clin Invest* 1996; 98:5-7.

11. Albert CM, Cooke NR, et al. Effect of folic acid and B vitamins on risk of cardiovascular events and total mortality among women at high risk for cardiovascular disease: a randomized trial. *JAMA* 2008; 299:2027-2036.

12. Stanger O, Herrmann W, et al. Clinical Use and rational management of homocysteine, folic acid, and B vitamins in cardiovascular and thrombotic diseases. *Z Kardiol* 2004 Jun; 93(6):439-53.

13. Pearson TA, Mensah GA, et al. Markers of inflammation and cardiovascular disease: a statement for healthcare professionals from the Centers for Disease Control and Prevention and the American Heart Association. *Circulation* 2003; 107:e2-e5.

14. Pradhan AD, Manson JE et al. C-reactive protein, interleukin 6, and the risk of developing type 2 diabetes mellitus. *JAMA* July 2001; 286(3):327-34.

15. Danesh J, Wheeler JG, et al. C-reactive protein and other circulating markers of inflammation in the prediction of coronary heart disease. *N Engl. J. Med* 2004 April; 350(14):1387-97.

16. Madison Miles. Beverly Hills Periodontal Institute. *Personal account.*

17. Salzberg TN, Overstreet BT, et al. C-reactive protein levels in patients with aggressive periodontitis. *J Periodontol* 2006 Jun; 77(6):933.

18. D'Aiuto F, Parkar M et al. Periodontitis and systemic inflammation: control of the local infection is associated with a reduction in serum inflammatory markers. *J Dent Res* 2004 Feb; 83(2):156-60.

19. Loesche WJ, Lopatin DE. Interactions between periodontal disease, medical diseases, and immunity in the older individual. *Periodontol 2000* 1998 Feb; 16 80-105. Review.

20. Wick G, Perschinka H et al. Atherosclerosis as an autoimmune disease: an update. *Trends Immunol* 2001 Dec; 22(12):665-9. Review.

21. Ballantyne CM, Hoogeveen RC, et al. Lipoprotein-Associated Phospholipase A2, high sensitivity C-reactive protein, and risk for incident stroke in middle-aged men and women in the Atherosclerosis Risk in Communities (ARIC) Study. *Arch Intern Med* 2005; 165:2479-2484.

22. Brilakis ES, McConnell JP, et al. Association of lipoprotein-associated phospholipase A2 levels with coronary artery disease risk factors, angiographic coronary artery disease, and major adverse events at follow-up. *Eur Heart J* 2005; 26:137-144.

23. May HT, Home BD, et al. Lipoprotein-associated phospholipase A2 independently predicts the angiographic diagnosis of coronary artery disease and coronary death. *Am Heart J* 2006; 152:997-1003.

24. Davidson MH, Corson MA, et al. Consensus panel recommendation for incorporating lipoprotein-associated A2 testing into cardiovascular disease risk assessment guidelines. *Am J Cardiol* 2008 Jun 16; 101(12A):51F-57F.

25. Schindhelm RK, van der Zwan LP, et al. Myeloperoxidase: a useful biomarker for cardiovascular risk stratification? *Clinical Chemistry* 2009 Aug; 55(8):1462-1470.

26. Baldus S, Heeschen C, et al. Myeloperoxidase serum levels predict risk in patients with acute coronary syndromes. *Circulation* 2003 Sept; 108:1440-1445.

27. Kesaniemi YA, Ehnholm C, et al. Intestinal cholesterol absorption efficiency in man is related to apoprotein E phenotype. *J Clin Invest* 1987 Aug; 80(2):578-581.

28. Tammi A, Ronnemaa T et al. Apolipoprotein E phenotype regulates cholesterol absorption in healthy 13-month-old children-The STRIP Study. *Pediatr Res* 2001 Dec; 50(6):688-91.

29. Bennet AM, di Angelantonio E, et al. Association of apolipoprotein E genotypes with lipid levels and coronary risk. *JAMA* 2007 Sept; 298(11):1300-1311.

30. Wilson PW, Schaefer EJ, et al. Apolipoprotein E alleles and risk of coronary disease. *Arteriosclerosis, Thrombosis, and Vascular Biology* 1996 Oct; 16:1250-1255.

31. Haan MN, Mayeda ER. Apolipoprotein E genotype and cardiovascular disease in the elderly. *Curr Cardiovasc Risk Rep* 2010 Sep; 4(5):361-368.

32. Mahley RW. Apolipoprotein E: from cardiovascular disease to neurodegenerative disorders. *J Mol Med (Berl)* 2016 Jul; 94(7):739-46.

33. Michaelson DM. APOE e4: the most prevalent yet understudied risk factor for Alzheimer's disease. *Alzheimers Dement* 2014 Nov; 10(6):861-8.

34. Li Y, Iakoubova OA, et al. KIF6 polymorphism as a predictor of risk of coronary events and of clinical event reduction by statin therapy. *Am J Cardiol* 2010 Oct 1; 106(7):994-8.

35. Hopewell JC, Parish S, et al. No impact of KIF6 genotype on vascular risk and statin response among 18,348 randomized patients in the heart protection study. *J Am Coll Cardiol* 2011 May 17; 57(20):2000-7.

36. Musunuru K. Lack of association of KIF6 genotype with vascular disease and statin response. *Circulation: Cardiovascular Genetics* 2011; 4:467-468.

37. Palomaki GE, Melillo S, et al. Association between 9p21 genomic markers and heart disease: a meta-analysis. *JAMA* 2010 Feb 17; 303(7):648-56.

38. Dekker JM. Fibrinogen, viscosity, and ischaemic heart disease risk. *Eur Heart J* 1996; 17:1780-81.

39. Krishnan RM, Adar SD, et al. Vascular responses to long- and short- term exposure to fine particulate matter: MESA Air (Multi-Ethnic Study of Atherosclerosis and Air Pollution). *J Am Coll Cardiol* 2012 Nov; 60(21); DOI:10.1016/j.jaac.2012.08.973.

40. Brook R, Rajagopalan S. Chronic air pollution exposure and endothelial dysfunction: what you can't see can harm you. *J Am Coll Cardiol* 2012; DOI:10.1016/j.jacc.2012.08.974.

REFERENCES

Chapter 22

1. Stress Working Party. Stress and cardiovascular disease: a report from the National Heart Foundation of Australia. *Med J Aust* 1988;148:510-513.
2. Bunker SJ, Tonkin AM, et al. "Stress" and coronary heart disease: psychosocial risk factors. *Med J Aust* 2003 Mar 17; 178(6):272-276.
3. Musselman DL, Evans DL et al. The relationship of depression to cardiovascular disease: epidemiology, biology, and treatment. *Arch Gen Psychiatry* 1998; 55:580-592.
4. Eriksen W. The role of social support in the pathogenesis of coronary heart disease: a literature review. *Fam Pract* 1994; 11:201-209.
5. Friedman M, Roseman RH. *Type A Behavior and Your Heart*. New York: Knopf Publishing, 1974.
6. Rozanski A, Blumenthal JA et al. Impact of psychological factors on the pathogenesis of cardiovascular disease and implications for therapy. *Circulation* 1999; 99:2192-2217.
7. Harvard Heart Letter. Stress and heart disease: How you think, feel, and love affects your heart. *Harvard Heart Publications* June 2005.
8. Nordestgaard BG. Elevated levels of C-reactive protein appear associated with psychological distress, depression. *Arch Gen Psychiatry* Published online December 24, 2012.
9. Menenschijn L, Schaap L et al. High long-term cortisol levels, measured in scalp hair, are associated with a history of cardiovascular disease. *JCEM* 2013 May; 98(5):2078-2083.
10. Hemingway H, Marmot M. Psychosocial factors in the aetiology and prognosis of coronary heart disease: systematic review of prospective cohort studies. *BMJ* 1999 May 29; 318(7196):1460-1467.
11. Johnson JV, Stewart W, et al. Long-term psychosocial work environment and cardiovascular mortality among Swedish men. *Am J Public Health* 1996; 86:325-331.
12. Marmot M, Bosma H, et al. Contribution of job control and other risk factors to social variations in coronary heart disease incidence. *Lancet* 1997; 350:235-239.
13. Wassertheil-Smoller S, Applegate WB, et al. Change in depression as a precursor of cardiovascular events. *Arch Intern Med* 1996; 156:553-561.
14. Linden W, Stossel C, et al. Psychosocial interventions in patients with coronary artery disease. *Arch Intern Med* 1996; 156:745-752.
15. Bucher HC. Social support and prognosis following first myocardial infarction. *J Gen Int Med* 1994; 9:409-417.
16. Yanek LR, Kral BG, et al. Effect of positive well-being on incidence of symptomatic coronary artery disease. *Am J Cardio* 2013 October; 112(8):1120-**1125.**

17. National Institutes of Health. Psychological stress and cancer. *National Cancer Institute: Fact Sheet* 2012 Dec.
18. Moreno-Smith M, Lutgendorf SK, et al. Impact of stress on cancer metastasis. *Future Oncology* 2010; (12):1863-1881.
19. Sloan EK, Priceman SJ, et al. The sympathetic nervous system induces a metastatic switch in primary breast cancer. *Cancer Research* 2010 ;70 (18): 7042-7052.
20. Lutgendorf SK, Sood AK, et al. Host factors and cancer progression: biobehavioral signaling pathways and interventions. *J Clin Oncol* 2010 Sep 10; 28 (26):4094-9.
21. Chida Y, Hammer M, et al. Do stress-related psychosocial factors contribute to cancer incidence and survival? *Nature Reviews Clinical Oncology* 2008 August; 5:466-475.
22. Eysenck HJ. *Smoking, personality, and stress: Psychosocial factors in the prevention of cancer and coronary heart disease.* New York: Springer-Verlag Publishing, 1991.
23. Reiche EMV, Nunes SOV, et al. Stress, depression, the immune system, and cancer. *Lancet Oncol* 2004; 5:617-25.

PART 4

Chapter 28

1. Mozaffarian D, Ludwig D. The 2015 US Dietary Guidelines-Ending the 35% limit on total dietary fat. *JAMA* 2015 Jun 23-30; 313(24):2421-2422.
2. Hooper K, Martin, et al. Reduction in saturated fat intake for cardiovascular disease. *Cochrane Database Syst Rev* 2015 June 10; (6):CD011737.
3. De Souza RJ, Mente A, et al. Intake of saturated and trans unsaturated fatty acids and risk of all cause mortality, cardiovascular disease, and type 2 diabetes: systematic review and meta-analysis of observational studies. *BMJ* 2015 Aug 11; 351: h3978.
4. Siri-Tarino PW, Sun Q, et al. Meta-analysis of prospective cohort studies evaluating the association of saturated fat with cardiovascular disease. *American Journal of Clinical Nutrition* 2010 March; 91 (3):535-546.
5. Chowdhury R, Warnakula S et al. Association of dietary, circulating, and supplement fatty acids with coronary risk: a systematic review and meta-analysis. *Ann Intern Med* 2014 May 6; 160(9):658.
6. Schwab U, Lauritzen K, et al. Effect of the amount and type of dietary fat on risk factors for cardiovascular diseases, and risk of developing type 2 diabetes, cardiovascular diseases, and cancer: a systematic review. *Food Nutr Res* 2014 Jul 10:58.

REFERENCES

7. Dreon DM, Fernstrom HA, et al. Change in dietary saturated fat is correlated with change in mass of large low-density-lipoprotein particles in men. *Am J Clin Nutr* 1998 May; 67(5):828-36.

8. Bonjour, JP. Protein intake and bone health. *Int J Vitam Nutr Res* 2011 Mar; 81(2-3):134-42.

9. Simopoulos AP. The importance of the ratio of omega-6/omega-3 essential fatty acids. *Biomed Pharmacother* 2002 Oct; 56 (8):365-79.

10. Simopoulos AP. Omega-3 fatty acids in health and disease and in growth and development. A*m J Clin Nutr* 1991 Sep; 54(3):438-63.

11. Dyson PA, Beatty S, et al. A low carbohydrate diet is more effective in reducing body weight than healthy eating in both diabetic and non-diabetic subjects. *Diabet Med* 2007; 24:1430-1435.

12. Santos FL, Esteves SS, et al. Systematic review and meta-analysis of clinical trials of the effects of low carbohydrate diets on cardiovascular risk factors. *Obes Rev* 2012; 13(11):1048-1066.

13. Bazzano LA, Hu T, et al. Effects of low-carbohydrate and low- fat diets: a randomized trial. *Ann Intern Med* 2014 Sept 2; 161(5):309-18.

14. Giugliano D, Ceriello A, et al. The effects of diet on inflammation: emphasis on the metabolic syndrome. *J Am Coll Cardiol* 2006 Aug15; 48(4):677-85.

15. Estruch R, Ros E, et al. Primary prevention of cardiovascular disease with a Mediterranean Diet. *N Engl J Med* 2013 April 4; 368:1279-1290.

16. Salas-Salvado J, Fernandez-Ballart, J et al. Effect of a Mediterranean Diet supplemented with nuts on metabolic syndrome status. *Arch Intern Med* 2008; 168(22):2449-2458.

17. Montserrat F, Guxens M,et al. Effect of traditional Mediterranean diet on lipoprotein oxidation. *Arch Intern Med* 2007; 167(11):1195-1203.

18. Salas-Salvado J, Bullo M, et al. Reduction in the incidence of type 2 diabetes with the Mediterranean diet: results of the PREDIMED-Reus nutritional intervention randomized trial. *Diabetes Care* 2011 Jan; 34(1):14-19.

19. Estruch R, Martinez-Gonzalez MA. Effects of a Mediterranean-style diet on cardiovascular risk factors. *Ann Intern Med* 2006 Jul 4; 145(1):1-11.

20. De Lorgeril M, Salen P, et al. Mediterranean diet, traditional risk factors, and the rate of cardiovascular complications after myocardial infarction: final report of the Lyon Heart Study. *Circulation* 1999 Feb 16; 99(6):779-85.

21. Lindeberg S, Jonsson T, et al. A palaeolithic diet improves glucose tolerance more than a Mediterranean-like diet in individuals with ischaemic heart disease. *Diabetologia* 2007 Sep; 50(9):1795-1807.

22. Osterdahl M, Kocturk T, et al. Effects of a short-term intervention with a paleolithic diet in healthy volunteers. *Eur J Clin Nutr* 2008 May; 62(5):682-5.

23. Jonsson T, Granfeldt Y, et al. Beneficial effects of a paleolithic diet on cardiovascular risk factors in type 2 diabetes: a randomized cross-over pilot study. *Cardiovascular Diabetology* 2009 Jul; 8(35).
24. Frassetto LA, Schloetter M et al. Metabolic and physiological improvements from consuming a paleolithic, hunter-gatherer type diet. *Eur J Clin Nutr* 2009 Aug; 63(8) 947-55.
25. Ryberg M, Sandberg S, et al. A paleolithic-type diet causes strong tissue-specific effects on ectopic fat deposition in obese postmenopausal women. *J Int Med* 2013; 274(1):67-76.
26. Lieberman, Shari, *The Gluten Connection: How Gluten Sensitivity May Be Sabotaging Your Health* (Rodale 2007).
27. Dong A, Scott SC. Serum B12 and blood cell values in vegetarians. *Ann Nutr Metab* 1982; 26:209-216.
28. Lord C, Chaput IP, et al. Dietary animal protein intake: association with muscle mass index in older women. *J Nutr Health Aging* 2007; 11(5):383-387.
29. Campbell WW, Barton ML Jr, et al. Effects of an omnivorous diet compared with a lactoovovegetarian diet on resistance-training-induced changes in body composition and skeletal muscle in older men. *Am J Clin Nutr* 1999 Dec; 70(6):1032-9.
30. Belanger A, Locong A, et al. Influence of diet on plasma steroids and sex hormone-binding globulin levels in adult men. *J Steroid Biochem* 1989 Jun; 32(6):829-33.
31. Benton D, Donohoe R. The influence of creatine supplementation on the cognitive functioning of vegetarians and omnivores. *British Journal of Nutrition* 2011 Apr; 105(7):1100-1105.
32. Burke DG, Chilibeck PD et al. Effect of creatine and weight training on muscle creatine and performance in vegetarians. *Med Sci Sports Exerc* 2003 Nov; 35(11):1946-55.
33. Hipkiss A. Chapter 3: Carnosine and its possible role in nutrition and health. *Advances in Food and Nutrition Research* 2009; 57:87-154.
34. Ornish D, Scherwitz LW, et al. Intensive lifestyle changes for reversal of coronary heart disease. *JAMA* 1998 Dec 16; 280(23):2001-2007.
35. McLean R, Qiao N, et al. Dietary acid load is not associated with lower bone mineral density except in older men. *J Nutr* 2011 Apr; 141(4):588-594.
36. Fenton TR, Eliasziw M, et al. Low urine pH and acid excretion do not predict bone fractures or the loss of bone mineral density: a prospective cohort study. *BMC Musculoskeletal Disorders* 2010 May; 11:88.
37. Robey I. Examining the relationship between diet-induced acidosis and cancer. *Nutrition & Metabolism* 2012; 9:72.
38. Gasior M, Rogawski M, et al. Neuroprotective and disease-modifying effects of the ketogenic diet. *Behav Pharmacol* 2006 Sep; 17(5-6):431-439.

REFERENCES

39. Westman EC, Yancy WS, et al. The effect of a low-carbohydrate, ketogenic diet versus a low-glycemic index diet on glycemic control in type 2 diabetes mellitus. *Nutr Metab (Lond)* 2008; 5:36.

40. Hemingway C, Freeman JM, et al. The ketogenic diet: a 3-to 6-year follow-up of 150 children enrolled prospectively. *Pediatrics* 2001 Oct; 108(4):898-905.

41. Brehm BJ, Seeley RJ, et al. A randomized trial comparing a very low carbohydrate diet and a calorie-restricted low-fat diet on body weight and cardiovascular risk factors in healthy woman. *J Clin Endocrinol Metab* 2003 Apr; 88(4):1617-23.

42. Johnstone AM, Horgan GW, et al. Effects of a high-protein ketogenic diet on hunger, appetite, and weight loss in obese men feeding ad libitum. *Am J Clin Nutr* 2008 Jan; 87(1):44-55.

43. Mannien AH. Very-low-carbohydrate diets and preservation of muscle mass. *Nutr.Metab (Lond)* 2006 Jan; 3:9.

44. Boden G, Sargrad K et al. Effect of a low-carbohydrate diet on appetite, blood glucose levels, and insulin resistance in obese patients with type 2 diabetes. *Ann Intern Med* 2005 Mar 15; 142(6) 403-11.

45. Gumbiner B, Wendel DA, et al. Effects of diet composition and ketosis on glycemia during very-low-energy-diet therapy in obese patients with non-insulin-dependent diabetes mellitus. *Am J Clin Nutr* 1996 Jan; 63(1):110-5.

46. Westman EC, Mavropoulos J, et al. A review of low-carbohydrate ketogenic diets. *Curr Atheroscler Rep* 2003 Nov; 5(6):476-83.

47. Klement RJ. Calorie or carbohydrate restriction? The ketogenic diet as another option for supportive cancer treatment. *Oncologist* 2013; 18(9):1056.

48. Zhou W, Mukherjee P, et al. The calorically restricted ketogenic diet, an effective alternative therapy for malignant brain cancer. *Nutr Metab (Lond)* 2007; 4:5.

49. McPherson PA, McEneny J. The biochemistry of ketogenesis and its role in weight management, neurological disease, and oxidative stress. *J Physiol Biochem* 2012 Mar; 68(1):141-51.

50. Jabre MG, Bejjani BP. Treatment of Parkinson disease with diet-induced hyperketonemia; a feasibility study. *Neurology* 2006 Feb 28; 66(4):617.

51. Mavropoulos JC, Yancy WS, et al. The effects of a low-carbohydrate, ketogenic diet on the polycystic ovary syndrome: A pilot study. *Nutr Metab (Lond)* 2005; 2:35.

52. Phinney SD, Bistrian BR, et al. The human response to chronic ketosis without caloric restriction: preservation of submaximal exercise capability with reduced carbohydrate oxidation. *Metabolism* 1983 Aug; 32(8):769-76.

53. Longo VD, Mattson MP. Fasting: Molecular mechanisms and clinical applications. *Cell Metab* 2014 Feb 4; 19(2):181-192.

54. Hartman ML, Veldhuis JD, et al. Augmented growth hormone (GH) secretory burst frequency and amplitude mediate enhanced GH secretion during a two-day fast in normal men. *J Clin Endocrinol Metab* 1992 Apr; 74(4):757-65.

55. Heilbronn LK, Smith SR, et al. Alternate-day fasting in nonobese subjects: effects on body weight, body composition, and energy metabolism *Am J Clin Nutr* 2005 Jan; 81(1):69-73.

56. Mizushima N, Levine B, et al. Autophagy fights disease through cellular self-digestion. *Nature* 2008 Feb 28; 451(7182):1069-1075.

57. Zhu Y, Yan Y, et al. Metabolic regulation of Sirtuins upon fasting and the implication for cancer. *Curr Opin Oncol* 2013 Nov; 25(6):630-6.

58. Martin B, Mattson M, et al. Caloric restriction and intermittent fasting: Two potential diets for successful brain aging. *Ageing Res Rev* 2006 Aug; 5(3): 332-353.

59. Wei MW, Brandhorst S, Longo VD, et al. Fasting-mimicking diet and markers/risk factors for aging, diabetes, cancer, and cardiovascular disease. *Sci Transl Med* 2017 Feb; 9(377):1-12.

60. Eenennaam AL, Young AE. Prevalence and impacts of genetically engineered feedstuffs on livestock populations. *J Anim Sci* 2014 Oct; 92(10):4255-78.

61. Domingo JL, Giné Bordonaba J. A literature review on the safety assessment of genetically modified plants. *Environ Int* 2011 May; 37(4):734-42.

Chapter 29

1. National Institute of Health. Should you take dietary supplements? *NIH News in Health* August 2013.

2. Molfino A, Gioia G, et al. The role for dietary omega-3 fatty acids supplementation in older adults. *Nutrients* 2014 Oct 3; 6(10):4058-73.

3. Papanikolaou Y, Brooks J, et al. U.S. adults are not meeting recommended levels for fish and omega-3 fatty acid intake: results of an analysis using observational data from NHANES 2003-2008. *Nutrition Journal* 2014; 13:31.

4. Singh M. Essential fatty acids, DHA and human brain. *Indian J Pediatr* 2005 Mar; 72(3):239-42.

5. Siriwardhana N, Kalupahana NS, et al. Health benefits of n-3 polyunsaturated fatty acids: eicosapentaenoic acid and docosahexaenoic acid. *Adv Food Nutr Res* 2012; 65:211-22

6. Terry PD, Terry JB, et al. Long-chain (n-3) fatty acid intake and risk of cancers of the breast and the prostate: recent epidemiological studies, biological mechanisms, and directions for future research. *J Nutr* 2004 Dec; 134(12 Suppl):3412S-3420S.

7. Sublette ME, Ellis SP, et al. Meta-analysis of the effects of eicosapentaenoic acid (EPA) in clinical trials in depression. *J Clin Psychiatry* 2011 Dec; 72(12):1577-84.

REFERENCES

8. Osher Y, Belmaker RH. Omega-3 fatty acids in depression: a review of three studies. *CNS Neurosci Ther* 2009 Summer; 15(2):128-33.
9. Morris MC, Evans DA, et al. Fish consumption and cognitive decline with age in a large community study. *Arch Neurol* 2005 Dec; 62(12):1849-5310.
10. Joint FAO/WHO Expert Consultation on Fats and Fatty Acids in Human Nutrition. Interim study of conclusions and dietary recommendations on total fat and fatty acids. 10-14 November 2008, WHO, Geneva.
11. EFSA Panel on Dietetic Products, Nutrition and Allergies (NDA). Scientific opinion on the tolerable upper intake level of eicosapentaenoic acid (EPA), docosahexaenoic acid (DHA) and docosapentaenoic acid (DPA). *EFSA Journal* 2012; 10(7):2815.
12. Sinatra Stephen. *Coenzyme Q10 and the Heart: A Miracle Nutrient for the Prevention and Successful Treatment of Heart Disease.* (Keats/Contemporary Publishing Group, Inc.) 1999.
13. Forrest KY, Stuhldreher WL. Prevalence and correlates of vitamin D deficiency in US adults. *Nutr Res* 2011 Jan; 31(1):48-54.
14. Linnebur SA, Vondracek SF, et al. Prevalence of vitamin D insufficiency in elderly ambulatory outpatients in Denver, Colorado. *Am J Geriatr Pharmacother* 2007 Mar; 5(1):1-8.
15. Lee JH, Gadi R, et al. Prevalence of vitamin D deficiency in patients with acute myocardial infarction. *Am J Cardiol* 2011 Jun 1; 107(11):1636-8.
16. Witte KK, Byrom R, et al. Effects of vitamin D on cardiac function in patients with chronic HF: the VINDICATE study. *JACC* 67(22):2593-2603
17. Dobnig H. A review of the health consequences of the vitamin D deficiency pandemic. *J Neurological Sciences* 2011 Dec 15; 311(1-2):15-18.
18. Holick MF, Chen TC. Vitamin D deficiency: a worldwide problem with health consequences. *AM J Clin Nutr* 87(4):1080S-1086S.
19. Braun A, Chang D, et al. Association of low serum 24-hydroxyvitamin D levels and mortality in the critically ill. *Crit Care Med* 2011 Apr; 39(4):671-7.
20. Pilz S, Dobnig H, et al. Low 25-hydroxyvitamin D is associated with increased mortality in female nursing home residents. *J Clin Endocrinol Metab* 2012 Apr; 97(4):E653-7.
21. University of Missouri-Columbia. Vitamin D deficiency related to increased inflammation in healthy women. *ScienceDaily* 14 Apr 2009.
22. Yin K, Agrawal D. Vitamin D and inflammatory diseases. *J Inflamm Res* 2014 May; 7:69-87.
23. Rosanoff A, Weaver CM, et al. Suboptimal magnesium status in the United States: are the health consequences underestimated? *Nutr Rev* 2012 Mar; 70(3):153-64.

24. De Baaij JH, Hoenderop JG, et al. Magnesium in man: implications for health and disease. *Physiol Rev* 2015 Jan; 95(1):1-46.
25. Nielsen FH, Lukaski HC. Update on the relationship between magnesium and exercise. *Magnes Res* 2006 Sep; 19(3):180-9.
26. Setaro L, Santos-Silva PR, et al. Magnesium status and the physical performance of volleyball players: effects of magnesium supplementation. *J Sports Sci* 2014; 32(5):438-45.
27. Serefko A, Szopa A, et al. Magnesium in depression. *Pharmacol Rep* 2013; 65(3):547-54.
28. Tarleton EK, Littenberg B. Magnesium intake and depression in adults. *J Am Board Fam Med* 2015 Mar-Apr; 28(2):249-56.
29. Eby GA, Eby KL. Rapid recovery from major depression using magnesium treatment. *Med Hypotheses* 2006; 67(2):362-70.
30. Dong JY, Xun P, et al. Magnesium intake and risk of type 2 diabetes: meta-analysis of prospective cohort studies. *Diabetes Care* 2011 Sep; 34(9):2116-22.
31. Rodriguez-Moran M, Guerrero-Romero F. Oral magnesium improves insulin sensitivity and metabolic control in type 2 diabetic subjects: a randomized double-blind controlled trial. *Diabetes Care* 2003 Apr; 26(4):1147-52.
32. Hatzistavri LS, Sarafidis PA, et al. Oral magnesium supplementation reduces ambulatory blood pressure in patients with mild hypertension. *Am J Hypertens* 2009 Oct; 22(10):1070-5.
33. Kawano Y, Matsuoka H, et al. Effects of magnesium supplementation in hypertensive patients: assessment by office, home, and ambulatory blood pressure. *Hypertension* 1998 Aug; 32(2):260-5.
34. Nielsen FH. Effects of magnesium depletion on inflammation in chronic disease. *Curr Opin Clin Nutr Metab Care* 2014 Nov; 17(6):525-30.
35. Nielsen FH. Magnesium, inflammation, and obesity in chronic disease. *Nutr Rev* 2010 Jun; 68(6):333-40.
36. Simental-Mendia LE, Rodriguez-Moran M, et al. Oral magnesium supplementation decreases C-reactive protein levels in subjects with prediabetes and hypomagnesemia: a clinical randomized double-blind placebo-controlled trial. *Arch Med Res* 2014 May; 45(4):325-30.
37. Walker AF, De Souza MC, et al. Magnesium supplementation alleviates premenstrual symptoms of fluid retention. *J Womens Health* 1998 Nov; 7(9):1157-65.
38. Facchinetti F, Borella P, et al. Oral magnesium successfully relieves premenstrual mood changes *Obstet Gynecol* 1991 Aug; 78(2P):177-81.
39. Koseoglu E, Talaslioglu A, et al. The effects of magnesium prophylaxis in migraine without aura. *Magnes Res* 2008 Jun; 21(2):101-8.
40. Shechter M. Magnesium and cardiovascular system. *Magnes Res* 2010 Jun; 23(2):60-72.

REFERENCES

41. Falco CN, Grupi C, et al. Successful improvement of frequency and symptoms of premature complexes after oral magnesium administration. *Arq Bras Cardiol* 2012 Jun; 98(6):480-7.

42. Nielsen FK, Johnson LK, et al. Magnesium supplementation improves indicators of low magnesium status and inflammatory stress in adults older than 51 years with poor quality sleep. *Magnes Res* 2010; 23(4):158-68.

43. Abbasi B, Kimiagar M, et al. The effect of magnesium supplementation on primary insomnia in elderly: a double-blind placebo-controlled clinical trial. *J Res Med Sci* 2012 Dec; 17(12):1161-9.

44. Raffelmann T, Ittermann T, et al. Low serum magnesium concentrations predict cardiovascular and all- cause mortality. *Atherosclerosis* 2011 Nov; 219(1):280-4.

45. Rowe WJ. Correcting magnesium deficiencies may prolong life. *Clin Interv Aging* 2012; 7:51-4.

46. O'Hara AM, Shanahan F. The gut flora as a forgotten organ. *EMBO Rep* 2006 Jul; 7(7):688-693.

47. Caricilli AM, Castoldi A, et al. Intestinal barrier: A gentleman's agreement between microbiota and immunity. *World J Gastrointest Pathophysiol* 2014 Feb 15; 5(1):18-32.

48. Sekirov I, Russell S, et al. Gut microbiota in health and disease. *Physiological Reviews* 2010 Jul; 90(3):859-904.

49. DiBaise JK, Zhang H, et al. Gut microbiota and its possible relationship with obesity. *Mayo Clinic Proceedings* 2008 Apr; 83(4):460-469.

50. Musso G, Gambino R, et al. Interactions between gut microbiota and host metabolism predisposing to obesity and diabetes. *Annual Review of Medicine* 2011 Feb; 62:361-380.

51. Tuohy KM, Fava F, et al. 'The way to a man's heart is through his gut microbiota'- dietary pro- and prebiotics for the management of cardiovascular risk. *Proc Nutr Soc* 2014 May; 73(2):172-85.

52. Naseer MI, Bibi F, et al. Role of gut microbiota in obesity, type 2 diabetes, and Alzheimer's disease. *CNS Neurol Disord Drug Targets* 2014 Mar; 13(2):305-11.

53. Dinan TG, Cryan JF. Melancholic Microbes: a link between gut microbiota and depression? *Neurogastroenterol & Motil* 2013 Sep; 25(9):713-719.

54. Ritchie ML, Romanuk TN. A meta-analysis of probiotic efficacy for gastrointestinal disease. *PLoS One* 2012; 7(4):e34938

55. Hempel S, Newberry SJ, et al. Probiotics for the prevention and treatment of antibiotic-associated diarrhea: a systematic review and meta-analysis. *JAMA* 2012 May9; 307(18):1959-69.

56. Moayyedi P, Ford AC, et al. The efficacy of probiotics in the treatment of irritable bowel syndrome: a systematic review. *Gut* 2010; 59:325-332.

57. Park SH, Kangwan N, et al. Non-microbial approach for Helicobacter pylori as faster track to prevent gastric cancer than simple eradication. *World J Gastroenterol* 2013 Dec21; 19(47):8986-95.

Chapter 30

1. Hills AP, Street SJ, et al. Physical Activity and Health: "What is old is new again". *Adv Food Nutr Res* 2015; 75:77-95.

2. Warburton D, Nicol C, et al. Health benefits of physical activity: the evidence. *CMAJ* 2006 Mar 14;174(6):801-809.

3. Lavie CJ, Arena R, et al. Exercise and the cardiovascular system: clinical science and cardiovascular outcomes. *Circ Res* 2015 Jul 3; 117(2):207-19.

4. Goedecke JH, Mickelsfield LK. The effect of exercise on obesity, body fat distribution and risk for type 2 diabetes. *Med Sport Sci* 2014; 60:82-93.

5. Carter MI, Hinton PS. Physical activity and bone health. *Mo Med* 2014 Jan-Feb; 111(1) 59-64.

6. Center for Disease Control and Prevention. Adult participation in aerobic and muscle-strengthening physical activities-United States, 2011. *Morbidity and Mortality Weekly Report (MMWR)* 2013 May 3; 62(17) 326-330.

7. Hayes SM, Alosco ML, et al. Physical activity is positively associated with episodic memory in aging. *J Int Neuropsychol Soc* 2015 Nov; 21(10):780-90.

8. Baker LD, Frank LL, et al. Effects of Aerobic Exercise on Mild Cognitive Impairment: A controlled trial. *Arch Neurol* 2010; 67(1):71-79.

9. Angevaren M, Aufdemkampe G, et al. Physical activity and enhanced fitness to improve cognitive function in older people without known cognitive impairment. *Cochrane Database Syst. Rev* 2008 Apr 16; (2):CD005381.

10. Cai Y, Abrahamson K. How exercise influences cognitive performance when mild cognitive impairment exists: A literature review. *J Pyschosoc Nurs Ment Health Serv* 2016 Jan; 54(1):25-35.

11. Heymsfield SB, Gonzalez MC, et al. Weight loss composition is one-fourth fat-free mass: a critical review and critique of this widely cited rule. *Obes Rev* 2014 Apr; 15(4):310-21.

12. Beavers KM, Beavers DP, et al. Effect of an 18-month physical activity and weight loss intervention on body composition in overweight and obese older adults. *Obesity (Silver Spring)* 2014 Feb; 22(2):325-31.

13. Garrow JS, Summerbell CD. Meta-analysis: effect of exercise, with or without dieting, on the body composition of overweight subjects. *Eur J Clin Nutr* 1995 Jan; 49(1):1-10.

14. American Heart Association. American Heart Association recommendation for physical activity in adults and kids. Last updated Apr 18, 2018.

15. Mersey DJ. Health benefits of aerobic exercise. *Postgrad Med* 1991 Jul; 90(1):103-7.

16. Ismail I, Keating SE, et al. A systematic review and meta-analysis of the effect of aerobic vs. resistance exercise training on visceral fat. *Obes Rev* 2012 Jan; 13(1):68-91.

REFERENCES

17. Westcott WL. Resistance training is medicine: effects of strength training on health. *Curr Sports Med Rep.* 2012 Jul-Aug; 11(4):209-16.
18. Willoughby DS. Resistance training and the older adult. *ACSM Current Comment*
19. Sequin R, Nelson ME, et al. The benefits of strength training for older adults. *Am J Prev Med* 2003 Oct; 25(3 Suppl 2):141-9.
20. Hunter GR, Byrne NM, et al. Resistance training conserves fat-free mass and resting energy expenditure following weight loss. *Obesity (Solver Spring)* 2008 May; 16(5):1045-51.
21. Zurlo F, Larson K, et al. Skeletal muscle metabolism is a major determinant of resting energy expenditure. *J Clin Invest* 1990 Nov; 86(5):1423-7.
22. Page P. Current concepts in muscle stretching for exercise and rehabilitation. *Int J Sports PT* 2012 Feb; 7(1):109-119.
23. McHugh MP, Cosgrave CH. To stretch or not to stretch: the role of stretching in injury prevention and performance. *Scand J Med* 2010 Apr; 20(2):169-81.

Chapter 32

1. Jin K. Modern Biological Theories of Aging. *Aging and Disease* 2010 Oct; 1(2):72-74.
2. Davidovic M, Sevo G, et al. Old age as a privilege of the "selfish ones" *Aging and Disease* 2010; 1:139-146.
3. Rozemuller AJ, van Gool WA, et al. The neuroinflammatory response in plaques and amyloid angiopathy in Alzheimer's disease: therapeutic implications. *Curr Drug Targets CNS Neurol Disord* 2005; 4:223-233.
4. Bjorksten J. The crosslinkage theory of aging. *J Am Geriatr Soc* 1968; 16:408-427.
5. Bjorksten J, and Tenhu H. The crosslinking theory of aging-added evidence. *Exp Gerontol* 1990; 25:91-95.
6. Harman D. Aging: a theory based on free radical and radiation chemistry. *J Gerontol* 1956; 11:298-300.
7. Afanas'ev I. Signaling and damaging functions of free radicals in aging-free radical hormesis, and TOR. *Aging and Disease* 2010; 1:75-88.
8. Writing Group for the Woman's Health Initiative Investigators. Risks and benefits of estrogen plus progestin in healthy postmenopausal women. *JAMA* 2002 July 17; 288(3):321.
9. Klaiber EL, Vogel W, et al. A critique of the Women's Health Initiative hormone therapy study. *Fertility and Sterility* 2005 Dec; 84(6)1589-1601.
10. Smith, PW. HRT: The Answers, *A Concise Guide for Solving the Hormone Replacement Therapy Puzzle.* Healthy (Living Books, Inc.) 2003.

11. Hotze SF, Ellsworth DP. Point/counterpoint: the case for bioidentical hormones. *Journal of American Physicians and Surgeons* 2008; 13(2)43-45.

12. Somers, Suzanne. *The Sexy Years: discover the hormone connection: the secret to fabulous sex, great health and vitality for women and men.* (Crown Publishers) 2004.

13. Somers, Suzanne. *Ageless: the naked truth about bioidentical hormones.* (Crown Publishers) 2006.

14. Huggins C and Hodges C. Studies on prostate cancer. 1. The effect of castration, of estrogen and of androgen injection on serum phosphatases in metastatic carcinoma of the prostate. *Cancer Res* 1941 Apr; 1(4):293-297.

15. Dobs AS, Morgentaler A. Does testosterone therapy increase the risk of prostate cancer? *Endocr Pract* 2008 Oct; 14(7):904-11.

16. Morgentaler A. Testosterone and prostate cancer: an historical perspective on a modern myth. *European Urology* 2006 Nov; 50(5):935-39.

17. Vigen R, O'Donnell CI, et al. Association of testosterone therapy with mortality, myocardial infarction, and stroke in men with low testosterone levels. *JAMA* 2013; 310(7):1829-1836.

18. Finkle WD, Greenland S, et al. Increased risk of non-fatal myocardial infarction following testosterone therapy prescription in men. *PLoS One* 2014 Jan 29; 9(1):e85805.

19. English K, et al. Men with coronary artery disease have lower levels of androgens than men with normal coronary angiograms. *EUR Heart Jour* 2000; 21(11):890-4.

20. Vermeulen A. Androgen replacement therapy in the aging male-a critical evaluation. *Jour Clin Endocrinol Metabol* 2001; 86:2380-90.

21. Malkin C, et al. Low testosterone and increased mortality in men with coronary artery disease. *Heart* 2010; 96:1821-25.

22. Turhan S, et al. The association between androgen levels and premature coronary artery disease in men. *Coron Artery Dis* 2007; 18(3):159-62.

23. Svartberg J, et al. Low testosterone levels are associated with carotid atherosclerosis in men. *Jour Int Med* 2006; 269(6):576-82.

24. Haring R, et al. Low serum testosterone levels are associated with increased risk of mortality in a population-based cohort of men aged 20-79. *Eur Heart J* 2010; 31(12):1494-1501.

25. Channer K, et al. Cardiovascular effects of testosterone: implications of the "male menopause?" *Heart* 2003 Feb; 89(2):121-22.

26. English K, et al. Low-dose transdermal testosterone therapy improves angina threshold in men with chronic stable angina. *Circulation* 2000 Oct; 102(16): 1906-11.

27. Malkin C, et al. The effect of testosterone replacement on endogenous inflammatory cytokines and lipid profiles on hypogonadal men. *Jour Clin Endocrinol Metab* 2004 Jul 1; 89(7):3313-18.

REFERENCES

28. Toma M, McAlister F, et al. Testosterone supplementation in heart failure: A Meta Analysis *Circ Heart Failure* 2012; 5:315-21.

29. Basaria S, Harman SM, et al. Effects of testosterone administration for 3 years on subclinical atherosclerosis progression in older men with low or low-normal testosterone levels: A randomized trial. *JAMA* 2015; 314(6):570-81.

30. Abbott A, et al. Serum estradiol and risk of stroke in elderly men. *Neurology* 2007; (8):563-68.

31. Mohamad M. Serum levels of sex hormones in men with acute myocardial infarction. *Neuro Endocrinol Lett* 2007; 28(2):182-86.

32. Tripathi Y, et al. Serum estradiol and testosterone levels following acute myocardial infarction in men. *Jour Physiol Pharmacol* 1998; 42(2):291-94.

33. Sudhir K, et al. Cardiovascular actions of estrogens in men. *Jour Clin Endocrinolol Metab* 1999; 84(10):3411-15.

34. Bassil N, et al. *Erythrocytosis in Hematopathology. 2nd Ed.* His., E, (Ed.) Philadelphia: (Elsevier/ Saunders.) 2012.

35. Skogastiema C. et al. A supraphysiological dose of testosterone induces nitric oxide production and oxidative stress. *Eur Jour Prev Cardio* 2013; March 7.

36. Ohlsson C, Labrie F, et al. Low serum levels of dehydroepiandrosterone sulfate predict all-cause and cardiovascular mortality in elderly Swedish men. *J Clin Endocrinolol Metab* 2010 Sept; 95(9):4406-14.

37. Tivesten A, Vandenput L, et al. Dehydroepiandrosterone and its sulfate predict the 5-year risk of coronary heart disease. *J Am Coll Cardiol* 2014 Oct28; 64(17):1801-10.

38. Shufelt C, Bretsky P, et al. DHEA-S levels and cardiovascular disease mortality in postmenopausal women: Results from the National Institutes of Health-National Heart, Lung, and Blood Institute (NHLBI)-sponsored Women's Ischemia Syndrome Evaluation (WISE). *J Clin Endocrinolol Metab* 2010 Nov; 95(11):4985-92.

39. Jimenez MC, Sun Q, et al. Low dehdroepiandrosterone sulfate is associated with increased risk of ischemic stroke among women. *Stroke* 2013 Jul; 44(7):1784-9.

40. Buford TW, Willoughby DS, et al. Impact of DHEA(S) and cortisol on immune function in aging: a brief review. *Appl Physiol Nutr Metab* 2008 Jun; 33(3): 429-33.

41. Von Muhlen D, Laughlin GA, et al. Effects of dehydroepiandrosterone supplementation on bone density, bone markers, and body composition in older adults: the DAWN trial. *Osteoporosis Int* 2008 May; 19(5):699-707.

42. Sun Y, Mao M, et al. Treatment of osteoporosis in men using dehydroepiandrosterone sulfate. *Chin Med J (Engl)* 2002 Mar; 115(3): 402-4.

43. Villareal DT, Holloszy JO, et al. Effect of DHEA on abdominal fat and insulin action in elderly women and men: a randomized controlled trial. *JAMA* 2004 Nov 10; 292(18):2243-8.

44. Lasco A, Frisina N, et al. Metabolic effects of dehydroepiandrosterone replacement therapy in postmenopausal women. *Eur J Endocrinol* 2001 Oct; 145(4):457-61
45. Zawilska JB, Skene DJ, et al. Physiology and pharmacology of melatonin in relation to biological rhythms. *Pharmacol Rep* 2009 May-June; 61(3):383-410.
46. Korkmaz A, Topal T, et al. Role of melatonin in metabolic regulation. *Reviews in Endocrine & Metabolic Disorders* 2009 Dec ;10(4):261-70.
47. Reiter RJ, Paredes SD, et al. Melatonin combats molecular terrorism at the mitochondrial level. *Interdiscip Toxicol* 2008 Sep; 1(2):137-49.
48. Esposito E, Cuzzocrea S. Antiinflammatory activity of melatonin in central nervous system. *Curr Neuropharmacol* 2010 Sep; 8(3):228-42.
49. Srinivasan V, Pandi-Perumal SR, et al. Melatonin, immune function, and cancer. *Endocr Metab Immune Drug Discov* 2011 May; 5(2):109-23.
50. Gruber J, Schaffer S, et al. The mitochondrial theory of aging- where do we stand? *Front Biosci* 2008 May 1; 13:6554-79.
51. Hekimi S, Lapointe J, et al. Taking a "good look" at free radicals in the aging process. *Trends Cell Biol* 2011 Oct; 21(10):569-76.
52. Reiter RJ, Tan DX, et al. Beneficial effects of melatonin in cardiovascular disease. *Ann Med* 2010 May 6; 42(4):276-85.
53. Pawlikowski M, Winczyk K, et al. Oncostatic action of melatonin: facts and questions marks. *Neuro Endocrinolol Lett* 2002; 23:S24-9.
54. Srinivasan V, Spence DW, et al. Therapeutic actions of melatonin in cancer possible mechanisms. *Integr Cancer Ther* 2008 Sep; 7(3):189-203.
55. Srinivasan V, Pandi-Perumal SR, et al. Melatonin in Alzheimer's disease and other neurodegenerative disorders. *Behavioral and Brain Functions* 2006; 2:15.
56. Kotlarczyk MP, Lassila HC et al. Melatonin osteoporosis prevention study (MOPS); a randomized, double-blind, placebo-controlled study examining the effects of melatonin on bone health and quality of life in perimenopausal women. *Pineal Res* 2012 May; 52(4):414-26.
57. Pandi-Perumal SR, BaHammam AS, et al. Melatonin antioxidative defense: therapeutic implications for aging and neurodegenerative processes. *Neurotox Res* 2013 Apr; 23(3):267-300.
58. Reiter RJ, Sainz RM, et al. Melatonin ameliorates neurologic damage and neurophysiologic deficits in experimental models of stroke. *Ann N Y Acad Sci* May; 993:35-47; discussion 48-53.
59. Ayer RE, Sugawara T, et al. Effects of melatonin in early brain injury following subarachnoid hemorrhage. *Acta Neurochir Suppl* 2008; 102:327-30.
60. Hwang AB, Jeong DE, et al. Mitochondria and Organismal Longevity. *Current Genomics* 2012 Nov; 13(7):519-532.

REFERENCES

61. Franceschi C, Garagnani P, et al. Inflammaging: a new immune-metabolic viewpoint for age-related diseases. *Nature Reviews Endocrinology* 2018; 14:576-590.
62. Fahy GM, Brooke RT, et al. Reversal of epigenetic aging and immunosenescent trends in humans. *Aging Cell* 2019 Sept 8; 18(6):1-27.

Made in the USA
Las Vegas, NV
15 June 2023